Countdown to Armageddon

CHARLES RYRIE
Consulting Editor
JOE JORDAN and TOM DAVIS
General Editors

HARVEST HOUSE PUBLISHERS
Eugene, Oregon 97402

Cover by Terry Dugan Design, Minneapolis, Minnesota

COUNTDOWN TO ARMAGEDDON
Copyright © 1999 by Word of Life Fellowship, Inc.
Published by Harvest House Publishers
Eugene, Oregon 97402

Library of Congress Cataloging-in-Publication Data

Countdown to Armageddon / Charles Ryrie, consulting editor;
Joe Jordan and Tim Davis, general editors.
      p.   cm.
   Includes bibliographical references.
   ISBN 0-7369-0014-4
   1. Bible–Prophecies–Armageddon.   2. Armageddon–Biblical teaching.
I. Ryrie, Charles Caldwell, 1925–   .   II. Jordan, Joe, 1946–   .
III. Davis, Tim, 1957–   .
BS649.A68C68   1999
236'.9–dc21   98–47206
                                                                   CIP

Printed in the United States of America

            99   00   01   02   03   /BP/   10   9   8   7   6   5   4   3   2   1

This book is dedicated in memory of Jack Wyrtzen, founder of Word of Life Fellowship, a man who motivated many to a diligent study of prophecy through his own enthusiasm for future events and his earnest commitment to rightly divide the Word of truth. Jack showed through his associations (men like Harry Ironside, William Pettingill, Lehman Strauss, Charles Ryrie), his activities (evangelism and discipleship), and his attitudes (a passion for holy living) that the study of prophecy affects not only our creed but equally our conduct.

CONTENTS

foreword

Interest in the future has captivated the minds of people for centuries. Old Testament prophets inquired diligently about the coming Messiah. Just before the ascension of our Lord the disciples wondered when He would restore Israel's kingdom. The Thessalonian believers wanted to know what would happen to their loved ones who had died before the Lord's return. The Corinthians showed uncertainty about facets of the resurrection.

I have lived long enough to have seen interest and curiosity about the future wax and wane. When things are going well, the comforts and pleasures of the present life on earth cast prophecy into the shadows. Why think about the end of the world when the contemporary world is so comfortable? However, when wars erupt, especially in the Middle East, then people want to know what significance they might have and whether they portend the end of the world.

Scenarios about the end of the world differ among Bible students. Some think the world will (continue to) get better and better through the efforts of the church, and then the Lord will come to raise and judge the dead and to usher in eternity. Others see defection and evil as characterizing the years before the return of Christ to end this world as we know it and begin eternity. Still others agree that the Bible teaches the world will not get better but worse, climaxing in seven years of a unique time of tribulation on the earth before the Lord returns to inaugurate His kingdom on this earth for 1,000 years after which eternity will begin.

These different scenarios turn on one's view of how plainly we should understand the prophecies of the Bible. Evangelicals do not fudge on understanding the prophecies of the first coming of Christ plainly. When it comes to predictions about the future, however, then all kinds of deliteralizing takes place. The tribulation, they say, happened in the early centuries of the church under Roman emperors. But horrible as some of those times were, the persecutions were not worldwide, nor concentrated in seven years, as the Scriptures plainly teach. Too, they say, the only kingdom is a spiritual one in our hearts now, and we should not expect any literal kingdom on earth in the future, as the Scriptures plainly teach. But how can one defend such inconsistency and selectivity in the use of a normal hermeneutic when interpreting the Bible?

I have also lived long enough to see well-meaning literal interpreters "see" almost weekly some current event as a portent, if not a fulfillment, of some prophecy. On the opposite extreme others seem to be insensitive to legitimate signs of the times. The contributors to this book are not wild-eyed date setters but thoughtful and seasoned interpreters of the prophetic Scriptures. The advent of a new millennium has understandably stirred interest in many circles in what lies ahead. The timely truth in this book guarantees to reward all who read it.

Charles C. Ryrie

Searching what, or what manner of time the Spirit of Christ which was in them did signify, when it testified beforehand the sufferings of Christ, and the glory that should follow.

1 PETER 1:10

Sadly, because of an Athenian spirit (the desire just to hear something new solely for the purpose of satiating one's carnal curiosity or intellect), the present generation has deemed the study of prophecy irrelevant for the present-day church. Yet, a study of church history and the Scriptures would show otherwise. If there ever was a day when the Church of the Lord Jesus Christ needed to know God's purposes and plan for our future, it is today. In a day of such insecurity, the study of prophecy underlines the authority of God's Word and gives us the assurance and comfort we need.

Chapter 1

Profiting from Prophecy

Joe Jordan

"If you can look into the seeds of time, and say which grain will grow and which will not; speak then to me."[1]

These words penned by William Shakespeare in *Macbeth* pose a question concerning prophecy and its value to man. Shakespeare, of course, had no concept of the profitability of the only type of prophecy that truly matters, and is truly reliable, Bible prophecy. Yet, the question is posed, in what way will Bible prophecy bring profit to the lives of those who are engaged in its study?

As the aged Apostle Paul was nearing the end of his life, the Spirit of God guided him to direct his last letter to young Timothy. In 2 Timothy 3, after speaking of the last days (the period between the time of the writing of the apostle's letter and the Lord's return) with all of its dangers, he points to the profitability of the Scripture when he said: "All Scripture is given by inspiration of God, and is profitable ..." (2 Timothy 3:16).

The word *profitable* in this text speaks of something useful, helpful, or advantageous. Without a doubt, we can say that prophecy truly is profitable because approximately one-fourth of all Scripture was prophetic when it was written. It is useful, it is helpful, and it is advantageous. To eliminate the study of prophecy would be to eliminate a great portion of our Bible, which is useful, helpful, advantageous, and, of course, very profitable.

Sadly, because of an Athenian spirit (the desire just to hear something new solely for the purpose of satiating one's carnal curiosity or intellect), the present generation has deemed the study of prophecy irrelevant for the present-day church. Yet, a study of church history and the Scriptures would show otherwise. If there ever was a day when the church of the Lord Jesus Christ needed to know God's purposes and plan for our future, it is today. Although there are many ways a proper study of prophecy can bring much profit to the church, we will highlight three key areas that are vital to the life of the believer in Christ.

The first area examines the problem of ignorance of the Scriptures, the Word of God. The second area considers our service for God (the work of God) and addresses the problem of inactivity. The third area focuses on our Savior (the worship of God) and critiques the problem of indifference.

The Scriptures: The Problem of Ignorance

It is impossible for one to have a complete view of the Scriptures and the knowledge of God without having a complete view of prophecy. One of God's key purposes of prophecy is to reveal to us what will happen before it happens. By the sheer fact of the abundance of space that the Spirit of God devotes to prophecy, it is easy to see the importance God gives to this vital truth. Thinking about prophecy and focusing on the Second Coming of Christ in Scripture, we observe the following statistics:

- Approximately one-fourth of the Bible was prophetic when it was written.

- Of the 333 prophecies concerning Christ, only 109 of them were fulfilled at His First Coming, leaving 224 yet to be fulfilled at His Second Coming.

- There are a total of 1,527 Old Testament passages referring to the Second Coming.

- In the New Testament, 330 verses refer directly to the Second Coming of Christ.

- The Lord Himself refers to His return 21 times in Scripture.

To be ignorant of such a significant amount of the Word of God opens the door to all types of false doctrines and false hopes. As the Apostle Paul wrote to the church of Thessalonica: "I would not have you to be ignorant, brethren" (1 Thessalonians 4:13).

Because the believers of Thessalonica were very concerned about their loved ones who had died, several questions came to their minds. What would happen to them should the Lord return? What would happen to their dead loved ones in Christ? This prophetic portion of Paul's letter to the Thessalonian church was designed to remove their ignorance concerning the return of Christ, the resurrection of the dead in Christ, and the Rapture of the church.

The profit that this knowledge brought to the Thessalonian believers can be ours, too, as we commit our hearts and minds to the study of the prophetic Word. The words of C.I. Scofield support this truth:

> We open the pages of the prophetic Word, and we see passing before us the magnificent panorama of the

> future of the nations. Our God unfolds to us that which
> He is doing here and there in this world; and not only
> that, He lifts the veil and shows us that which He is
> going to do in the future. Through the prophetic Word,
> and through that alone, we look over into the great
> hereafter, and see that which is to be. We look into an
> open Heaven with all its joys and glories, the goal of
> our own desire; and we look into an open Hell. All this
> is in the prophetic Word. The mightiest subjects, the
> greatest thoughts that can possibly fill the mind are
> those with which the prophetic Word is occupied.[2]

The proper study of prophecy also sheds light on false prophets and their heretical teachings. Concerning these false prophets, the Apostle Peter said: "Knowing this first, that there shall come in the last days scoffers, walking after their own lusts, and saying, Where is the promise of his coming? for since the fathers fell asleep, all things continue as they were from the beginning of creation" (2 Peter 3:3,4).

Speaking about this portion of Scripture, E. Schuyler English said:

> The last days are already here, dear friends, but we are
> not in the darkness that the day of the Lord's coming
> should overtake us as a thief. Through reading the
> Scriptures, we have been permitted to step behind the
> curtain of the future to discover ahead of time how the
> drama begins and unfolds.[3]

Without a doubt, one of the great advantages of studying prophecy is that it helps remove our ignorance concerning the Scriptures, protecting us from destructive heresies. In a day of such insecurity, the study of prophecy underlines the authority of God's Word and gives us the assurance and comfort we need.

The importance of addressing the problem of ignorance is demonstrated by the ministry of the apostle in Thessalonica where he possibly remained only three or four weeks.

Yet, in that period of time, Paul gave them an extensive study in prophecy.

Lewis Sperry Chafer refers to this in his introduction to eschatology:

> In the limited time of his stay in that city, he was con-
> fronted with heathenism but was able to make contacts
> with individuals and not only to lead them to Christ but
> to teach them enough truth that he would afterwards
> write the two Thessalonian Epistles to them with the
> expectation that they would understand them. In the
> second Epistle where the reference is made to the
> falling away, the "man of sin" who will sit in the
> restored Jewish temple declaring himself to be God and
> the destruction of the "man of sin" by the glorious
> appearing of Christ, Paul declares "remember ye not
> that when I was yet with you I told you these things."
> Assuredly, no clear evidence could be desired to estab-
> lish the truth that both Christ and Paul gave to the right
> understanding of prophecy a foremost place. There is
> no license granted here for a teacher to be a faddist in
> prophetic truth, nor is there any permission granted to
> men to ignore the field of prophetic revelation.[4]

A thorough study of prophecy addresses the problem of ignorance of God's Word and also forms a barricade against the barrage of false teaching from the many cults that have invaded Christendom today.

Dave Breese says in his book, *The Marks of a Cult:*

> The chief reason for the success of cults is the spiritual
> naïveté on the part of people. Far too many Christians
> are content with the superficial knowledge of the Word
> of God, thinking themselves spiritually intelligent.
> Nothing could be further from the truth. The Christian
> must give himself to a detailed study of Scripture and
> understand the Bible from a doctrinal point of view.[5]

Thinking of the tremendous profit of prophecy in rela-
tion to the Scriptures, the words of the Apostle Paul to young

Timothy are very apropos: "Study to shew thyself approved unto God, a workman that needeth not to be ashamed, rightly dividing the word of truth" (2 Timothy 2:15).

The Service of God: The Problem of Inactivity

The next benefit from a proper study of Bible prophecy is that it addresses the problem of inactivity in the work of God. As we study the great prophecies of the coming of our Lord Jesus Christ, we are moved to action. The study of prophecy should not produce a divisive spirit or a dormant spirit but a dynamic spirit resulting in service for our Lord. Some of the greatest evangelistic and missionary movements in this past century were born out of great prophetic conferences that motivated the participants of those conferences to share their faith and sound out the message of the coming of Christ. The truth that the study of prophecy should produce not inactivity, but activity, is underscored through Paul's very stern admonition in 2 Thessalonians 3:6 when he says: "Now we command you, brethren, in the name of our Lord Jesus Christ, that ye withdraw yourselves from every brother that walketh disorderly, and not after the tradition which he received of us."

Some members of the church at Thessalonica took the study of prophecy and the return of Christ as an opportunity for inactivity, leaving their jobs and living off the church. This was met with a strong word of correction from the Apostle Paul saying that those who did not work must not eat. Prophecy should never produce laziness or inactivity. Concerning this truth, Warren Wiersbe says:

> Misinterpretations and misapplications of the truths of God's Word can cause endless trouble. History records the foolishness of people who set dates, sell their possessions and sit on mountains waiting for the Lord to return. Any teaching that encourages us to disobey another divine teaching is not Bible teaching.[6]

Paul goes on to say in 2 Thessalonians 3:11: "For we hear that there are some which walk among you disorderly, working not at all, but are busybodies."

Not only does the proper study of prophecy produce work or service for God, but it produces the right type of work. Interestingly, we see in this text a play on words because the word *busybody* means to work all around, bustle about, to be occupied but as busybodies. That is, everywhere doing everything, but accomplishing nothing. An important benefit of prophetic study is that it produces not busybodies but people who are busy in the body of Christ, building it up, not burdening it down. This great truth is underscored as Paul writes to the church at Rome saying: "And that, knowing the time, that now it is high time to awake out of sleep: for now is our salvation nearer than when we believed" (Romans 13:11).

The understanding of the future culmination of our salvation at the return of our Lord Jesus Christ should motivate us to a life of productivity and purity. This was the very heartbeat of Paul as he wrote to Titus in Titus 2:11-15.

The study of prophecy is totally related to our spiritual walk and our work for Christ in this present age. Academics should never be divorced from activity in the service of our Savior. Roy B. Zuck says it well: "To have the academic without the spiritual is like having a car without gasoline or like having wood on a cold day with no match for a fire."[7]

B.B. Warfield said it another way: "Knowledge of the Word is a powerful thing ... and so is a locomotive a powerful thing providing it has steam in it."[8]

The study of prophecy must produce the steam of productivity in the work of God. Unequivocally, the pursuit of prophecy in my life has made me a more passionate preacher and productive worker in the service of my Savior. The words of the Lord Jesus Christ ring in my ears: "I must work the works of him that sent me, while it is day: the night cometh, when no man can work" (John 9:4).

The Savior and Worship of God:
The Problem of Indifference

One of the greatest profits or benefits from our study and application of Bible prophecy is that it focuses our lives on the Savior, the precious Son of God, and produces within our soul what A.P. Gibbs called the Christian's highest occupation, worship. This addresses the problem of indifference. Someone has said that history is "His story." As we look through history in the light of Bible prophecy we center on one Person, the Lord Jesus Christ, and as we focus on Him, we fall on our knees and worship Him.

The concept that worship must flow from our study of prophecy was heralded by Wiersbe when he said: "When worship and prophecy are divorced, the result is mere religious curiosity."[9]

On January 29, 1948, Jim Elliott, the soon-to-be missionary martyr at the hands of the Auca Indians, wrote in his diary while studying Genesis 35:

> Lord, I would recenter my spiritual life as Jacob does in this portion. Instead of Bethel he centers his experience on El-Bethel. Not the house of God, but the God of that house. Praise God, the Savior is exalted in heaven and there given His deserved place. As in earth, so in heaven. Even so come, Lord Jesus.[10]

Yes, the center of our worship is the God of the house of God. So it is not just prophecy, but the key person spotlighted by prophecy, the Lord Jesus Christ Himself, who calls us to worship. This becomes so clear as we read Revelation 19:10: "... the testimony of Jesus is the spirit of prophecy."

Concerning this passage, John Walvoord says: "This means that prophecy at its very heart is designed to unfold the beauty and loveliness of our Lord and Savior Jesus Christ.... Christ is not only the major theme of the Scriptures but also the central theme of prophecy."[11]

Concerning the importance of studying prophecy and its benefit of worship in the life of the believer, Charles Ryrie says: "It will help to make the unseen real and create within the believer's life the very atmosphere of heaven. One cannot do other than worship in reading the Revelation."[12]

A study of the book of Revelation should bring us to reverence the One who is the focus of Revelation, Jesus Christ Himself. Commenting on this truth, Gibbs states:

> The remembrance feast points toward a time when the Lord shall return, for we eat the bread and drink the cup only till He comes. The great hope of the church is the literal and personal coming again of the Lord Jesus Christ. It is a significant fact that about one-sixth of the New Testament is taken up with this great event and its far-reaching consequences to the church, to Israel, and to the world. Throughout the vast, eternal ages, the redeemed shall worship the Lamb that was slain and that liveth again.[13]

This causes us to sing the old hymn:

> Lord of glory, we adore thee, Christ of God, ascended high. Heart and soul we bow before thee, glorious now beyond the sky. Thee we worship, thee we praise, excellent in all thy ways. Lord of life, to death once subject, bless, yet a curse once made of thy Father's heart the object, yet in depth the anguish laid. Thee we gaze on, thee we call, bearing here our sorrows all. Royal robes shall soon invest thee, royal splendors crown thy brow. Christ of God, our souls confess thee, King and Sovereign, even now. Thee we reverence, thee obey, own thee Lord in Christ alway.[14]

The spotlight of prophecy turns to a future song of worship that the redeemed will sing around His throne. The words are as follows:

> ...Thou art worthy to take the book, and to open the seals thereof: for thou wast slain, and hast redeemed us

to God by thy blood out of every kindred, and tongue, and people, and nation; and hast made us unto our God kings and priests: and we shall reign on the earth....Worthy is the Lamb that was slain to receive power, and riches, and wisdom, and strength, and honour, and glory, and blessing (Revelation 5:9,10,12).

Wiersbe states:

Twenty-eight times in the book of Revelation, Jesus is referred to as the Lamb. The Greek word means a little pet lamb. The kind you would not want to see slain for any reason. The major themes of Revelation are all related to the Lamb. God's wrath is the wrath of the Lamb (6:16). The tribulation saints are washed in the blood of the Lamb (7:14). The story is consummated with the marriage of the Lamb (19:7) and the church is the Bride, the Lamb's wife (21:9). The heavenly throne is the throne of God and of the Lamb (22:1,3). Eliminate the Lamb and redemption from the Book of Revelation and there is very little left. We worship Him not only for who He is, and where He is, but also what He has done for us. The fact that He was slain indicates that He first took upon Himself a human body, for God as Spirit cannot die. When we worship the Lamb we are bearing witness to the incarnation as well as the atonement.[15]

One of the great by-products of a true worship of our Lord Jesus Christ is that it produces within our hearts a fervent desire to live a holy life for Him. In 2 Peter 3:11 the Apostle Peter expresses it this way: "Seeing then that all these things shall be dissolved, what manner of persons ought ye to be in all holy conversation and godliness."

Speaking to the fact of how true worship produces holy conduct, Scofield stated:

Let me say here that there is not such a thing as an abstract doctrine in Scripture. There is not a proposition of truth which is not intended by Almighty God to have an influence upon conduct. We know, and believe, and expect we shall be like Him when He shall appear; that we shall see Him as He is, and every man that hath this hope in Him purifieth himself even as He is pure.[16]

Yes, there can be much profit from studying prophecy. It addresses the whole problem of ignorance; increases our knowledge of the Scriptures, the Word of God; and enables us not only to have concepts but clarity in God's program and plan for the ages. Also, it will address the problem of inactivity in the service and work of God. The true study of prophecy will motivate us to be actively involved in His work. Last, but not least, the proper study of prophecy will lead us to worship the central figure of all prophecy, the Lord Jesus Christ Himself. As you move through the following pages of this book in your study of prophecy, may they be used to enlighten you in His Word, to enlist you in His Work, and to enthrall you in His Worship as we all bow before Him and sing with inflamed hearts of love, "Worthy is the Lamb that was slain, to receive power, and riches, and wisdom, and strength, and honor, and glory, and blessing."

For the testimony of Jesus is the spirit of prophecy.

REVELATION 19:10B

It might be asked, why is it so important to have the right interpretation of Bible prophecy? First, to not understand what the Spirit actually said would deprive us of one-third of the information contained in the Bible. Also, a proper understanding of prophetic interpretation is crucial to the understanding of several other doctrines, including evangelism and missions. The starting point is a commitment to the literal interpretation of Scripture. By this we mean one that is determined by the textual statements and includes corresponding historical references as determined in the text and as intended by the Divine author.

Chapter 2

How to Interpret Bible Prophecy

Charles U. Wagner

In a day when so many people are curious about the future, when people confer with crystal balls and tea leaves and even consult Ouija boards, it is important to note that the only voice of certainty about the future is God's voice, which comes from the Bible.

Bible prophecy is unique because only God knows and can declare the future. Isaiah, the prophet, wrote: "Who has declared this from ancient time? Who has told it from that time? Have not I, the LORD? And there is no other God besides Me" (Isaiah 45:21 NKJV).

Prophecy, which means both forth tell (proclaim) and foretell (predict the future) is God's way of communicating the future before it happens. It is foolish to think that prophecy is the product of men's intelligence or initiative because Scripture clearly states that the author of prophecy is God Himself. The Apostle Peter made this so clear: "no prophecy of the Scripture is of any private interpretation. For the prophecy came not in old time by the will of man:

but holy men of God spake as they were moved by the Holy Ghost" (2 Peter 1:20,21).

Concerning this concept, Stephen Olford states: "The body of prophetic teaching throughout the Bible is not of man's devising. On the contrary, holy men were so caught up by the Holy Spirit that they wrote supernaturally and infallibly. At times they wrote above and beyond their own experience."[1]

It is obvious that in studying Bible prophecy there must be a firm conviction that God has actually spoken and that all Scripture is God-breathed and given to us for doctrine, for reproof, for correction, for instruction and righteousness (2 Timothy 3:16). Concerning this conviction, Roy Zuck writes: "As a divine book, the Bible contains predictions of the future, which only God could provide. Many of the Bible's predictions of the future have been fulfilled, especially in the life of Christ. And yet numerous prophecies, some of them in startling detail, await fulfillment in connection with and following His return."[2]

The vastness of this study is aptly stated by Zuck:

> The range of prophetic subject matter in the Bible is wide. The Scriptures include predictions about Gentile nations, the nation Israel, individuals, the Messiah, planet earth, the tribulation, the millennium, life after death, and the eternal state. Some predictions pertain to events that were soon fulfilled, whereas others pertain to events that were or will be fulfilled dozens or even hundreds of years after the predictions. The former are sometimes called "near" prophecies and the others are referred to as "far" prophecies. Examples of "near" prophecies are these: Samuel prophesied the death of Saul (1 Samuel 28:16-19), Jeremiah prophesied the 70-year captivity in Babylon (Jeremiah 25:11), Daniel predicted that Belshazzar's kingdom will be taken over by the Medes and the Persians (Daniel 5:25-30), Jesus predicted that Peter would deny Him (Matthew 26:34), and

that Judas would betray Him (Matthew 26:23-25), Agabus prophesied that Paul would be arrested (Acts 21:10-11).[3]

In order to truly understand the Scriptures, a student must not only have the firm conviction that the Bible is the Word of God but also be converted or born again. This is clearly stated by the Apostle Paul: "But the natural man receiveth not the things of the Spirit of God" (1 Corinthians 2:14a).

But conversion alone is not enough, for the proper understanding of God's Word is only available to those who by their own will have made themselves bondslaves of the Lord Jesus Christ. It is interesting to note that *bondslave* is a word that many New Testament writers used to describe themselves. They call themselves servants of the Lord Jesus Christ or bondslaves. This is one who has submitted his will to the will of God and is resting not on his human intellect to understand Scripture but on the illuminating ministry of the Holy Spirit of God who is the Divine author of Holy Scripture. At this point it would be interesting to note the words of Jesus Christ: "If any man will do his will, he shall know of the doctrine, whether it be of God, or whether I speak of myself" (John 7:17).

Therefore, in the study of Bible prophecy, there must be a firm conviction that God has actually spoken and the one who desires to understand this prophecy must be converted and also committed to do the will of God.

The Importance of a Right Interpretation

The starting point for the proper understanding and interpretation of prophecy is a commitment to the literal interpretation of Scripture. By literal interpretation of Scripture, we mean one that is determined by the textual statements and includes corresponding historical references as determined in the text and as intended by the Divine author.

This is aptly stated by Elliott Johnson:

In the literal tradition there is this maxim: "The biblical text says what it means and means what it says, uniting what the text says (focusing on the verbal statement) to what the text means (focusing on the interpretation in communication)." Accordingly, there is no division of textual statements and construed meanings. The maxim is a warning against interpreting biblical statements equivocally in the sense of a single text sponsoring multiple, unrelated meanings.[4]

Johnson also states: "Literal interpretation formulates a system that takes what the Bible claims to be true of itself as a necessary framework for interpretation."[5]

It might be asked, why is it so important to have the right interpretation of Bible prophecy? First, to not understand what the Spirit actually said would deprive us of one-third of the information contained in the Bible. Also, a proper understanding of prophetic interpretation is crucial to the understanding of several other doctrines, including evangelism and missions.

Feinberg cites Lehman as follows:

Ultimately these differences (that is, in the matter of interpretation) affect evangelism and missions. The results are indeed far-reaching, and they extend into every phase of theological study. It has been pointed out that there is an affinity between premillennialism and fundamentalism and that the greatest strength of the liberal point of view finds its support in postmillennial and amillennial circles.[6]

The reason for this seems obvious. The abandonment of the literal interpretation of Scripture throws open the door to error. The rejection of the literal understanding of the Word of God leaves the meaning of the text to every man's imagination. The tendency, then, is to conform the text to a preconceived opinion.

Why Is There So Much Confusion?

In the post-apostolic age, many interpreters were influenced by the Greek theory of inspiration. For example, various allegorical interpretations of Homer's poetry were postulated. This allegorical method impacted the interpretations of the Old Testament by Alexandrian Christians such as Clement and Origen.

F.F. Bruce writes:

> To them, [Clement and Origen] much in the Bible that was intellectually incredible or morally objectionable if understood literally could be made intelligible and congenial if it was allegorized. By allegorization it was believed the intention of the Spirit who spoke through the prophets and apostles could be penetrated. But his approach was largely arbitrary, because the approved interpretation depended so largely on the interpreter's personal preference, and in practice it violated the original intention of the Scriptures and almost obliterated the historical relatedness of the revelation they recorded.[7]

This problem occurs when the interpreter seeks a deeper meaning in the text. He is in danger of reading into the text what he perceives to be that deeper meaning, rather than seeking the literal understanding of the text itself. This is especially true when studying prophetic Scripture.

Three Basic Views

Although much could be said about the different views of interpreting Bible prophecy, there are three basic views of the 1,000-year reign of Christ ("millennium") that need to be considered.

The Amillennial View

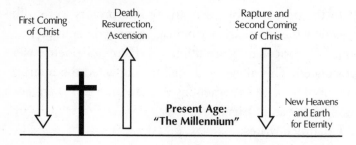

Those holding this view do not believe prophecy can be taken literally and that therefore there will be no literal millennium (amillennialism means "no millennium"). Prophecy is basically spiritualized. The book of Revelation, for example, becomes simply a description of the persecuted church. The amillennial view originated in the heretical school of theology in Alexandria, Egypt, at the close of the second century. Origen claimed that the Bible is one huge allegory and that it cannot be taken literally. Both Origen and Augustine applied the allegorical approach to the interpretation of prophecy and taught amillennialism. Amillennialism was later held by Luther and Calvin. The early church fathers rose up and emphatically refuted the allegorical interpretation of the Bible. They were able to restore the interpretation of nonprophetic Scripture to its normal, literal, natural, grammatical, historical meaning. Because the prophetic passages awaited fulfillment, however, it was more difficult to prove their literal fulfillment, and, unfortunately, many settled for a literal interpretation of salvation passages but a nonliteral interpretation of prophetic portions.

The Postmillennial View

Postmillennialism was developed by Daniel Whitby (1638–1725). He proposed that the world would grow progressively better until human history would climax in a

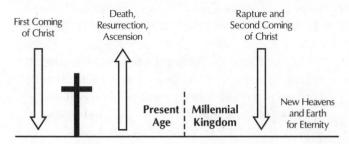

golden age of 1,000 years during which the gospel would be triumphant. He claimed that the preaching of the gospel would gradually improve the world until the conditions were so good they would be considered "millennial." This golden age would be consummated with the return of Christ to complement and reward His triumphant church. Sadly, this was accepted by many conservative theologians in the eighteenth and nineteenth centuries. This position also appealed greatly to liberal scholars who saw in its optimism a "biblical" counterpart to biological evolution.

A Brief Look at History. A brief survey of history shows how this postmillennial optimism came to an end. The first world war was to be "the war to end all wars." There was hope that through social change, a perfect utopia would materialize and the kingdom promised in Scripture would be realized. But, it was insisted, this depended upon man's best efforts and works. Wilbur Smith quotes James Snowden, a popular postmillennialist, illustrating the ridiculous claims and hopes of one holding this position:

> Man is hitching all his wagons to the great, golden, driving wagon of the sun … but now all such fetters are broken…. The majestic march of modern knowledge is one highway by which it [the kingdom of God] is coming unto the world … the sense of truth is growing finer and more exacting. Barbarism has been almost swept from the globe, and no slave now crouches

beneath any civilized flag. The world has found out the
natural worth of man; and the right of every man to
himself is now woven into the very texture of its civilization…. Property rights are being subordinated to
human rights…. Conscience is coming to its splendid
coronation. Politics is being subjected to higher ethical
standards than in former days, and is growing cleaner
and more honorable. Public opinion appears to be
growing purer and more powerful…. The world is
developing a world supreme court of international
law…. Humanity is beginning to realize its brotherhood…. After this war, Christianity will have a freer
field, and the world will be built along Christian lines of
justice, and truth, righteousness and peace.[8]

Subsequent events in the twentieth century demonstrate
that things are not getting better but worse. Justice, truth,
righteousness, and peace are far from being established on
the earth. It is, therefore, doubly discredited—both by recent
history and also by its subjectivity, which leaves man to his
own ingenuity, and provides no firm ground for interpreting
Bible prophecy.

John Walvoord says it well:

Postmillennialism is based on the figurative interpretation of prophecy which permits wide freedom in finding
the meaning of difficult passages…. As a system of theology based upon a subjective spiritualizing of Scripture, postmillennialism lacks the central principles
necessary for coherence. Each postmillennialist is left
more or less to his own ingenuity in solving the problem of what to do with prophecies of a millenium on
earth…. The result is that postmillennialism has no unified front to protect itself from the inroads of other interpretations. At best postmillennialism is superimposed
upon systems of theology which were developed
without its aid.[9]

In recent years, the abandoned postmillennial model has been resurrected in a new form named, "Dominion Theology." "Dominion" refers to the rule of Christian men over the earth. It also goes by the name, "Reconstructionism," which refers to the goal of reforming the institutions of society. It has also been identified as Theonomic Neopostmillennialism. "Theonomic" means "God's law" and refers to the intent to make the Law of Moses the basis of this Christianized earth. "Neo" means "new"–the new postmillennialism. If postmillennialism was so faulty, why has there been a resurgence? The answer probably lies in the frustration spiritually minded individuals have with present-day promiscuity and the absence of spiritual values in modern life. Neopostmillennialism is reminiscent of the Puritans and their application of the Mosaic code to civil life.

The prospect of legislating righteousness on a nationwide basis and changing human behavior without changing the human heart is doomed to failure. What is needed is divine intervention–which is exactly what will take place when Christ comes to judge the world and to bring in a righteous kingdom.

Addressing this problem, Thomas Ice states: "They are working to build a society that God has not purposed. There is the danger that they will become wrongly involved in this world's system."[10]

The Premillennial View

The premillennial view is based on a literal interpretation of Scripture. We believe the premillennial view is the correct one because it is the result of the proper principles of interpretation. In premillennialism, prophetic Scripture is read in its literal sense and approached like any other nonprophetic passage. This position takes very literal the biblical distinction between Israel and the church. A dispensational premillennialist believes that the next event, prophetically, will

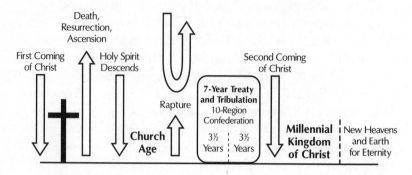

be the Rapture of the church followed by a period called the tribulation. Most of the book of the Revelation, when considered literally, describes Jeremiah's predicted "time of Jacob's trouble" (Jeremiah 30:7). After the tribulation runs its course, Christ will return with His church and will set up a literal kingdom on the earth. Several principles require this view to be the correct one.

Principles in Interpreting Prophecy

David Cooper, in *The World's Greatest Library Graphically Illustrated,* says it well: "When the plain sense of Scripture makes common sense, seek no other sense; therefore, take every word at its primary, ordinary, usual, literal meaning unless the facts of the immediate context, studied in the light of related passages and axiomatic and fundamental truths, indicate clearly otherwise."[11]

We should note that the early church held to a literal interpretation of Holy Scripture. This is well stated by Walvoord:

> From the first century, Bible scholars have held the Second Coming of Christ will be premillennial, that is, the Second Coming will be followed by a thousand years of Christ's literal reign on earth. This was a predominant view of the early church as witnessed by the early church fathers. By the third century, however, the Alexandria School of Theology, bringing in sweeping

allegorical interpretation of Scripture, succeeded in displacing the premillennial view. In the last centuries, however, premillennialism has been revived by biblical scholars and now is held by many who are orthodox in other respects. Unlike amillennialism and postmillennialism, the premillennialism interpretation has no liberal adherents as it builds on the concept that *the Bible is the Word of God and that prophecies are to be interpreted in their normal literal sense.*[12]

J. Dwight Pentecost, also supporting a literal interpretation of Scripture, writes:

> Perhaps the primary consideration in relation to the interpretation of prophecy is that, like all other areas of biblical interpretation, it must be interpreted literally. Regardless of the form through which the prophetic revelation is made, through that form some literal truth is revealed. It is the problem of the interpreter to discover the truth.... The reason a nonliteral method of interpretation is adopted is, almost without exception, because of a desire to avoid the obvious interpretation of the passage.[13]

The Biblical Imperative

What does Scripture itself say about the interpretation of prophecy? Again, the Apostle Peter's words come to mind:

> We have also a more sure word of prophecy; whereunto ye do well that ye take heed, as unto a light that shineth in a dark place, until the day dawn, and the day star arise in your hearts: Knowing this first, that no prophecy of the Scripture is of any private interpretation. For the prophecy came not in old time by the will of man: but holy men of God spake as they were moved by the Holy Ghost (2 Peter 1:19-21).

Both the negative and positive aspects are seen in this passage. Negatively, we are told prophecy is not of a private interpretation. Positively, we learn it came as holy men were moved by the Holy Spirit. "No private interpretation" means that one cannot come to a conclusion by one isolated passage. The whole has to be seen.

This is appropriately stated by Charles L. Feinberg:

> There are several well-defined laws for the interpreta-
> tion of prophecy. Scripture itself lays down the first and
> most essential of all. Peter tells us in his second letter
> that "...no prophecy of the Scripture is of any private
> interpretation." By this it is not meant that no private
> individual can interpret prophecy. The idea intended
> by the apostle is that no prophecy of the Word is to be
> interpreted solely with reference to itself *(idias spiluseos
> ou ginetai)*. But all other portions of the prophetic reve-
> lation are to be taken into account and considered.
> Every prophecy is part of a wonderful scheme of reve-
> lation; for the true significance of any prophecy the
> whole prophetic scheme must be kept in mind and the
> inter-relationship between the parts in the plan as well.[14]

The Time Perspective

When studying Scripture it should be remembered that often several events are listed in one passage. However, *time-wise* there may be great time periods between them. This is especially true as one studies the major prophets. I spent much of my ministry in Washington State. There, on a clear day, one could see several mountain peaks at one time from the Mount Rainier area. Although the mountains would be viewed as fairly close together, they were actually hundreds of miles apart. As there was a distance perspective in that picture with many miles apart, so there is a time perspective between the "mountain peaks" of Scripture. This is why the prophets inquired, "...what, or what manner of time the Spirit of Christ, which was in them did signify, when it tes-tified beforehand the sufferings of Christ, and the glory that should follow" (1 Peter 1:11). Often the two advents of Christ were listed together, when actually they were thousands of years apart. Time perspective is important.

Fulfilled Prophecy Shows the Way

Finally, it should be remembered that we need to look at prophetic truth and its fulfillment from the perspective of prophecy already fulfilled. Feinberg writes:

> In the interpretation of prophecy that has not yet been fulfilled, those prophecies which have been fulfilled are to form the pattern. The only way to know how God will fulfill prophecy in the future is to ascertain how He has done it in the past. All the prophecies of the suffering Messiah were literally fulfilled in the first advent of Christ. *We have no reason to believe that the predictions of a glorified and reigning Messiah will be brought to pass in any other manner.*[15]

While interpreting Bible prophecy, it is also important to consider the use of symbolic language and how it is used in Scripture. We must maintain a balance in the handling of symbols in the Bible. Some totally disallow symbolism and others read symbols into all of Scripture through their own wild imaginations.

Feinberg writes concerning this important balance:

> The language of prophecy is relatively free from symbolic language and is not smothered into incomprehensibility by so much symbolic drapery. Indeed, far too great liberties have been taken with prophetic truth; the like practice with regard to salvation truth would long have rendered it void as to the actual teaching of God's Word. We do not wish to be misunderstood in this particular, however, for we do believe that some prophecy is conveyed to us by means of symbolic language. But whenever such is the case, the symbols are explained in the immediate context, in the book in which they occur, or elsewhere in the Word, no room

being left to the imaginations of men to devise expla-
nations.[16]

We would be amiss if we did not mention that all of history is "His" story. Throughout Bible prophecy God desires
to put the spotlight on the Lord Jesus Christ. Perhaps the
focal point of all Bible prophecy is the coming earthly reign
of Jesus Christ as the long-promised Messiah. Relating to
this truth, Walvoord writes:

> Theologians have often pointed out that Jesus Christ is
> the center of theology because all the great purposes of
> God depend on Him—His Person and His Works. What
> is true of theology as a whole is especially true of escha-
> tology. Biblical prophecies about Jesus Christ begin in
> Genesis with the Garden of Eden and climax in the last
> book of the Bible, with its theme, "The Revelation of
> Jesus Christ" (Revelation 1:1). Accordingly, while
> prophecy in its broadest revelation deals with such great
> scenes as the history of the world, the divine program
> of God for Israel, and His plan for the church, central
> in all these great themes is Jesus Christ, the Savior, the
> ultimate Judge of all men, the final Victor over sin and
> death. All prophecy, whatever its theme, is ultimately
> connected in some way or other to the purposes of God
> in and through Christ.[17]

To sum up the principles for interpreting Bible prophecy,
we have considered the importance of following a historical, grammatical, literal interpretation of Scripture; the
importance of taking words of prophecy in the normal,
grammatical sense; the importance of recognizing the place
of figurative language but not abusing it; and the importance
of focusing on the coming Messiah and the establishment
of His literal earthly reign.

The sincere Bible student, with a right relationship with
the Lord, has the priceless privilege of reading prophetic
truth and understanding it as he applies the strict rules that
govern the literal, historical, contextual, grammatical inter-

pretation of Scripture. The study, then and only then, can be applied to his own life. Through a proper study of Bible prophecy the student will be comforted and encouraged with the truth that God is in complete control of the events of history. He need not speculate or wonder what God has said nor depend on some subjective allegorizing in order to find the meaning of the text. When Scripture tells him to "look for that blessed hope" he can do so with a confidence that allows this hope to impact his life spiritually. His pace in evangelism and missions is quickened knowing that he is commanded to serve the Lord while waiting for the Son from heaven (see 1 Thessalonians 1:10). He does so with a vision that is not vague, a hope that is not in vain, and an assurance that when Christ comes there will be ultimate and final victory.

Seventy weeks are determined upon thy people [O Daniel]...to bring in everlasting righteousness....

DANIEL 9:24

After Assyria and Babylon this Gentile dominion over Israel continued through Medo-Persia, Greece, and Rome. During the days of Roman dominion, Jesus Christ spoke the following ominous words, "Jerusalem shall be trodden down of the Gentiles, until the times of the Gentiles be fulfilled" (Luke 21:24). This statement implied that Israel would continue to be subject to Gentile domination into the future beyond the first century A.D.

Chapter 3

The Times of the Gentiles

John F. Walvoord

The Definition of the Times of the Gentiles

Very early in Israel's history God presented the nation with two distinct prospects for its future (Deuteronomy 28-30). First, God promised that He would bless the nation abundantly if it would "hearken diligently unto the voice of the LORD thy God, to observe and to do all his commandments." God would set Israel "on high above all nations of the earth." He would make that nation "the head, and not the tail." It would "be above only," and "not be beneath" (Deuteronomy 28:1,13). In other words, in return for Israel's obedience God would make it the dominant head nation above all the Gentile nations of the world.

Second, God also promised to curse Israel abundantly if it would "not hearken unto the voice of the LORD thy God, to observe to do all his commandments and his statutes" (Deuteronomy 28:15). For example, God would scatter the people of Israel among the nations "from one end of the earth even unto the other" (Deuteronomy 28:64). During that dispersion they would despair for life itself (Deuteronomy 28:63-67). In other words, in return for Israel's disobedience God would bring it under the domination of the Gentile nations of the world.

Concerning these two distinct prospects for Israel's future as a nation, God said, "I call heaven and earth to record this day against you, that I have set before you life and death, blessing and cursing: therefore choose life, that both thou and thy seed may live" (Deuteronomy 30:19).

Tragically, for centuries after God presented the nation with these two prospects, Israel repeatedly chose the second prospect of disobedience. God graciously sent prophets to the nation to warn it of the serious consequences of this choice, but the majority of the people of Israel did not heed the warnings (Jeremiah 7:21-28). As a result, during the eighth to the sixth centuries B.C., God used Assyria and Babylon as His instruments to conquer the people of Israel, remove most of them from their land, and scatter them as captives among Gentile nations (Isaiah 7:17-20; 8:7,8; 10:5,6; Jeremiah 20:4,5; 25:8-11; Ezekiel 23:1-30). This was the beginning of Gentile dominion over the nation of Israel.

After Assyria and Babylon this Gentile dominion over Israel continued through Medo-Persia, Greece, and Rome. During the days of Roman dominion, Jesus Christ spoke the following ominous words, "Jerusalem shall be trodden down of the Gentiles, until the times of the Gentiles be fulfilled" (Luke 21:24). This statement implied that Israel would continue to be subject to Gentile domination into the future beyond the first century A.D.

In light of what has been observed, the following conclusion can be drawn: The expression "the times of the Gentiles" refers to the extensive period of history when the Gentiles are the dominant world powers and the people of Israel are subject to those powers. In line with this, Norval Geldenhuys wrote, "It refers rather to the whole period during which the Gentile world-powers are in command, until the time comes for the 'saints of the Most High' to possess the kingdom (cf., Daniel 7:27)."[1]

During the time that Babylon was the dominant power, God gave significant revelation concerning "the times of the Gentiles." Some of this revelation came in the dream recorded in Daniel 2.

King Nebuchadnezzar's Dream

The Setting of the Dream (Daniel 2:1-30)

In 603 B.C. King Nebuchadnezzar, the greatest of ancient Babylon's kings, had a dream that disturbed him so much that he could not continue to sleep.[2] The king demanded that his wise men tell him both the content and interpretation of the dream. The wise men could not fulfill the king's demand (verses 1-13).

Daniel, a Hebrew prophet who was in Babylon as a result of the Babylonian captivity of the people of Israel, asked God to reveal the content and interpretation of the king's dream to him. God granted Daniel's request. As a result, Daniel was able to go before the king to fulfill his demand. Daniel told the king that it was the God of heaven (not the pagan gods of the Babylonians, which they believed came from the earth[3]) who had given him his dream. Daniel also stated that the dream revealed what would happen in the future ("the latter days" and "hereafter," verses 14-30,45).

The Content of the Dream (Daniel 2:31-35)

Daniel signified that the dream consisted of two major objects: an image and a stone. The image was human in form and was terrifying to see because of its huge size and brilliance. It had a head of gold, arms and breast of silver, belly and two thighs of bronze, two legs (from the knees to the ankles) of iron, and feet and toes that were a mixture of iron and clay.

The stone had been cut out of the side of a mountain without hands (cf. verse 45). This indicated that it was not human in origin. The stone struck the feet of the image with such force that the feet were crushed and the substances of the image disintegrated into the consistency of chaff. The wind blew away every remnant of the image. Then the stone became a large mountain that filled the whole earth.

The Interpretation of the Dream (Daniel 2:36-45)

It should be noted that in the interpretation Daniel moved progressively from the top to the bottom of the image. This downward movement represented the passage of time. Thus, the upper parts of the image portrayed earlier time, and the lower parts represented later time.

Daniel signified that the head of gold represented both the Babylonian kingdom and its great king (verses 38-39a).[4] Orientals regarded kings and their kingdoms as being synonymous with each other.

God represented Babylon with gold for two reasons. First, Marduk, the chief god of Babylon, was called the god of gold.[5] Second, Babylon used gold extensively in its buildings, images, and shrines. Herodotus, who visited Babylon 90 years after the era of Nebuchadnezzar, was astonished at the amount of gold there. Even walls and buildings were overlaid with gold.[6]

Babylon was to be succeeded by a second Gentile kingdom, represented by the image's two arms and breast of silver (verse 39a). That kingdom was Medo-Persia. Two arms coming together to form one breast pictured this kingdom well. Two distinct peoples, the Medes and the Persians, were united together in 550 B.C. under the same king to form one great power.[7]

Silver was an accurate representation of the Medo-Persian kingdom, because in ancient times silver signified money. Silver was the standard of value and the medium of exchange. Medo-Persia was noted for basing its power on money that was collected through an extensive tax system (Ezra 4:13; Daniel 11:2).[8]

Daniel stated that Medo-Persia would be inferior to Babylon. It was not inferior in military strength, for it conquered Babylon. It was not inferior in size, because Medo-Persia was a much larger kingdom than Babylon. It was inferior in one respect. As a partnership kingdom, it lacked the absolute unity that Babylon enjoyed.[9]

This part of the prophetic dream was fulfilled when Medo-Persia conquered Babylon in 539 B.C.[10]

Medo-Persia was to be succeeded by a third Gentile kingdom represented by the image's belly and thighs of bronze (verse 39b). This was the kingdom of Greece under Alexander the Great and his successors. One belly subdivided into two thighs was an accurate portrayal of the Grecian kingdom. After Alexander had unified his kingdom, he died at a young age. His kingdom was then divided among his four leading generals. But only two of those divisions played important roles in history. They headquartered in Syria and Egypt.[11]

God represented the Greek kingdom with bronze, because He knew that the Greeks would develop this metal and use it extensively in their implements of war.[12]

Daniel said that Greece would rule over all the earth, referring to the world then known to Daniel and his contemporaries. Alexander's kingdom ruled considerably more of the earth than did Babylon and Medo-Persia. This part of the prophetic dream was fulfilled when Greece conquered the Medo-Persian kingdom in 331 B.C.[13]

Greece was to be succeeded by a fourth Gentile kingdom represented by the image's two legs of iron and feet and toes of iron and clay (verses 40-43). This proved to be the Roman

Empire. Two legs were an apt portrayal of Rome, for the ancient Roman Empire ruled extensive areas of both the western and eastern divisions of the world. As a result of becoming huge in size, it was divided into two political divisions in A.D. 364—the Western Roman Empire with Rome as its capital and the Eastern Roman Empire with Constantinople as its capital.[14]

Iron was an excellent designation for the ancient Roman Empire for at least two reasons. First, ancient Rome was noted for its use of iron in its military weapons.[15] Second, Daniel indicated that, just as iron is able to crush gold, silver, and bronze because of its superior strength, so Rome would crush and shatter the ancient world (verse 40). Ancient Rome did that through its great military strength. This aspect of the prophetic dream was fulfilled when Rome conquered Greece by 146 B.C.[16]

As noted earlier, Daniel's downward movement on the image represented the passage of time. Thus, when he interpreted the last part of the image—the feet and toes—he was dealing with the final form of Gentile world dominion in time. The language of verse 41 indicates that the feet and toes were part of the portrayal of the Roman kingdom. Thus, they represented the Roman Empire in its final stage of existence in contrast with its earlier leg stage.

The legs of this fourth Gentile kingdom consisted of iron, but the feet and toes were a mixture of iron and clay. This distinction in substance also indicated that the Roman Empire would experience at least two distinct stages of existence—an earlier and a later stage.

Daniel interpreted the iron and clay mixture as follows: Just as iron is strong, so the final stage of the Roman Empire would be strong militarily. Just as clay is characterized by brittleness, so the final stage of the Roman Empire would be characterized by division. Different groups of people would combine with one another to form the final stage of the empire, but they would not adhere completely to one another, just as iron and clay do not combine completely with each other (verses 41-43).

It would appear, then, that the final stage of the Roman Empire would consist of a federation of several divisions. These divisions would federate for the sake of military strength, but they would not integrate to the extent of losing their ethnic and cultural identities. Because the image of the dream was human in form, it would have had ten toes. This indicated that the final stage of the Roman Empire would consist of a ten-division federation. Indeed, Daniel 7:23,24 signified that eventually the Roman kingdom would consist of a federation of ten divisions with ten equal rulers (cf., Revelation 17:12).

When was this feet-and-toes stage of the Roman Empire to exist? Because the Roman Empire never consisted of a ten-division federation with ten equal rulers in past history, one is forced to conclude that this stage of Rome's existence must take place in the future.

Sometime beyond the present there will be a revived form of the Roman Empire established. The empire that died in western Europe in A.D. 476 will be brought to life again in the form of a ten-division federation. It appears that the European Union will develop into that future revived Roman Empire. Leaders of the member nations of that union have been working toward such a federation for economic and even military strength, but with ethnic and cultural distinctions being maintained.

Daniel indicated that the Roman Empire was to be succeeded by a fifth kingdom represented by the stone in the dream (verses 44,45). This kingdom would be set up by the God of heaven, not by man. The characteristics of this kingdom would be as follows: It would never be destroyed; no other kingdoms would ever succeed it; it would end and destroy all the Gentile kingdoms portrayed in the image of the dream; and it would endure forever. These characteristics of God's kingdom would contrast sharply with those of the Gentile kingdoms.

Babylonian theology associated mountains with things divine. They called their chief god, Marduk, "The Great Mountain."[17] They believed that their gods came from the sacred mountain of the earth–the mountain they called "the Mountain of the Lands."[18] Their ziggurat temples were intended to imitate mountains.[19] In light of this Babylonian mindset, God portrayed His future kingdom first as a stone cut out of a mountain and second as a stone that becomes a great mountain (verse 35). He did this to make Nebuchad-nezzar understand that the fifth kingdom in the dream would be divine rather than human in origin. To emphasize this divine origin, God portrayed the stone as cut out of a mountain without human hands. But to prevent the king from concluding that this divine kingdom would be set up by Babylonian gods, Daniel made it clear that the God of heaven would establish it.

In the dream the stone struck the huge image on its feet, thereby causing the entire image to disintegrate. This indi-cated several things. First, the coming of the kingdom of God would take place when the last stage of Rome–the revived Roman Empire–is in existence. Second, when the kingdom of God comes, it will destroy the revived Roman Empire. Third, when God's kingdom destroys the last stage of the Roman Empire, it thereby will destroy all of Gentile world dominion.

In the dream after the stone crushed the entire image, the wind blew away every remnant of it. The Babylonians believed that wind is a divine activity. They called Marduk "Lord of the Wind."[20] This part of the dream was designed to make Nebuchadnezzar understand that divine activity would rid the earth of Gentile domination.

After every remnant of the image was removed from the earth, the stone became a great mountain and filled the whole earth (verse 35). The Babylonians pictured the earth as a great mountain. They called the earth "Mountain-house."[21] In light of this Babylonian concept, God portrayed His kingdom as a great mountain that filled the earth to make one thing clear—although the fifth kingdom will be set up by the God of heaven, it will be a kingdom on earth just as the four Gentile kingdoms have been. It will rule the earth of its day just as the Gentile kingdoms ruled the known earth of their days.

As noted earlier, the ancient Orient regarded kings and kingdoms as being synonymous. In light of this, the stone of the dream must represent not only the future kingdom of God, but also its king. Other prophetic passages of the Bible indicate that that king will be the person who is called the Messiah (Psalm 2:2,6), the Son of God (Psalm 2:4-12), and the Son of Man who comes with the clouds of heaven (Daniel 7:13,14). The Bible also indicates that Jesus Christ is that person (Matthew 16:16; 26:63,64). It can be concluded, then, that the stone represented both the future kingdom of God and Jesus Christ. It is significant that more than once the Bible refers to Jesus as "the stone" (Matthew 21:33-45; 1 Peter 2:4-8).

Because the stone represented both the kingdom of God and Jesus Christ, its appearance in the dream portrayed the coming of Christ to establish that kingdom. The fact that the Bible presents two comings of Christ prompts an important question: Would Christ establish the future kingdom of God during His First or Second Coming? Some have concluded that the divine kingdom of Daniel 2 was established by Christ during His First Coming, and that the kingdom is totally spiritual in nature. According to this view, the kingdom consists either of the church or the spiritual rule of Christ in human hearts, and the Gentile kingdom that was crushed by the kingdom of God was the ancient Roman Empire, not a future revived Roman Empire.

Others assert that the future kingdom of God foretold in Daniel 2 has already been established by Christ in a spiritual sense during His First Coming, but that it has not yet been established in its political sense. According to this view, Christ will not establish the kingdom in its political sense until His Second Coming.

Several things militate against both of these views. First, according to the imagery and Daniel's interpretation of the king's dream, the stone did not appear and destroy the image until the feet-and-toes stage (the ten-division federation stage) of the fourth kingdom (Rome). Earlier it was observed that this stage of the Roman Empire must yet be future, because that empire never consisted of a ten-division federation in the past. This prompts the conclusions that the coming of Christ portrayed by the dream must be His future Second Coming, and that the dream was indicating that the future kingdom of God would not be established until that coming.

Second, Daniel stated that the future kingdom of God would be set up "in the days of these kings" (verse 44). Because this statement was part of Daniel's interpretation of the feet-and-toes stage of the Roman Empire, "these kings" must be a reference to the kings who will rule the future federated revived Roman Empire (cf. Daniel 7:23,24; Revelation 17:12,13). Thus, Daniel's statement signified that Christ would come to establish God's kingdom when the future revived Roman Empire would be dominating the world, not when the ancient Roman Empire was the dominant Gentile power.

Third, the imagery of the king's dream suggested that there would be no coexistence of the Roman Empire and the future kingdom of God. The appearing of the stone represented the coming of Christ to establish God's kingdom. After the stone crushed the image, every remnant of the image was blown away before the stone became a great mountain and filled the whole earth (verses 34,35). This indicated that every remnant of Gentile world dominion, including its last form (the Roman Empire), would be gone before the future kingdom of God would be established to rule the earth.

In contrast with this imagery, both views that assert that the future kingdom of God foretold in Nebuchadnezzar's dream was established (in at least some form) during Christ's First Coming would require several centuries of coexistence of the Roman Empire and the future kingdom of God. It is a fact of history that the Western Roman Empire lasted more than four hundred years after Christ's First Coming, and the Eastern Roman Empire lasted more than fourteen hundred years after that coming.

Fourth, the imagery of the dream corresponds with the Apostle John's description of Christ's Second Coming and millennial rule. In Revelation 19 and 20, John indicates that Christ will crush Gentile world power at His Second Coming and then will rule the earth for a thousand years.

Fifth, those views that assert that the future kingdom of God foretold in the king's dream was established (in at least some form) during Christ's First Coming teach that the throne of God on which Christ presently sits with the Father in heaven is the throne on which He was to sit when He would rule over the kingdom of God (cf. Isaiah 9:6,7; Jeremiah 23:5; Luke 1:31-33). By contrast, several decades after Christ's First Coming and ascension to heaven He drew a distinction between the throne of God on which He presently sits with the Father in heaven and the throne on which He will sit in the future (Revelation 3:21). In addition, during His First Coming Christ indicated that He would take His seat on His throne when He comes in His glorious Second Coming and when He will give people entrance into the kingdom of God (Matthew 25:31,34).

Conclusion

Through the prophetic dream that He gave to King Nebuchadnezzar, God revealed that "the times of the Gentiles," which began in the eighth to the sixth centuries B.C., would continue until the Second Coming of Jesus Christ to the earth. This means that the Gentiles would be the dominant world powers and the people of Israel would be subject to those powers for an extended period of time. That period has continued now for more than two and one-half millennia and will continue yet for some time into the future. In spite of the fact that a nation-state of Israel was reestablished in its ancient homeland in 1948, approximately two-thirds of all the Jewish people alive at the end of the twentieth century are still scattered among the Gentile nations of the world and, therefore, are subject to the authority of those nations. In addition, in spite of its independent status, the state of Israel is often pressured to submit to the desires and criticisms of the Gentile world powers.

Not until the Second Coming of Christ will Gentile domination of the world be ended. Then, during His rule of the earth in the future kingdom of God, the nation of Israel will be the spiritual and political center of the world (Isaiah 2:2-4; 61:6; Micah 4:1-3; Zechariah 8:22,23; 14:16-19).[22]

... behold a fourth beast, dreadful and terrible, and strong exceedingly; and it had great iron teeth: it devoured and brake in pieces, and stamped the residue with the feet of it....

DANIEL 7:7

The beast that represented the Roman Empire was so terrifying and ferocious that there was no living animal that could represent it. The major thing emphasized concerning this beast was its overwhelming destructive power. With iron teeth it devoured and crushed everything in its way and trampled all else under its feet. This was an apt description of the ancient Roman Empire, for it was able to crush and shatter the ancient world in an unparalleled way through its great military strength.

CHAPTER 4

Revival of the Roman Empire

Renald E. Showers

A Significant Prophecy

More than 2,500 years ago God gave the prophet Daniel a significant prophecy in the form of a dream or vision. It is recorded in Daniel 7. In this prophecy God revealed the future course of Gentile world dominion from Daniel's time to the Second Coming of Messiah. The vision portrayed four great beasts coming out of a sea one after the other.

God used this imagery of beasts to reveal the following progression of Gentile world powers: Babylon (represented in the vision by a winged lion, verse 4), the great power in Daniel's day, would be succeeded by Medo-Persia (represented by a bear, verse 5). Medo-Persia would be followed by Greece (represented by a four-winged, four-headed leopard, verse 6). Greece would be conquered by Rome (represented by a dreadful nondescript beast, verses 7,8).[1]

The beast that represented the Roman Empire was so terrifying and ferocious that there was no living animal that could represent it. The major thing emphasized concerning this beast was its overwhelmingly destructive power. With iron teeth it devoured and crushed everything in its way and trampled all else under its feet. This was an apt description of the ancient Roman Empire, for it was able to crush and shatter the ancient world in an unparalleled way through its great military strength.

This unusual beast had ten horns on its head (verse 7). An angel told Daniel that the ten horns represented "ten kings" (verse 24). Orientals regarded kings and their kingdoms as being synonymous with each other (see Daniel 2:38-39 where Daniel equated King Nebuchadnezzar with his kingdom). Thus, the ten horns represented ten rulers and their realms. The fact that the ten horns were on the head of the fourth beast and were, therefore, part of it, indicated that the ten rulers and their realms belong to the Roman Empire.

The angel told Daniel that these ten rulers (and, thus, their realms) would arise out of the Roman Empire (verse 24). This statement implied that the Roman Empire would experience more than one phase of history. The first phase would be the beast or conquering phase (the ancient Roman Empire). A later phase would be the ten-ruler or ten-division phase.

The language of verses 8, 20, and 24 implied that the ten rulers would all be ruling at the same time. This, together with the fact that the ten rulers and their realms would belong to the Roman Empire, indicated that in this later phase of its history the Roman Empire would consist of a ten-division federation.

In a parallel prophetic dream that God gave to King Nebuchadnezzar of Babylon (Daniel 2), this later phase of the Roman Empire was portrayed as a mixture of iron and clay (verses 41-43). Daniel interpreted the iron and clay mixture as follows: Just as iron is strong, so the Roman Empire in this later phase would be strong. Just as iron and clay do not naturally mix with each other, so this later phase of the

Roman Empire would be characterized by divisions. Different realms of people would federate together to have influential strength, but they would not completely integrate or adhere to one another.

The combination of concepts from Daniel 2 and 7 signifies that this later phase of the Roman Empire's history would consist of a ten-division federation with ten equal rulers co-ruling at the same time. Ten realms would federate for the sake of strength in the world, but they would not integrate to the extent of losing their ethnic and cultural identities.

It should be noted that the Roman Empire in the past never consisted of a ten-division federation with ten equal co-rulers. That prompts the conclusion that this later phase of the Roman Empire is yet to come. In other words, there will be a revived form of the Roman Empire in the future.

A Significant Dream

The western half of the ancient Roman Empire fell in A.D. 476. Over the centuries since that time western European leaders have persistently held on to the dream of trying to continue or revive the Roman Empire. Several examples will be noted.

Between A.D. 768 and 800 Charlemagne, King of the Franks, brought more of western Europe under his rule than had been under one man since A.D. 476. It appeared that he would revive the Roman Empire. In fact, on Christmas Day, A.D. 800, the Pope crowned Charlemagne "Emperor of the Romans."[2] However, Charlemagne's realm fell apart after he died in A.D. 814.[3]

The idea of the Roman Empire was revived again in A.D. 962 when the German ruler, Otto the Great, started the Holy Roman Empire. This lasted until 1806 when Napoleon ended it.[4]

Napoleon craved the restoration of the forms of Roman imperialism, considered himself to be a Roman, and wanted to be an emperor. He thought that Europe should be ruled by one emperor who would have kings under him.[5] He laid plans "to reunite Europe in the bonds of an indissoluble federation"[6] which he referred to as "a United States of Europe."[7] On December 2, 1804, Napoleon crowned himself "Emperor" with a Roman crown of gold leaves.[8] Later he said, "I am a Roman emperor, in the best line of the Caesars."[9] But Napoleon's empire disintegrated after his defeat at Waterloo in 1815.

The idea of a Roman Empire was revived again when Bismarck, the Iron Chancellor of Germany, conquered France in 1870. In 1871 the Germans called their new empire "the Second Reich." They regarded it to be the continuation of the old Holy Roman Empire (962–1806).[10] The emperor of the Second Reich, Wilhelm I, was given the title "Kaiser" (the German form of Caesar). The Second Reich ended, however, in 1918 after Germany's surrender to allied forces of World War I.

On February 15, 1930, Winston Churchill published an article entitled "The United States of Europe" in *The Saturday Evening Post*. He encouraged a federation of European nations on the continent.[11]

Mussolini dreamed about a revival of the ancient glory of Rome.[12] When his black shirt troops occupied Rome in 1921, he said, "It is destiny that Rome again takes her place as the city that will be the director of the civilization of all western Europe."[13] On May 9, 1936, Mussolini proclaimed "the reappearance of the Empire on the fated hills of Rome."[14] Hitler declared that the Roman Empire had been resurrected through the efforts of Mussolini.[15] But by 1943 the course of World War II had gone so strongly against Italy and Mussolini that he was dismissed from office and imprisoned by decree of King Victor Emmanuel on July 25.[16] "So fell, ignominiously, the modern Roman Caesar."[17]

In July 1944, national resistance movements of Europe issued a joint declaration stating that "Federal union alone could ensure the preservation of liberty and civilization on the continent of Europe."[18]

In 1944 several German generals plotted to overthrow Hitler and Nazism. If successful, they planned to ask the western allies for an armistice and hoped for the establishment "of a 'constructive peace' within the framework of a United States of Europe."[19]

On September 19, 1946, Winston Churchill talked about Europe's ills at the University of Zurich: "What is the sovereign remedy? It is to recreate the European family, or as much of it as we can, and to provide it with a structure under which it can dwell in peace, safety, and freedom. We must build a kind of United States of Europe."[20]

From May 7 to May10, 1948, 750 delegates from all over free Europe gathered at The Hague and established the Congress of Europe for the purpose of unifying Europe.[21]

On March 25, 1957, statesmen from six western European nations met on the Capitoline Hill in Rome and established the European Economic Community (more popularly known as the Common Market and later called the European Union). Western European leaders expressed the hope that the Common Market would become the nucleus of a future United States of Europe.[22]

Konrad Adenauer, chancellor of postwar West Germany, stated, "I want to stay alive longer for only one reason—to see a United States of Europe in my time."[23] "The integration of Europe must be achieved. I am convinced that it is the sole salvation for the Christian West."[24] "The necessity for union for economic, political, and military reasons is incontestable."[25]

One observer of the movement for European unity stated that it "has reconceptualized and brought up-to-date the historic ideal of European unity, dating back to Roman times."[26]

It is interesting to note how many leaders over the years have dreamed of a federation of nations in Europe (a federation very similar to that revealed in Daniel 2 and 7) and have associated that federation with a continuation or revival of the Roman Empire (just as Daniel 2 and 7 associated their federation with a later phase of the Roman Empire's history).

A Significant Prospect

Developments within the European Union (EU) increasingly make it a significant prospect to fulfill both the revelation in Daniel concerning a future revived Roman Empire and the dream of western European leaders over the centuries. In the late 1980s, as the EU was actively pursuing the fulfillment of its goal of economic unity, one analyst stated that the European Union "is potentially the richest market the world has ever known."[27] Another declared that Europe "will finally be restored to the first rank of economic powers."[28]

Some analysts observed that a common economy could be the forerunner of a common political system. One writer stated that a common economy "is the absolute precondition for accomplishing the long-term European dream: a real political union that will restore Europe to its role as a world power."[29] Concerning some European leaders, Caspar Weinberger said, "the more ambitious of these planners really want a new, single country, the United States of Europe."[30]

In 1990 a Canadian television documentary, entitled "Birth of a Superstate," gave the following evaluation of the direction of western Europe: "Europe is moving to become the economic, political center of the world. It will also develop great military strength. One Europe, under one flag, will perhaps be the super power that will challenge the world of the twenty-first century." It also asserted that the common market is "evolving toward a European federation," and declared, "That ancient dream of one Europe diverse, yet strong and whole, seems to speak to this new age" and prompts "visions of a new golden age."[31]

In this documentary Jacques Delors, the president of the European Community Commission, which directs the European Union, stated, "My objective before the end of the decade is a real federation of Europe."[32]

During the weekend of December 15, 1990, leaders of the member nations of the European Union met in Rome and "reached an unprecedented agreement that will bring their elusive goal of a 'United States of Europe' closer than ever to reality." This agreement aimed "to develop a single European nation with its own form of money as fast as possible, and sooner than anyone thought likely."[33] Concerning this agreement, Jacques Delors said, "We have a rendezvous with destiny."[34]

The television documentary presented interview statements of key European leaders concerning the direction of western Europe. One person said, "A new empire is taking shape." A second asserted, "The world will never be the same." Another declared, "This is a major turning point of history." A fourth responded, "This is the end of an epoch and the beginning of another." Still another said, "If it works, it will be one of the most remarkable achievements of civilized human beings."[35]

In December 1991, leaders of the European Union crafted the treaty of Maastricht, which called for "a common central bank and single currency" for the EU by 1999.[36] In line with this, on May 1, 1998, 11 of the 15 member nations of the European Union committed themselves to the establishment of "an unprecedented new common currency."[37] The new currency was named the "euro." It was determined that, although the euro would not replace national currencies until 2002, businesses and governments would start using it in their transactions beginning January 1, 1999. In addition, it was determined that the new currency system would involve the supervision of one European Central Bank.[38]

The fact that the majority of member nations of the EU could establish a common currency that soon surprised many analysts. In fact, some doubted that they would ever be able to accomplish such a feat. In light of this, one analyst stated that "the achievement of the Europeans is impressive" and "the truth is, the euro is the greatest financial experiment in the past quarter century, and no one can foresee its consequences."[39]

Political union may be one consequence. Some European leaders are convinced that a common currency is essential for such union. For example, Helmut Kohl, the chancellor of Germany when the commitment to a common currency was made, stated, "Without economic and monetary union there will be no political union."[40]

A Significant World Ruler

In the prophetic dream of Daniel 7, an eleventh horn pushed its way up through the head of the fourth beast and uprooted three of the ten horns that were already there (verse 8). Verse 24 provides the interpretation of this imagery. It indicates that, sometime after the establishment of the future ten-division revived Roman Empire, an eleventh ruler will rise to power from within it while the original ten rulers will be co-ruling. This new ruler will overthrow three of those rulers. This implies that he will thereby gain the dominant position of authority over the empire and in essence become its emperor.

Daniel 7 and other prophetic passages signify that this ruler (now commonly called the Antichrist) will be an arrogant, blasphemous, absolute dictator during the last seven years prior to the Second Coming of Christ to earth. In the middle of that period he will set himself up as God in a new temple in Jerusalem (Daniel 9:27; 11:36,37; 2 Thessalonians

2:3,4), then will severely persecute Israel and those who refuse to worship him (Daniel 7:21,25; 9:27; Revelation 13:4-8; 20:4). His goal will be to bring the whole world under his rule on behalf of his master, Satan (Daniel 11:38-45; Revelation 13:1-8; 16:13-16; 19:19).

In light of this aspect of the prophecy concerning the future revived Roman Empire, several things should be noted. First, some western European leaders who were interviewed in the Canadian television documentary expressed the fear that the direction of the European Union is away from democracy. One stated that the present arrangement is not democratic because the European Community Commission that is leading western Europe toward unity is responsible to no one. It consists of a small body of leaders who make decisions totally apart from the voice of hundreds of millions of people who will be tremendously affected by those decisions. Another leader expressed the following irony: While eastern European nations are struggling to move from more than four decades of dictatorial oppression *toward* democracy, western Europe, which has enjoyed democracy for those same decades, is *moving away* from it. Concerning this trend, a third leader said, "I am shocked and afraid."[41]

Second, in 1994 three news reporters stationed in western Europe co-authored an article to the effect that western Europe is "disenchanted with democracy."[42]

Third, in the 1990 Canadian television documentary Jacques Delors stated, "We must have in Europe one political executive which can draw out common interests and fight for them."[43]

Fourth, Nadji Tehrani, publisher and editor-in-chief of *Telemarketing* magazine, asserted that, because of the cultural and social differences that exist in the member nations of the European Union, "A united Europe will need a *leader*—only *one* overall leader—to function effectively."[44]

In light of the Daniel 7 prophecy concerning Antichrist's rise to power from within the future revived Roman Empire, these statements, together with the shift away from democracy in western Europe, may convey an ominous implication for the European Union. The direction of Europe deserves close watch.

A Significant Number

Finally, the Bible consistently signifies that the future revived Roman Empire will consist of ten divisions (Daniel 7:7,20,24; Revelation 13:1; 17:3,7,12,16). By contrast, the European Union consists of more than ten member nations. In light of this contrast, how can the European Union be a significant prospect to fulfill the biblical revelation concerning a future revived Roman Empire? This contrast does pose a problem.

One possible solution to the problem is that some nations may drop out. A second possible solution may be found in the following statements from a western European bank advertisement in *Forbes* magazine: "The experts all agree; the Europe of the future will continue to be characterized by contrast and complexity. Not only because of its great linguistic and cultural diversity, but because Europe is about to be transformed into a continent of regions rather than of separate nations."[45]

In light of this, it may be that the biblical number ten is a reference to ten regions rather than ten nations.

Looking for that blessed hope, and the glorious appearing of the great God and our Saviour Jesus Christ....

TITUS 2:13

Even a casual reading of the revelation concerning the Second Coming (Revelation 19:11-16) demonstrates how dramatically different the Second Coming is from the Rapture. The Rapture apparently is not a public demonstration watched by the entire world as it happens suddenly and is quickly accomplished. On the other hand, the Second Coming will be a dramatic procession of Christ, saints, and angels from heaven to earth. This triumphant march will be seen by all earthdwellers, probably taking many hours, as Revelation 19:19 indicates that the armies of the world have time to set their strategy as they watch the Lord descending. The primary purpose of the Rapture is to remove the church from the earth to avoid the horrors of the judgments of the tribulation. By contrast, the purpose of the Second Coming is plainly stated as a time of judgment on the world and a preparation for the millennial kingdom.

CHAPTER 5

The Pretribulational Rapture

John F. Walvoord

One of the pressing theological questions facing the church today is the relationship between the church and the time of tribulation preceding the Second Coming of Christ. Amillennialists (and to some extent, postmillennialists) teach that the church will go through this time of trouble, looking forward to deliverance by the Rapture at the close of the tribulation and the return of Christ. By the time of the Second Coming, both the amillennialists and postmillennialists say the millennium will be completed. Therefore, in their view, the resurrection of the dead in Christ and the translation of the living church are events that immediately precede the final judgments (the Great White Throne Judgment and the Judgment Seat of Christ). It is only within the premillennial interpretation of prophecy that much attention has been paid to the doctrine of the Rapture.

What is true of premillennialism in contrast to amillennialism is also true of the pretribulational view in contrast to midtribulationalism and posttribulationalism. It is impossible to hold to posttribulationalism or midtribulationalism without introducing, to a considerable degree, the principles of spiritualization of prophecy. It is interesting to note how the specifics of the tribulation are often ignored by midtribulationalism and posttribulationalism. We must note, however, that even within pretribulationalism some do not keep Israel and the church distinct as to their Divine programs. Though widespread variation exists in interpretation of end-time events, the tendency has been for posttribulationalism to spiritualize the tribulation; whereas, pretribulationalism interprets it literally.

An important argument in favor of the pretribulational position is the fact that the Rapture is presented in the Bible as an imminent event. In none of the passages that predict the translation of the living saints and the resurrection of the dead in Christ are any events interposed as signs or indications of the approaching Rapture. In classic passages on the Rapture such as 1 Thessalonians 4:13-18 and 1 Corinthians 15:51-58, it is viewed as the immediate expectation of those who put their hope and trust in Christ.

This is made clear by the fact that the night before Jesus' crucifixion the disciples were greatly concerned when He said He was about to leave them. "Simon Peter said unto him, Lord, whither goest thou? Jesus answered him, Whither I go, thou canst not follow me now; but thou shalt follow me afterwards" (John 13:36). Then Christ told the disciples not to worry for He would return and take them to heaven. He said, "Let not your heart be troubled: ye believe in God, believe also in me. In my Father's house are many mansions: if it were not so, I would have told you. I go to prepare a place for you. And if I go and prepare a place for you, I will come again, and receive you unto myself; that where I am, there ye may be also" (John 14:1-3).

Although the promise was given by Christ in John's gospel, the full revelation of the Rapture of the church was given to the Apostle Paul. As we consider his teachings, it becomes evident that the Rapture of the church occurs before the tribulation period.

The Rapture in 1 Thessalonians 4:13-18: A Major Revelation

In determining the character of the Rapture, it is important to observe what 1 Thessalonians 4:13-18 does and does not reveal about it. In John 14:1-3, Christ revealed for the first time that He would come again to take believers, who were still alive, to heaven. The disciples were deeply troubled because Christ, after more than three and a half years of kingdom teaching, was not bringing in the prophesied kingdom as they had expected. They were further confused when He announced that He was going to leave them and that He would be betrayed by one of them. It did not fit their thinking at all that He would leave them before the kingdom was brought down to earth as prophesied in the Old Testament. Christ indicated plainly that He would be in heaven for a period of time, but that eventually He would return to take them to be with Him.

The disciples were totally surprised by this revelation as it was not what they originally had anticipated because at that time they had not even understood the difference between the First and Second Comings of Christ. It was not the appropriate time for Christ to explain to them that the Rapture is something different from the Second Coming. Accordingly, it was not until later that Paul revealed the Rapture doctrine as he does here in 1 Thessalonians 4:13-18.

In the background of this declaration in the Thessalonian epistle, other Scriptures make clear that after Paul's conversion, God took him into the wilderness and taught him some basic doctrines that he needed to learn, such as the church as the body of Christ composed of both Jews and Gentiles; the doctrine of salvation by grace; and also the truth of His coming for them. Accordingly, Paul in his missionary journeys emphasized two basic truths: first, that Christ died for our sins and rose again and provided salvation; and second, that He was coming again to take His own from the earth to heaven.

In 1 Thessalonians 4:13 he began by declaring, "But I would not have you to be ignorant, brethren, concerning them which are asleep, that ye sorrow not, even as others which have no hope." It is most significant that he addresses them as "brethren" because the doctrine of the Rapture, though not essential to salvation, is very important. God does not want Christians to be ignorant concerning the Rapture. The reason God gives us is that He does not want them to grieve when Christians die, because they have the certain hope that Christ might come at any time and take them all to heaven.

Paul states the certainty of this expectation in 1 Thessalonians 4:14, "For if we believe that Jesus died and rose again, even so them also which sleep in Jesus will God bring with him."

There was a time when the death and resurrection of the Messiah was prophecy in the Old Testament but now it is history. And although prophecy and history are equally certain, it has left no room for unbelief concerning His death and resurrection. He states that if they believe this, they can also believe with equal certainty the doctrine that Christ is coming for Christians who have fallen asleep, as well as for those who are living. In the verses that follow he explains what the Rapture is going to be like: first, in 1 Thessalonians 4:15, he states that it came to him by special revelation, "the word of the Lord"; and then he describes in the verses that follow what will actually happen. The Thessalonians wondered what would happen to the believers who had already died. They apparently had the idea that somehow they would have to wait for sometime after the Rapture before their resurrection.

Paul sets them straight. He points out what could be expected. He states,

> For this we say unto you by the word of the Lord, that we which are alive and remain unto the coming of the Lord shall not prevent [precede] them which are asleep. For the Lord himself shall descend from heaven with a shout, with the voice of the archangel, and with the trump of God: and the dead in Christ shall rise first: Then we which are alive and remain shall be caught up together with them in the clouds, to meet the Lord in the air: and so shall we ever be with the Lord (1 Thessalonians 4:15-17).

First of all, he points out that believers who have fallen asleep or who have died will be resurrected just a moment before living Christians will be instantly changed. First Corinthians 15:51-53 declares that Christians, whether living or dead at the time of Christ's coming, will be instantly changed to a resurrection body suited for heaven. Therefore, at that time, they will not have to wait for some future resurrection to see their dead loved ones.

Paul also describes what will actually happen. He points out that Christ is going to descend from heaven and command Christians everywhere to be resurrected if dead, or remarkably changed, if living. This is going to be accompanied by the voice of the archangel Michael, who has been fighting the forces of the demon world for thousands of years, and now a great victory is assured when the church is raptured. There is also the sound of the trumpet which 1 Corinthians 15:52 calls "the last trump." It is not the "last" trumpet chronologically in Scripture as there are other trumpets to follow, such as the one in Matthew 24:31, and the seven trumpets in Revelation 8:2-13; 11:15. This is, however, the last trump for the church. It will mark the departure of the church from earth to heaven. Christians are declared to be "caught up together with them." This could be translated "raptured together with them" as an accurate rendition of the New Testament's original statement. As a result of this, we will be with the Lord forever. Whether in heaven or on the millennial earth; in the new heaven, new earth, or New Jerusalem; they will be with Christ. On the basis of this, Christians are exhorted, "Wherefore comfort one another with these words" (1 Thessalonians 4:18).

We sometimes overlook a very important aspect of this revelation—what it does not say. The Rapture is presented here and uniformly throughout the New Testament as an event that could occur at any time. A preceding event is not mentioned in any Rapture passage. This is also true in 1 Thessalonians 5:1-11 and in 2 Thessalonians 2:1-12.

The Rapture Contrasted to the Second Coming

Even a casual reading of the revelation concerning the Second Coming (Revelation 19:11-16) demonstrates how dramatically different the Second Coming is from the Rapture. The Rapture apparently is not a public demonstration watched by the entire world as it happens suddenly and is quickly accomplished. On the other hand, the Second Coming will be a dramatic procession of Christ, saints, and angels from heaven to earth. This triumphant march will be seen by all earthdwellers, probably taking many hours, as Revelation 19:19 indicates that the armies of the world have time to set their strategy as they watch the Lord descending.

Also, in the Rapture (as opposed to the Second Coming), with the exception of Michael, there is no mention of angels or any disturbances in the heavens. At the Rapture, the movement is from earth to heaven, not heaven to earth. The Second Coming will be uniquely characterized by the heavens ablaze with the glory of God (Matthew 24:27).

The Purpose of the Rapture

Obviously, the primary purpose of the Rapture is to remove the church from the earth to avoid the horrors of the judgments of the tribulation. By contrast, the purpose of the Second Coming is plainly stated as a time of judgment on the world and a preparation for the millennial kingdom (Revelation 19:11-16). It is significant that there is neither a translation (Rapture) of saints nor a resurrection of saints at the time of the Second Coming, although there must be a resurrection of the martyred dead, apparently a few days after the Second Coming, to fulfill the promise to the martyrs in Revelation 20:4-6.

No Rapture at the Time of the Second Coming

Only One Rapture at the Beginning of the End Times

Though there are a number of resurrections in the New Testament (beginning with the resurrection of Christ and concluding with a seventh resurrection, namely, the resurrection of the wicked at the end of the millennium) on the day of the Second Coming itself, there is no resurrection and certainly no translation.

The Resurrection Following the Second Coming

According to Revelation 20:4-6, after the Second Coming of Christ, the martyred dead of the tribulation will be resurrected to reign with Christ for a thousand years (Revelation 20:4). They will have been killed (beheaded) a few years before the Second Coming because they would not worship the Antichrist as God. They are resurrected to enjoy and to serve in the millennial kingdom. Those who deny a literal millennium have a hard time trying to explain this passage. They have adopted a literary device, claiming that a recapitulation of church history begins in chapter 20, as if the prophecy reverts back to the First Coming of Christ. There is absolutely no textual support for this supposition, and the facts revealed in chapter 20 do not fit the present church age.

Revelation 20:1-3 says that Satan is to be bound for 1,000 years. This did not occur at the First Coming of Christ because Satan is not bound in the present age. It has always been true that Satan is restricted in his activities and could go only as far as the Lord permits (cf. the book of Job). His widespread activity, however, is clearly revealed in many passages in the New Testament, especially in 1 Peter 5:8, where Peter alerts us that "your adversary the devil, as a roaring lion, walketh about, seeking whom he may devour." We are exhorted to resist him. There is no indication that his situation changed with the death and resurrection of Christ, except that he is now condemned to a deferred execution. Several resurrections occur in the end times. The resurrection of the two witnesses (Revelation 11:11,12) occurs within the tribulation period. The martyred dead are raised several days after the Second Coming. The Old Testament saints may be raised along with the martyred dead (Revelation 20:4-6, cf. Daniel 12:2).

The word *first* is qualitative. It refers to the goodness of this kind of resurrection—it is a resurrection to everlasting life. The resurrection of the damned is not even referred to as a second resurrection, but rather the "second death" (Revelation 20:14). The use of the word *first,* therefore, does not preclude a prior resurrection, but simply identifies the respective natures of the two resurrections in this passage.

A further confirmation that there is no Rapture at the Second Coming, or in the days that follow, is found in Matthew 25:31-46, where the sheep and the goats are still intermingled several days after the Second Coming. If the Rapture takes place at the Second Coming or immediately before, the sheep would have already been taken out of the world, leaving only the goats for judgment at the Second Coming. The fact that they are intermingled some time after the Second Coming demonstrates that there will have been no Rapture at the time. As a matter of fact, these flesh and blood believers cannot be raptured because they are the ones who populate the millennial earth. This natural continuance of human biological life is pictured in Isaiah 65, wherein millennial saints plant crops, build houses, bear children, live, die, and even sin.

The Imminency of the Rapture

No Signs of the Rapture

The Bible never gives a sign of the Rapture but instead instructs us to be looking for His coming (cf. Titus 2:11-13). We are never encouraged to look for the day of the Lord. We are never encouraged to look for the Antichrist or any of the other events that lead up to the Second Coming. Instead, the Rapture is pictured as the next major event that will take us from earth to heaven. Conversely, there are signs of the Second Coming, such as the Antichrist erecting the abomination of desolation in the temple three and one-half years before the Second Coming (Matthew 24:15), but no Rapture is associated with the Second Coming. There are signs for the Second Coming, but none for the Rapture.

No Rapture in any Second Coming Passage

Adherents to the posttribulation view often appeal to Matthew 24 as proof that there will be a Rapture at the end of the tribulation. A close examination of Matthew 24 reveals no indication of either resurrection or Rapture, and this idea has been read into the passage without justification or support. Many interpreters confidently refer to the disciples as knowing all about the Rapture, but there is no proof of this whatsoever. In fact, the disciples were so focused on the establishment of a physical kingdom here on the earth that they demonstrate no understanding of a difference between the Rapture and the Second Coming as would be necessary in the posttribulational view.

Appeal is sometimes made to Matthew 24:36-42 where the Second Coming is likened to the days of Noah when the flood came and took away those who were not in the ark, as though this is a reference to the Rapture. To do this, however, completely reverses the illustration of the flood because at the flood the ones "taken away" were "taken" in judgment and put to death as Matthew 25 indicates will happen to the goats. Further, in Luke 17:34-37, a parallel passage, the disciples asked the Lord where those taken are to be found. When they asked this question, he replied in verse 37, "Wheresoever the body is, thither will the eagles be gathered together." In other words, those taken are put to death and their bodies will be eaten by the vultures. It is clear that this passage in Matthew is just the reverse of the Rapture where the one taken is taken in salvation and the one left is left for the tribulation. In contrast here, the one taken, is taken in judgment, and the one who is left, is the saint who is going to enter into the millennial kingdom.

The Day of the Lord

Further study of 1 and 2 Thessalonians reveals support for an imminent pretribulational Rapture. First Thessalonians 5:1 impacts the timing of the Rapture. In the context, it is stated that the day of the Lord will begin only after the church is safely removed in the Rapture. Paul writes,

> But of the times and the seasons, brethren, ye have no need that I write unto you. For yourselves know perfectly that the day of the Lord so cometh as a thief in the night. For when they shall say, Peace and safety; then sudden destruction cometh upon them, as travail upon a woman with child; and they shall not escape. But ye, brethren, are not in darkness, that that day should overtake you as a thief (1 Thessalonians 5:1-4).

In his discussion of the doctrine of the day of the Lord, he states that he does not need to write to them concerning the "times and the seasons," that is, the general sequence that leads up to the coming of the day of the Lord. This is in contrast to 1 Thessalonians 4:13, where he implies that they *were* ignorant of the timing and nature of the Rapture. Here in 1 Thessalonians 5:1-11, he tells them that they already know the facts concerning the times and the seasons, namely, that (a) the coming of the day of the Lord will be abrupt ("like a thief," verse 2) and (b) the removal of the church precedes the day of the Lord (verses 4 and 9).

The expression, "the day of the Lord," is a common one in both Old and New Testaments. It refers to that extended period of time when the Lord deals directly with human sin through various forms of Divine judgment. The Old Testament commonly speaks of the day of the Lord as a period characterized as "a day of darkness and gloominess, a day of clouds and thick darkness" (Joel 2:2). When "all the inhabitants of the land tremble" (Joel 2:1); when there will be warfare and destruction of the land (see Joel 2:3-9); when "the earth shall quake before them; the heavens shall tremble: the sun and moon shall be dark, and the stars shall withdraw their shining" (Joel 2:10).

As Joel explains, the day of the Lord is "great and very terrible; and who can abide it?" (Joel 2:11). It is, therefore, a period of Divine judgment preceding the return of Christ to the earth. However, according to Zephaniah 3:14-20, it will also include a time of rejoicing which will follow the day of judgment (Zephaniah 1:14-18). From these various passages it is concluded that the day of the Lord includes not only a time of the tribulation subsequent to the Rapture but also the entire 1,000-year reign of Christ on earth.

In the perspective of a Thessalonian church, they were living in the day of grace, the present dispensation during which God is gathering out both Jews and Gentiles to form one body—the church. When the Rapture occurs, this work of God will be brought to a close and the day of the Lord will begin. Though not all of the major events will take place immediately, the period will extend from the Rapture to the end of the millennium. This, in turn, will be followed by the "day of God" (2 Peter 3:12) when the heavens and the earth are destroyed with fire and a new heaven and a new earth are created. This destruction, predicted by Peter as occurring in the day of the Lord, is actually the transition from the day of the Lord to the eternal day of God.

Between 1 and 2 Thessalonians apparently false teachers came into the Thessalonian church and told them that their sufferings meant they were already in the day of the Lord. This disturbed the Thessalonians greatly because they wondered if they had missed the Rapture. When Paul heard this he wrote 2 Thessalonians to refute the rumor that they were already in the day of the Lord. In 2 Thessalonians 2:1 Paul states emphatically that the day of the Lord has not begun and will not until the lawless (the Antichrist) is revealed.

> Now we beseech you, brethren, by the coming of our Lord Jesus Christ, and by our gathering together unto him, that ye be not soon shaken in mind, or be troubled, neither by spirit, nor by word, nor by letter as from us, as that the day of Christ is at hand. Let no man deceive you by any means: for that day shall not come, except there come a falling away first, and that man of sin be revealed, the son of perdition; who opposeth and exalteth himself above all that is called God, or that is worshipped; so that he as God sitteth in the temple of God, shewing himself that he is God. Remember ye not, that, when I was yet with you, I told you these things? (2 Thessalonians 2:1-5).

Careful distinction should be made here between the day of the Lord beginning and the day of the Lord coming, a distinction overlooked by many interpreters. It can be said that the day of the Lord "comes" with the Rapture of the church, but it doesn't "begin" until the Antichrist signs the seven-year treaty with Israel (his "revelation" and the start of the judgments in Revelation). Chronologically, therefore, the day of the Lord *begins* after the Rapture. The interval between the Rapture and the start of the day of the Lord is undetermined in Scripture but apparently is only a short interval of time. With the moderating influence of the church removed, it will not take long for Satan to move in the hearts of unsaved men. The event that will mark the beginning of the day of the Lord is the emergence of the man of sin, the Antichrist (2 Thessalonians 2:3). Matthew 24:15, 2 Thessalonians 2:4, and Revelation 13:15 speak of his ultimate revelation as the "abomination of desolation"—the image of the Antichrist that is placed in the temple at the mid-point of the seven-year tribulation period, breaking his protection-treaty with Israel. However, a careful study reveals that he is actually revealed much earlier than the mid-point of the tribulation. First, the predicted covenant-breaker will also be the covenant-signer at the beginning of the seven years. Additionally, he has to have political power before he can make such a treaty. Daniel 7:7 says he will rise to power in the area of the ancient Roman Empire, initially overthrowing three kings and then dominating the seven remaining rulers, uniting ten countries or regions into a revived Roman Empire. This would have to occur more than seven years before the Second Coming and would unmistakably identify him as the one who is going to rule the world during the tribulation period. According to Paul, this man cannot be revealed before the church is raptured (because the Holy Spirit–empowered church constrains the activities of Satan). Therefore, the Rapture must take place more than seven years before the Second Coming. This eliminates all views except pretribulationalism.

Though this is emphatically denied by many, it seems to be the key to understanding the great prophecies concerning the Rapture as an imminent event.

Paul adds a second emphatic reason for saying that they were not in the tribulation in 2 Thessalonians 2:5-12. Paul states in verse 6 that they know that what is holding back sin is that the sinfulness of man can be revealed in the proper time, "And now ye know what withholdeth that he might be revealed in his time." He adds, "For the mystery of iniquity doth already work: only he who now letteth will let, until he be taken out of the way. And then shall that Wicked be revealed, whom the Lord shall consume with the spirit of his mouth, and shall destroy with the brightness of his coming: Even him, whose coming is after the working of Satan with all power and signs and lying wonders, and with all deceivableness of unrighteousness in them that perish" (2 Thessalonians 2:7-10a). Although there has been considerable discussion as to whom this restrainer is, it seems that the only restraint adequate to control Satan is the power of the Holy Spirit. Since Pentecost, the Holy Spirit has indwelt believers and the church in a unique and powerful way. This Holy Spirit-empowered entity has been God's major tool for holding back the tide of wickedness.

Paul states that the restrainer will be taken away. Because the Holy Spirit is everywhere as a spirit being, this obviously must be referring to the body the Holy Spirit empowers. The Holy Spirit will be "taken away" as the bodies He indwells are suddenly removed in the Rapture— a reversal of Pentecost! Earlier, Christ had told the disciples "for he dwelleth with you, and shall be in you" (John 14:17). In the period before Pentecost, the Holy Spirit ministered to people as one who was "with them." At Pentecost, due to the completed cross-work of Christ and as part of God's plan for this new organism, "the church," the Holy Spirit came in power and was "in them." At the Rapture of the church, apparently the ministry of the Spirit returns to what it was prior to the day of Pentecost, although certainly He works mightily through the two witnesses and the 144,000 so that countless millions are saved by His convicting power even in the world's darkest hour.

Accordingly, there are two major proofs provided in 2 Thessalonians 2 that they were not in the day of the Lord:

(a) the Antichrist had not been revealed, and (b) the Holy Spirit's tool of restraint had not been removed. Putting these facts together, the prophetic perspective, therefore, is for three general periods: the first, the day of grace or the present age; next, the day of the Lord from the Rapture to the end of the millennium; and then the day of God—the eternal day.

The Practical Value of the Rapture

It should be clear that only the imminent nature of the Rapture as taught in pretribulationalism allows the doctrine to be a source of joy (1 Thessalonians 4:18), encouragement (1 Corinthians 15:58), or warning to be ready so as not to be embarrassed when He comes (1 John 3:3). The total absence of any exhortation to look for events other than the Rapture is confirming proof that the Rapture is the next major event in God's prophetic timetable and precedes the massive end-time prophecies of which the Scriptures speak. We are told to look for the return of Jesus Christ, not the coming of the Antichrist!

Wherefore comfort one another with these words.

1 THESSALONIANS 4:18

Revelation 5 narrates a heavenly scene of Christ pictured as a slain, but victorious Lamb. The Lamb is pictured as worthy to open the seals on a scroll that result in judgment—the judgment described in the succeeding chapter as the seal judgments. In chapter 6, each one of the seal judgments commences as a result of the Lamb's breaking of each seal (Revelation 6:1,3,5,7,9, 12). Because all six seal judgments begin the same way, with the breaking of the seal by the Lamb, one should not be at all surprised that Revelation 6:16,17 summarize all six judgments as "the wrath of the Lamb" and "the great day of his wrath."

CHAPTER 6

An Examination of "The Pre-Wrath Rapture" View

Thomas D. Ice

In the 1980s, Robert Van Kampen, a Christian business-man, developed a new view of the timing of the Rapture. After eliminating pretribulationalism and then posttribula-tionalism,[1] he concluded that Christians will be raptured about three-quarters of the way through the seven-year tribulation period.[2] Mr. Van Kampen recruited Marvin Rosenthal, and they entitled their new view "the *pre-wrath* Rapture position."[3] Their new view was introduced to the public in 1990 through Mr. Rosenthal's book, *The Pre-Wrath Rapture of the Church*,[4] followed in 1992 by Mr. Van Kampen's *The Sign*.[5] In this short chapter, I will examine a few key, but crucial, mistakes—in light of Scripture—that have given rise to this recent prophetic error.

What Is the Pre-Wrath Rapture?

Although Van Kampen and Rosenthal produce a great deal of detail relating to many issues in their books, the thrust of their position is that the church will be raptured before God pours out His wrath upon the world about 21 months before Christ's Second Advent. Rosenthal writes:

> It will be demonstrated that the seals of Revelation 6 represent the climactic actions of unregenerate men and that believers will not be exempt from those difficult days. The trumpets and bowls, in contrast, originate with God—they are His final wrath on an unbelieving world. God's children will be delivered from that day. That is the "blessed hope."… the objective of this volume is to demonstrate that the day of the Lord is the time of divine wrath. It will be recognized as about to begin by the cosmic disturbances associated with the sixth seal (Joel 2:10,11, 30,31; Revelation 6:12-17; cf. Matthew 24:29) and will begin with the opening of the seventh seal (Revelation 8:1). The Rapture of the church will immediately precede the day of the Lord. The day of the Lord will begin sometime within the second half of Daniel's seventieth week.[6]

This view Van Kampen and Rosenthal term "the pre-wrath Rapture."

The essentials of this new teaching—the pre-wrath Rapture—could be summarized as follows:

- The church will be raptured before the time of God's wrath.

- The time of God's wrath is limited to the day of the Lord.

- The day of the Lord does not consist of the entire seven years of the seventieth week of Daniel, but only the final quarter (21 months).

The Van Kampen/Rosenthal innovation differs from the pretribulational view at key points. Pretribulationists agree with Van Kampen/Rosenthal that the church will escape the time of God's wrath. However, pretribulationalism begins the time of God's wrath and the day of the Lord with the beginning of the seven years of the seventieth week of Daniel. Thus, I believe that Scripture supports the pretribulational teaching that the church will be raptured before the entire seventieth week of Daniel.

Rapture Before Wrath

1 Thessalonians 1:10 admonishes the church "to wait for his [God's] Son from heaven," because Christ "delivered us from the wrath to come." 1 Thessalonians 5:9 echoes this promise when Paul tells the church that "God hath not appointed us to wrath, but to obtain salvation by our Lord Jesus Christ." Further, Paul tells the church in Romans 5:9 that in addition to "being now justified by his blood," believers "shall be saved from wrath through him." Our Lord, speaking through John promises the church: "I also will keep thee from the hour of temptation, which shall come upon all the world, to try them that dwell upon the earth" (Revelation 3:10). Van Kampen agrees with pretribulationists that the church will not pass through the time of God's wrath. He says,

> The pretribulation position argued that the church would not see the wrath of God, primarily using Romans 5:9, 1 Thessalonians 1:10, 5:9, and Revelation 3:10 as their proof-texts. I had no choice but to agree because that was what the Bible clearly appeared to teach.[7]

Although in agreement on the church's exemption from the time of God's wrath, Van Kampen believes that pretribulationists err in their understanding that "the entire seven-year tribulation period [is] the wrath of God."[8] This provides a major basis for disagreement between Van Kampen/Rosenthal and pretribulationalism.

God's Wrath

Van Kampen/Rosenthal chop the seven years of Daniel's seventieth week into a sequence of unwarranted compartments. They divide the seven years into the following parts:

- The first half is labeled the beginning of sorrows.
- The first half of the second half is called the Great Tribulation.
- The final 21 months are tagged the day of the Lord.[9]

For Van Kampen/Rosenthal only the final period—the day of the Lord—is a time of God's wrath. They see the first three-quarters as the wrath of man and Satan. But does the Bible make such distinctions? I do not believe it does.

Wrath in Zephaniah

Zephaniah 1:14-18 heaps together a number of terms that characterize the future day of the Lord. Verse 14 labels this time as "the great day of the Lord" and "the day of the Lord." Then verses 15-18 describe this time with the following description: "That day is a day of wrath, a day of trouble and distress, a day of wasteness and desolation, a day of darkness and gloominess, a day of clouds and thick darkness, a day of the trumpet and alarm....I will bring distress upon men....the day of the Lord's wrath." The context supports the conclusion that all these descriptives apply to the day of the Lord. Such biblical usage does not allow an interpreter to chop the day of the Lord into compartmental segments as Van Kampen/Rosenthal insist. The text plainly says that the day of the Lord is a time of both tribulation and God's wrath. All of the many descriptives in this passage provide a characterization of the day of the Lord that applies to the entire period. The Zephaniah passage clearly contradicts the basis upon which Van Kampen/Rosenthal attempt to build their recently developed theory. Zephaniah is not alone in providing an obstacle to the Van Kampen/Rosen-thal speculation.

Wrath in Revelation

Revelation 6:1-17 records the six seal judgments, which are the first reported judgments of the tribulation. Revelation 6 and the seal judgments also contradict the Van Kampen/Rosenthal formulation because the Bible describes all six judgments as "...the wrath of the Lamb: For the great day of his wrath is come...." (Revelation 6:16c-17a). Revelation 5 reveals that only the Lamb (Christ) was qualified to open the seals that would begin the first judgments of the tribulation. As we connect the dots of Revelation 5 and 6, there is no basis for saying that the events of the seal judgments are somehow disconnected from Scripture's characterization as God's wrath. The following observations about the seal judgments support such a connection:

- The Lamb is the individual who breaks, and thus initiates, all six of the seals (Revelation 6:1,3,5,7,9,12) clearly indicating that He (God) is the source of the events or wrath. These are explicit references to the wrath of God, not the wrath of man or Satan as taught by Van Kampen/Rosenthal.

- One-quarter of the earth's population is killed (Revelation 6:8).

- At the end of the six seal judgments an assessment is given as follows: "Fall on us, and hide us from the face of him that sitteth on the throne, and from the wrath of the Lamb: For the great day of his wrath is come; and who shall be able to stand?" (Revelation 6:16,17). "Him that sitteth on the throne" is God the Father as indicated in chapter 4, thus it is clearly God's wrath. It is also the Lamb's wrath (Christ). The passage clearly says "the great day of his wrath is come," meaning that all six of the seal judgments are classified as God's wrath.

Van Kampen/Rosenthal attempt to demonstrate that the events of the seal judgments are not really "God's" wrath, but the wrath of man. Rosenthal declares, "The word *wrath* occurs eight times in the book of Revelation. All eight occurrences follow the opening of the sixth seal. The word *wrath* is never used in connection with the first five seals."[10] It might seem, at first glance, that the fifth seal (which reveals the martyred souls in heaven) is clearly a case of man's or Satan's wrath. The issue here, however, is not how the martyrs died, but rather that their death will be avenged by the wrath of the Lamb—the topic of the whole chapter.

Rosenthal neglects to tell his readers that Revelation 6:16,17 is a summary statement of all the previous seal judgments. In spite of the Van Kampen/Rosenthal claim to follow the plain interpretation of the text,[11] I believe that Revelation 6:16,17 relates to all six seal judgments for the following reasons:

- Revelation 6:15-17 is a report of the human response to God's judgment. A similar evaluation is recorded after the trumpet judgments in Revelation 9:20,21. In both cases, humanity does not repent so God continues prosecution of the war. This argues in favor of associating this report with the preceding seal judgments.

- The controlling verb in verse 17, "is come" *(êlthen)*, "is aorist indicative, referring to a previous arrival of the wrath, not something that is about to take place."[12] Rosenthal's attempt to say that this verb is a future aorist[13] cannot be supported by the context. Such contextual support is necessary to adopt his unusual use of the aorist indicative. Further, if a future look was intended by the verb then John most likely would have used the future tense.

• Revelation 5 narrates a heavenly scene of Christ pictured as a slain, but victorious Lamb. The Lamb is pictured as worthy to open the seals on a scroll, which result in judgment—the judgment described in the succeeding chapter as the seal judgments. In chapter 6, each one of the seal judgments commences as a result of the Lamb's breaking of each seal (Revelation 6:1,3,5,7,9,12). Because all six seal judgments begin the same way, with the breaking of the seal by the Lamb, one should not be at all surprised that Revelation 6:16,17 summarize all six judgments as "the wrath of the Lamb," and "the great day of his wrath."

This information provides ample biblical proof that all six seal judgments are the wrath of God (the Lamb). The Van Kampen/Rosenthal view teaches, as do pretribulationists, that the first seal judgment (the rise of Antichrist) begins in the first part of the seventieth week of Daniel, right after the seven-year period commences.[14] Because all six seal judgments are designated in Scripture as God's wrath it means that the entire seventieth week of Daniel is called the wrath of God in Revelation 6. Therefore, this passage does not support the Van Kampen/Rosenthal interpretation. Because the church is promised deliverance from the wrath of God (Romans 5:9; 1 Thessalonians 1:10, 5:9; and Revelation 3:10), it is clear in light of Revelation 6 that the church will be raptured before the seventieth week of Daniel.

The Day of the Lord

Another key point has been noted by Robert Thomas about the language of the text in Revelation 6:17 that argues against the Van Kampen/Rosenthal theory. Thomas explains:

> It is difficult to capture the Greek wording in English without a periphrasis such as "the day, that great day." "The great day" is a title borrowed from the OT

> (Joel 2:11,31; Zephaniah 1:14; Malachi 4:5). . . . The
> primary passages from which John draws his images in
> the description of the sixth seal prove the reference of
> this phrase to be to the day of the Lord (Joel 2:11,
> 30,31; cf. Isaiah 2:10,11, 19-21; 13:9-13; 34:4,8; Ezekiel
> 32:7,8; Hosea 10:8).[15]

This passage links all the seal judgments to God's wrath, in contrast to Van Kampen/Rosenthal, and even associates it with the day of the Lord. Such biblical facts contradict the recent Rapture view of Van Kampen/Rosenthal. This would also support the pretribulational understanding that the day of the Lord includes the entire seventieth week of Daniel and thus a time of God's wrath from which the church is promised deliverance.

A biblically accurate summary of the day of the Lord is provided by Charles Ryrie who says:

> In the Bible, the day of the Lord always involves the
> broad concept of God's special intervention in human
> history. The concept includes three facets (1) a historical
> facet about God's intervention in Israel's affairs (Joel
> 1:15; Zephaniah 1:14-18) and in the affairs of heathen
> nations (Isaiah 13:6; Jeremiah 46:10; Ezekiel 30:3); (2)
> an illustrative facet, in which a historical incident of
> God's intervention also illustrates a future intervention
> (Isaiah 13:6-13; Joel 2:1-11); (3) an eschatological facet
> about God's intervention in human history in the future
> (Isaiah 2:12-19; 4:1; 19:23-25; Jeremiah 30:7-9). Only
> this third, the eschatological facet, pertains to our dis-
> cussion of the Rapture's timing.[16]

Rosenthal invests much in his belief that the day of the Lord is limited to the final quarter of the seventieth week of Daniel. "If expositors get the starting point of the day of the Lord right," insists Rosenthal, "the timing of the Rapture becomes clear."[17] This is true! But Rosenthal is not able to answer two major points relating to the day of the Lord and the timing of the Rapture as put forth by Ryrie.

First, how can the Rapture precede Armageddon and yet be a single event with the Second Coming, which puts a stop to Armageddon? Armageddon is not a single, confined battle; it is a war (Revelation 16:14). For the church to miss Armageddon, the Rapture cannot be a single, continuous event with the Second Coming.... Second, if the day of the Lord commences with the judgments at the end of the tribulation, then how can it begin with a time of peace and safety (1 Thessalonians 5:2,3)? Even a superficial knowledge of the tribulation does not give the impression that there will be any time of peace and safety, except perhaps at the very beginning; certainly not at the end.[18]

In order to make their view work in the abstract, Van Kampen/Rosenthal must redefine the nature and scope of terms like "the day of the Lord." Their work, however, does not fit when all of Scripture is considered. Further, their wrong understanding of the key biblical terminology sets the stage for their erroneous conclusion that the Rapture will occur three-quarters of the way through the seventieth week of Daniel, instead of before.

Internal Contradiction

The Van Kampen/Rosenthal view of the Rapture is not only built upon faulty interpretation of the Bible, as demonstrated previously, but also upon flawed data and logic. In 1990 Rosenthal released the first published expression of the Van Kampen/Rosenthal Rapture view. Reading the book revealed many problems, though one especially stuck out on pages 103-104. Rosenthal made the following statement: "The Greek word *thlipsis,* translated *tribulation* or *affliction* in many English Bibles, occurs twenty times in the New Testament."[19] Having done a word study of *thlipsis* just the week before, it was fresh on my mind and I knew that my computer concordance showed that it actually occurs

45 times in 43 New Testament verses. Why had he not even considered more than half of the New Testament references?

The point that Rosenthal was attempting to make when he committed such a glaring factual error was that the word *tribulation* is never used to refer to the first half of Daniel's seventieth week.[20] I don't believe that to be the case because Matthew 24:9 is an instance where *tribulation* (KJV = *afflicted*) refers to the first half of Daniel's seventieth week. John McLean explains:

> Rosenthal has not only overstated his case but has stated as true fact that which is clearly false. A cursory reading of a Greek concordance reveals that the word "tribulation" *(thlipsis)* is used in prophetic contexts to refer to both the first and second halves of the seventieth week of Daniel. Matthew 24:9, which chronologically relates to the first half of the seventieth week as evidenced by its preceding the midpoint of the abomination of desolation (Matthew 24:15-21) states: "Then they will deliver you to *tribulation [thlipsis],* and will kill you, and you will be hated by all nations on account of My name" (NASB, emphasis added). Clearly the biblical text describes the first half of the seventieth week as a time of *tribulation.* The second half of the seventieth week is also described as a time of tribulation. Second Thessalonians 1:6 uses the Greek word *thlipsin* while referring to the Second Coming of Christ which occurs during the second half of the seventieth week of Daniel: "For after all it is only just for God to repay with *affliction [thlipsin]* those who afflict you" (NASB, emphasis added). Therefore, it is proper and even biblical to refer to, and even describe, the seventieth week of Daniel as "The Tribulation," or "A Time of Tribulation."[21]

Interestingly, Rosenthal restricts the use of *thlipsin* "tribulation" to simply trials to be experienced[22] while at the same time locating such tribulation in the first half of Daniel's seventieth week.[23] Like McLean and pretribulationists,

Rosenthal equates Matthew 24:9 with the fifth seal judgment as stated in Revelation 6:9-11. This is exactly the understanding of pretribulationalism. Yet if Rosenthal admits the obvious logical conclusion—that the tribulation in Matthew 24:9 is the tribulation—then it would provide another item that contradicts his new view and would support the only true pre-wrath position that actually does harmonize all scriptural data—pretribulationalism. Instead, Rosenthal would rather foster an internal contradiction within his system that he apparently expects his followers to overlook.

Conclusion

The brand new innovation of the three-quarters Rapture view of Van Kampen/Rosenthal is a recent demonstration of just how important it is to build one's view of Bible prophecy upon an accurate biblical analysis of foundational items such as the nature and scope of the tribulation. As Van Kampen/Rosenthal demonstrate in their writings, if one errs at this crucial point then it paves the way for faulty conclusions. It should be clear that Van Kampen/Rosenthal must resort to strained characterizations of things like the day of the Lord, the tribulation, and the scope of God's wrath in order to first avoid pretribulationalism and second to support their new three-quarters Rapture view. Bible believing Christians should continue to draw strength and hope from the fact that our Lord could Rapture His church at any moment. We will not be left on earth when our Lord moves history to the point of the commencement of the seventieth week of Daniel. This is our true blessed hope. Maranatha!

And now, little children, abide in him; that, when he shall appear, we may have confidence, and not be ashamed before him at his coming.

1 JOHN 2:28

The issue at the Judgment Seat of Christ is not whether we are believers or not, or whether we will enter heaven or not. The fact is, whoever appears before the Judgment Seat of Christ is already in heaven. Forgiveness has been accomplished forever through redemption, and reconciliation with a holy God is assured. The punishment that everyone deserves has already been borne by Jesus when He shed His blood and died on the cross. He was made to be sin with our sin so we could be made righteous with His righteousness (2 Corinthians 5:21). Therefore whatever is evaluated at the Judgment Seat of Christ is not a question of sin and its relationship to eternal punishment. The purpose is to determine the worthiness or worthlessness of the believer's works. It is in its truest sense a reward seat.

CHAPTER 7

The Judgment Seat of Christ

Mark L. Bailey

The writer of the revelation of Jesus Christ portrays the results of the believer's works as the dress attire of a bride: "Let us be glad and rejoice and give Him glory, for the marriage of the Lamb has come, and His wife has made herself ready. And to her it was granted to be arrayed in fine linen, clean and bright, for the fine linen is the righteous acts of the saints" (Revelation 19:7-8 NKJV). If the works of the believer will be represented in the attire of the Bride of Christ when she accompanies the Lord as He returns to earth after the Great Tribulation, what will those saints be wearing if they have not served the Lord well through their righteous works? How embarrassing and inappropriate it would be to show up at a wedding celebration with inadequate or insufficient clothing befitting such a sacred occasion. If in some measure the glory of Christ will be reflected by the beauty of His Bride, how important it is that every believer have a clear understanding of how his or her works will be evaluated and rewarded.

Almost every religion has an idea of what will happen immediately after death. Most teach there will be some kind of an accounting or judgment based on a person's behavior. Religious persuasions differ on the number of judgments and the basis for each judgment. The Bible teaches that God will use a series of judgments to recompense every human being according to his deeds (Matthew 16:27; Revelation 22:12). Often there is confusion as it relates to these judgments and a failure to properly distinguish between the biblical truth as it pertains to salvation and eternal rewards. Such is a confusion between the gift of entrance into eternal life and the rewarded kingdom experience of those once they have arrived in the presence of Christ. One is the issue of faith and the other is the issue of faithfulness. Although salvation is always by grace through faith in what God has done in Christ (Ephesians 2:8,9), judgment is determined according to the works that a person has done (Matthew 16:27; 25:31-46).

There is a general principle of Scripture that every member of the human race is accountable to God (Jeremiah 17:10; 32:19). The unbeliever and the believer will both be judged. The judgment of all unbelievers will take place at the Great White Throne judgment described in Revelation 20:15. This judgment takes place after the millennial reign of Christ and is described as that final judgment prior to eternity future. The judgment of every believer is affirmed by Paul in 2 Corinthians 5:10: "For we must all appear before the judgment seat of Christ, that each one may receive the things done in the body, according to what he has done, whether good or bad" (NKJV).

That all are judged will justify the justice of God before all creatures. That any will be saved will be the greatest demonstration of God's grace the world could ever know. The judgment of the wicked will confirm their rejection of God's provision of salvation in His Son and will result in eternal condemnation. The judgment of the righteous will confirm their security in Christ and will determine their eternal rewards. The judgment on the wicked will be more or less "tolerable" in proportion to their wickedness (Matthew 10:15; 11:23,24; Luke 19:27). The judgment of the righteous will result in more or less rewards in proportion to their faithfulness (Luke 19:11-27). The particular topic of this essay is the nature of that judgment which every believer will undergo called the Judgment Seat of Christ.

The Background of the Word *Bema*

The seat of judgment as described by Paul is called the bema (2 Corinthians 5:10). By way of cultural background, the bema could refer to a step or a platform that might be used in both the political and the athletic arenas. Earthly bemas were raised platforms on which rulers or judges sat when making speeches (Acts 12:21) or adjudicating cases (Acts 18:12-17). In the Isthmian games (which was the forerunner to the Olympic games) the umpire presided from a raised platform called the bema (Judgment Seat). From there he watched the games and awarded the winners. With the variety of metaphors mentioned in the New Testament, the "Judgment Seat" is an appropriate term to capture both the judicial and athletic imageries used to describe the judgment to be administered by Christ.

A Word About the Judge

God has committed all judgment to the Son (John 5:27). This is what makes all of His judgments just. In the imagery of Revelation 4–5 Jesus is seen to have the right of judgment because He is both the Lion from the tribe of Judah and the Lamb of God who died and rose again. He who was judged has the right to judge all humanity because He is both the Sovereign and Savior. The Bible says that Jesus is the "righteous judge" and therefore all judgments will be fair and final (2 Timothy 4:8). As is characteristic of the Father, He will also judge "without respect of persons" (1 Peter 1:17). The attributes of Jesus Christ as the Son of God guarantee that all evidence is in and all has been carefully evaluated.

Who Will Be Judged at the Bema?

The issue at the Judgment Seat of Christ is not whether we are believers or not, or whether we will enter heaven or not. The fact is, whoever appears before the Judgment Seat of Christ is already in heaven. Any person who has trusted in Jesus Christ for his salvation will never be condemned for his sins (Romans 8:1). Justification by faith results in peace with God through Jesus Christ (Romans 5:1). Forgiveness has been accomplished forever through redemption, and reconciliation with a holy God is assured. The punishment that everyone deserves has already been borne by Jesus when He shed His blood and died on the cross. He was made to be sin with our sin so we could be made righteous with His righteousness (2 Corinthians 5:21). Therefore whatever is to be evaluated at the Judgment Seat of Christ is not a question of sin and its relationship to eternal punishment.

The message of the New Testament reveals certain foundational truths concerning those to be judged at the Judgment Seat of Christ. First, *only believers* will be judged. Every passage which directly mentions or indirectly alludes to the bema assumes those who will be judged will be believers. Second, *every* believer will stand before the Judgment Seat of Christ. The Bible says, "For we must all appear..." (2 Corinthians 5:10). Finally this judgment is not optional, every believer *must* appear for judgment. The judgment is obligatory and not optional. Because there is no way to avoid it, to be ready for such an evaluation is the better part of wisdom.

When and Where Will the Judgment Take Place?

1 Corinthians 3:13 speaks of "the Day" (NKJV) when the quality of each person's work will be revealed. Some passages

indicate that the "day of the Lord" is an extended period of time. Like the Jewish concept for "day," which is comprised of both darkness and light, the "day of the Lord" may refer to the entire period of both the judgment and blessing that will come upon the world: the tribulation and the millennium. The day of the Lord can also refer to the specific day on which He returns to the earth to change the night to day, to turn judgment into blessing, to make the transition from this present age to the age to come. That day and hour when the Lord will come to earth is unknown to all except the Father (Matthew 24:36).

The implications from various passages of Scripture seem to indicate that the evaluative judgment of the believer will take place in heaven between the resurrection and Rapture of the church and the personal return of Christ from heaven at the Second Advent. If the elders in heaven are representatives of the church age (cf. Revelation 4:4-10), they are seen in heaven with their crowns already in place. In addition, the church as the Bride of Christ is pictured as already clothed when she accompanies the Lord at His Second Coming to the earth (Revelation 19:7-9). The return to the earth is for the wedding banquet. It seems evident then that when Christ returns in judgment, the marriage and rewarding of the church will have already taken place. The rewarding of believers and the wedding between Christ and His Bride are heavenly events before the throne. The marriage feast with all the invited guests is described by Jesus as taking place on earth (Matthew 25:1-13). The imagery of the earthly kingdom as a wedding feast is therefore entirely appropriate.

That believers are not judged immediately at the time of their death is evident from 1 Corinthians 4:5, which seems to teach that before believers can be judged, Jesus must come back for His church. Therefore, after the Lord returns for the church and before He comes back to the earth to rule and reign, every saint of the church will have stood before the bema of Christ for their judgment and rewards.

What Will Be Judged?

The purpose for the judgment of believers at the Judgment Seat of Christ is to determine the worthiness or worthlessness of their works. That the judgment applies only to believers is further clarified in that, even if they suffer loss, those judged will be saved. The works that are evaluated are those done in their life as a Christian. Because we have been saved unto good works that God has prepared for the believer (Ephesians 2:10), it is only natural to expect Him to examine the faithfulness with which such service has been performed. Various passages of the New Testament affirm the evaluation of the life-performance of the Christian. This is evident from the fact that all who are judged are said to have built their lives on the true foundation, Jesus Christ Himself (1 Corinthians 3:11,12). The New Testament affirms that the Judgment Seat of Christ will evaluate various elements of the believer's life and work. All of our sin was judged at the cross. Those sins God "will remember no more" (Hebrews 10:17 NKJV). The Second Coming will not be in reference to the believer's sin (Hebrews 9:28). Therefore the Judgment Seat of Christ is not a judgment to determine salvation; it is a judgment of the saved with reference to their works. The evaluation of the believer's works will include the works themselves, the quality with which they have been done, and the motivation of the heart.

The Works

What one does for God really does count. Malachi 3:16 speaks of a "book of remembrance" in which God keeps track of all that has been done for Him. For differing works the Scripture records the promise of specific rewards. A couple of passages from the Gospels will be sufficient to indicate that rewards will be given for the accomplishment of individual works. Suffering insults, persecution, and false testimony for the sake of Christ and the cause of righteousness will bring great rewards in heaven (Matthew 5:11,12; cf. Luke 6:21,22). A receptive response to prophets or other righteous servants of the Lord guarantees a prophet's or righteous man's reward for such a response. Benevolent activity as illustrated by "a cup of cold water" in the name of a disciple will keep that respondent from losing a reward (Matthew 10:41,42). Luke 14:12-14 records the motivation of Jesus to the disciples to reach out to the underprivileged for which the disciples are promised, "you will be repaid at the resurrection of the righteous" (Luke 14:14 NASB). Although certain works are singled out in various passages, the implication is that for all works that are evaluated as having eternal value or merit, rewards are held out as both the promise or motivation for such activity.

The Quality

How work is done for Christ will also be tested for its genuineness of character. Paul wrote that the fire of God's judgment "will test each one's work, of what sort it is" (1 Corinthians 3:13 NKJV). The imagery of gold, silver, and precious stones as opposed to wood, hay, and stubble reveals that the quality of the works themselves will be tested. What distinguishes one from the other is their eternal value. Works that have no eternal significance do not merit eternal recognition. In Paul's illustration an adequate foundation, the quality of the materials, and the proper methods of building are the symbolic components for quality work for God. Works will be judged to be either good or bad (Greek = *agathos* or *phaulos)* at the Judgment Seat.

Good Works. Good works *(agathos)* may be defined as those which have been "manifested as having been wrought in

God" (John 3:21 NASB). These may also be categorized as "works of faith" (1 Thessalonians 1:3). As defined by God, good is designated as gold, silver, and precious stones, which is produced by a believer who is walking in fellowship and who is controlled by the Holy Spirit. Good works are also called "the fruit of righteousness which comes through Jesus Christ, to the glory and praise of God" (Philippians 1:11 NASB). The power to produce good works comes directly from God, not from within man (cf. Philippians 2:13).

Bad Works. Bad deeds *(phaulos),* refer to that which is worthless in the sight of God. These could be called dead works or works of the flesh. The danger of producing works of the flesh is that labor is said to be in vain (1 Corinthians 15:58), empty (1 Timothy 6:20; 2 Timothy 2:16), and worthless (Galatians 4:9; Titus 3:9; James 1:26). Bad works do not measure up to the standard and therefore are characterized as wood, hay, and stubble—commodities of little worth or durability. These are deeds produced by believers when they are in a carnal or fleshly state. These are produced in the energy of the flesh apart from the power of the Spirit. Works will also be shown to be bad if they were done for the wrong motives.

The Motivations

Why works are performed will also be determined by the judgment of Christ. On that day the motives of the believer will be exposed. Jesus said "But there is nothing covered up that will not be revealed, and hidden that will not be known. Accordingly, whatever you have said in the dark shall be heard in the light, and what you have whispered in the inner rooms shall be proclaimed upon the housetops (Luke 12:2,3 NASB). Purposes give birth to behavior. The purpose or motivation of the heart validates or invalidates the actions of one's life. An example from the Sermon on the Mount will illustrate. Jesus said what appears to be two opposite statements. On the one hand He exhorted believers to let their lives shine as lights in order to be seen by others who in turn will glorify the Father in heaven (Matthew 5:16). On the other, Jesus taught that activities such as prayer, offerings for the poor, and fasting should be done in secret to be seen by God alone and not before others lest one lose their reward in heaven (Matthew 6:1-21). Eternal rewards are not lost for good deeds seen by others, but they are lost when those works are done to be seen by others. First Corinthians 4:5 says that the hidden counsels of the heart will be exposed. What Jesus thinks about our works is more important than what anyone else thinks. Revelation 2:23 reminds us that God searches both minds and hearts in order to evaluate for the proper reward.

What Will Be the Results of the Judgment?

Rewards will be gained or lost at the Judgment Seat of Christ. Works enduring through the fire of God's judgment will be rewarded (1 Corinthians 3:14). Works that do not survive the fire of judgment will mean the loss of reward.

Losing Rewards

That rewards can be lost is evident by a number of Scriptures. John wrote about the possibility of being ashamed at the coming of Christ (1 John 2:28). The passive voice in the grammar of this passage suggests the self-realizing embarrassment of shame at the appearing of the Lord rather than any punitive shaming from the Lord. There will be no condemnation for the believer (Romans 8:1). John also taught that one could lose rewards for unfaithful living (2 John 8). He wanted his readers to get the "full reward" that was available to them for their faithful service. Paul also spoke of being "disqualified" by failing in the pursuit of a faithful life (1 Corinthians 9:24-27). In Paul's analogy of the house that is burnt, the works are consumed but the builder escapes with his life. Rewards are lost but the person is not. That which is forfeited is the recognition and reward that could have been achieved had the works been done according to the standards of God.

Ironically, ministry done for the wrong motives, which may result in the forfeiture of rewards, may even have eternal effects (Philippians 1:14-19). God's Word does not return void and may have an effect in spite of the person who for whatever reasons may have been doing their duty in the power of the flesh.

Gaining Rewards

The distribution of rewards will take place at the judgment. The rewards are never given for the ego-satisfaction of the person but for the praise and glory of the Christ who enabled such work to be accomplished (cf. Philippians 1:11). Rewards are promised for faithful service. If any works are ever evaluated as fruits of righteousness, whatever ultimate praise is given must be to the One who graciously provided the righteous standing in which the works of God could be manifested (cf. John 3:21).

A series of crowns are held up in the writings of the New Testament as motivations for godly behavior. The Bible speaks of two kinds of crowns. One is the "diadem" crown, which is given to one who reigns. Another is the victory crown (Greek = *stephanos*) given as the award to those who achieve great accomplishments. The latter is used for the crowns of reward that are promised to the believer for successful service for the Lord. With the imagery of the winners' crowns handed out in the sporting events and military ceremonies of the first century, the New Testament writers use the crowns to speak of the commendations to come to the Christian at the judgment of their works. Those crowns that were given to the athletes were woven vines or wreaths made of withered, wild celery. As Paul says in 1 Corinthians 9:25, "they do it to obtain a corruptible crown; but we an incorruptible." Four such crowns are mentioned in the Scripture.

The Crown of Life. This is the crown awarded to those who remain faithful through trials (James 1:2,3,12; cf. Revelation 2:10; 3:11). Two qualifications in these passages include the response of joy, which comes from viewing trials as sent from the Lord intended as opportunities for growth and stability, as well as a love for the Lord, which motivates the faithful behavior. Israel was guilty of wrongly responding to their wilderness trials and was charged with forgetting the powerful deliverance of the Lord throughout its history (Psalm 78:11,42). Their unfaithful response to trials caused them some pretty ridiculous doubtings of the care of a redeeming God. Spiritual forgetfulness will rob believers of their joy and raise the question of the sincerity of their love.

The Crown of Righteousness. This crown is reserved for all who anxiously await the Lord's return. In his later years Paul was more concerned with standing before the court of heaven than the court of Rome. Paul said,

> For I am already being poured out as a drink offering, and the time of my departure has come. I have fought the good fight, I have finished the course, I have kept the faith; in the future there is laid up for me the crown of righteousness, which the Lord, the righteous Judge, will award to me on that day; and not only to me, but also to all who have loved His appearing. (2 Timothy 4:6-8 NASB).

Loving the appearing of the Lord assumes a lifestyle of obedience. Such faithfulness provides a platform of confidence as one awaits the soon return of the Lord.

The Crown of Glory. This crown is promised to those who shepherd the flock of God with right motives (1 Peter 5:2-4). Godly shepherds worthy of reward are those who serve willingly rather than under compulsion. They model godly living rather than mandating it to their sheep. They recognize theirs is an entrusted stewardship for which they will give an account to the Chief Shepherd. Jesus, of course, is the ultimate model of the Good Shepherd who laid down His life for the sheep (John 10:11) and has become "the Shepherd and Guardian" of the souls of all believers (1 Peter 2:25). By the negative example of Israel's failure, Ezekiel taught that the real work of the shepherd toward the sheep was to feed, care for, restore, as well as to go search out the lost sheep (Ezekiel 34:2-4). Such is the nature of the pastoral ministry (cf. Acts 20:27-30).

The Crown of Rejoicing. This crown is the soul winner's crown. Paul wrote to the Thessalonians, "For who is our hope or joy or crown of exultation? Is it not even you, in the presence of our Lord Jesus at His coming? For you are our glory and joy" (1 Thessalonians 2:19,20 NASB). Again to the Philippians he said, "Therefore, my beloved brethren whom I long to see, my joy and crown, so stand firm in the Lord, my beloved" (Philippians 4:1 NASB). Evangelism of the lost is a deep desire of God and He has promised to reward those who will seek them on His behalf. Jesus taught the principle well in John 4. In the imagery of the reaper who will receive wages for his efforts at a later time Jesus said that those believers engaged in active evangelism are gathering fruit for eternal life. The effort is a team ministry because rarely does one both sow and reap. " 'One sows, and another reaps' " (John 4:37 NASB). The teamwork in evangelism among believers is so designed by Christ that "he who sows and he who reaps may rejoice together" (John 4:36 NASB).

The Glory of the Crowns

The crowns with which the saints have been rewarded will one day be used for the praise and worship of the Lord as they are laid before the throne of heaven (Revelation 4:10). Rewards also imply future responsibilities and future privileges. Though the crowns will be cast at Christ's feet, He might give them back as a part of the privileged positions faithful believers will fulfill because the Bible says they will be given responsibilities to reign.

How Can a Sinner Ever Produce Good Works?

Once we are saved, the Scripture says we are saved "unto good works." These good works are pleasing to God because they are a part of His "workmanship" for every believer (Ephesians 2:8-10). Jesus Christ makes these works acceptable to the Father. The Bible says that we are to "offer up spiritual sacrifices acceptable to God through Jesus Christ" (1 Peter 2:5). Romans 12:1,2 teaches that a dedicated life can present holy and acceptable service as an act of worship and can accomplish the perfect and acceptable will of God. That's why the Bible teaches people that if they are faithful they will be rewarded. Works do have merit in the sight of God. And it's very important to recognize that the way one lives today will have eternal repercussions.

Are Rewards a Legitimate Motivation?

Some may wonder whether the prospect of rewards might generate a mercenary mentality in one's service to the Lord. The question is often phrased, "Shouldn't one serve the Lord just because one loves the Lord?" Although God is worthy of worship and service whether the worshiper is rewarded or not, it must be remembered that the idea of eternal rewards was introduced and developed by Jesus. It is not wrong to be motivated by rewards as long as we realize that the main reward is to receive the approval of Christ and please Him. Even Jesus was motivated! Why? "Who for the joy that was set before Him endured the cross" (Hebrews 12:2). Other examples of biblical characters who were motivated to act because of the rewards that awaited them include Abraham, Moses, and Paul. Abraham "looked for a city which hath foundations, whose builder and maker is God" (Hebrews 11:10). Moses was motivated because he "looked to the coming reward" (Hebrews 11:26 NKJV). Paul said, "I run and I lay hold of the truth that I may not have run in vain" (see Philippians 2:16; 3:12). The Christian should look at rewards as the wonderful opportunity to prove his love and loyalty to the Lord.

Two Balancing Principles to Remember

The parable of the talents (Matthew 25:14-30) and the parable of the pounds (Luke 19:13-27) illustrate an important and balancing set of principles in God's reward program. The talents illustrate that each believer is delegated an unequal entrustment proportionately assigned according to ability. Not all believers enjoy the same natural talents, spiritual giftedness, intellect, educational opportunities, or sovereignly designed opportunities. They may, however, receive equal commendations and rewards from the Lord for their faithfulness. On the other hand, the parable of the pounds illustrates that in certain ways all believers share an equal entrustment before the Lord. Each one has one life to live and give to God, the Scriptures, a common faith, and the gospel message. Differing delegations of rule in God's kingdom are awarded according to proportionate faithfulness. Therefore both God's grace as well as human faithfulness are factors to be remembered as one anticipates rewards.

The Metaphors of Judgment

The Judgment Seat of Christ is portrayed throughout the Bible with metaphors. These word pictures are designed for both meditation and application. Biblical illustrations allow one to keep the truths in mind to probe deeper into their implications. In addition, the imageries carry their own built-in appeal. That which is necessary for the successful completion of the actions within the imageries helps teach what one needs to do to successfully prepare for the coming judgment.

Metaphor	Image of Evaluation	Application	Scriptures
Building	Quality of Material	Building Well	1 Corinthians 3:12
Athletic Race	Reward Stand	Strict Training Running Hard	1 Corinthians 9:24-27
Marriage	Bridal Beauty and Purity	Eliminating Flaws Staying Faithful	2 Corinthians 11:2
Auditor's Report	Record of Good Works	Producing Good Works	2 Corinthians 5:10
Work	Reimbursement	Heartfelt Service	Colossians 3:24
Farming	Harvest	Being Fruitful	John 4:36
Investment	Return on Money	Wise Stewardship	Luke 16:1-14
Favors	Return of Favor	Dedicated Service	Ephesians 6:8
Battles of War	Celebrated Return	Being Victorious	2 Corinthians 2:14-17
Working	Earned Wages	Working Hard	Revelation 22:12
Stewardship	Service to Master	Being Faithful	1 Corinthians 4:2
Boxing Match	Winning the Fight	Defeating Opponent	1 Corinthians 9:24-27

What Should Be Our Goals in Light of His Coming?

In light of the Lord's return and the coming judgment, the Scriptures are replete with applicational challenges. The following are suggested as a place to begin:

1. Be faithful with your God-given stewardships (1 Corinthians 4:2).

2. Make it the aim of your life to be pleasing to the Lord (2 Corinthians 5:9).

3. Do all works heartily as unto the Lord (Colossians 3:23).

4. Be diligent to be found by Him in peace, spotless and blameless (2 Peter 3:14).

5. Never try to evaluate another believer's production (Matthew 7:1,2; Romans 4:4).

6. Stay humble by realizing you are unworthy even to be a servant (Luke 10:7-10).

7. Maintain a steadfast and unmovable commitment to serving the Lord (1 Corinthians 15:58).

8. Avoid prejudging others who must answer for themselves to the Lord as their Master (Romans 14:10; 1 Corinthians 4:5).

9. Stop comparing yourself with others (2 Corinthians 10:12).

10. Cleanse yourself from all spiritual defilements and deceptions that would keep you from proper preparation for your marriage to Christ (2 Corinthians 11:2).

Reminder: "We must work the works of Him who sent Me, as long as it is day; night is coming, when no man can work" (John 9:4 NASB).

And he saith unto me, Write, Blessed are they which are called unto the marriage supper of the Lamb.

The figure of betrothal appears in Scripture to represent the spiritual reality of Christ and His church. For example, before we were born physically, we were betrothed by the Father to the Son. "Blessed be the God and Father of our Lord Jesus Christ, who hath blessed us with all spiritual blessings in heavenly places in Christ: According as He hath chosen us in him before the foundation of the world, that we should be holy and without blame before him in love" (Ephesians 1:3,4). When we look at this teaching, we see that the individual who has accepted Christ as Savior is part of what we refer to as the Bride of Christ. In the Oriental wedding the bride had little place. The bridegroom was in the place of prominence. They gathered, therefore, to honor him, not her. And the reason they honor Him is because "the marriage of the Lamb is come, and his wife hath made herself ready" (Revelation 19:7). John was speaking of an event that will take place at the Second Advent—the return of Christ to the earth. During the age in which we live, the Spirit has been calling out a bride; we have been betrothed to Him.

CHAPTER 8

The Marriage Supper of the Lamb

J. Dwight Pentecost

A "feast," a "wedding," a "marriage feast," and a "marriage supper," are all terms used throughout the New Testament that relate to a wedding event we call the Marriage Supper of the Lamb. In the Gospels and in particular, our Lord's parables, Christ makes references to these terms in order to teach truth concerning the prophetic program. Also, in many other New Testament passages we are shown the relationship between Christ and the church using the figures of the bridegroom and the bride (John 3:29; Romans 7:4; 2 Corinthians 11:2; Ephesians 5:25-33; Revelation 19:7,8). It is at the event known as the Rapture of the church that Christ appears as a Bridegroom to take His Bride (the church) unto Himself.

The Scriptures have a good deal to say concerning this marriage, which will be consummated in heaven. If we try to interpret this marriage in light of our modern western customs, however, we will miss most of the meaning. In order to picture the relationship we will have with Christ we must leave our twentieth-century culture and go back to the time when Christ lived.

During the time of Christ and in some Oriental countries today, there were three separate parts of a marriage. The first stage was called the betrothal. Marriage was by contract. There was no ceremony as we see today in our western civilization. Most often the arrangements were made by the parents in the absence of the bride and the bridegroom. There were times when parents *might* enter into the contract when asked to do so by a son, who saw a young woman, thought she was lovely, and expressed an interest in her as a wife, as in the case of Samson (Judges 14). More frequently though, the contract was drawn up by the fathers while the future bride and groom were still small children. Some records cite instances when a contract was drawn up before the couple was even born.

This contract, called the betrothal, was a legal enactment, duly signed before judges, which bound the parties to each other and could be broken only by a bill of divorcement. Both Matthew and Luke show that Joseph and Mary were betrothed. They had not been officially joined in marriage, and their union had never been consummated, but they were called husband and wife because of the betrothal. When it became evident that Mary was expecting a child that could not possibly belong to Joseph, Joseph had one of two choices. First, he could accuse her before the judges and subject her to the penalty of the law, which said that a person who was betrothed and then found to be unfaithful could be stoned to death. Second, he could "put her away privily," that is, he could give her a divorce. They were betrothed to each other, not married in our sense of the word, yet that betrothal could be broken only by a bill of divorcement.

The word used to describe the legal relationship of a young man and woman is also used to describe our relationship to Jesus Christ. The Apostle Paul, putting himself in the position of a spiritual father to the Corinthians, wrote,

"For I am jealous over you with godly jealousy: for I have *espoused you to one husband,* that I may present you as a chaste virgin to Christ" (2 Corinthians 11:2, emphasis added). The word *espoused* here is translated elsewhere in the New Testament as "betrothed." To Paul, the Corinthian believers were daughters in the faith, and Jesus Christ was a Bridegroom—a husband-to-be. Like a father, Paul had been instrumental in enacting a legal betrothal contract between his spiritual daughters and the Lord Jesus Christ. An indissoluble relationship had been instituted, and the apostle did not want the Corinthians to be drawn aside by false teachings. He feared they would be found unfaithful to their betrothed. Paul had betrothed, or espoused, them and he wanted them to continue in faithfulness until they were presented to the Groom.

The figure of betrothal appears in Scripture to represent the spiritual reality of Christ and His church. For example, before we were born physically, we were betrothed by the Father to the Son. "Blessed be the God and Father of our Lord Jesus Christ, who hath blessed us with all spiritual blessings in heavenly places in Christ: according as he hath chosen us in him before the foundation of the world, that we should be holy and without blame before him in love" (Ephesians 1:3). In this passage, Paul pictures God the Father as choosing those whom He will betroth to His Son. When we look at this teaching, we see that the individual who has accepted Christ as Savior is part of what we refer to as the Bride of Christ.

God is bringing together, into a living, vital union, every believer in His Son. The church in this sense is an organism. The true church of Jesus Christ is composed of every individual who receives the gift of eternal life that God offers through His Son. Those who are blood-bought and blood-washed are brought together into a relationship with one another, which we call the church, which is the Bride of Christ. As it is natural for a bride to anticipate her wedding day, it is natural for the church to anticipate the day her Groom will come and take her into His presence.

The second part of the wedding was called the "presentation." When a couple reached marriageable ages, the young man would say, "Father, you have made legal arrangements for my marriage. Now it is time to send for my bride so that this contract might be fulfilled." The father then would send a retinue of servants to the house of the bride. They would carry the legal contracts with them, present them to the father of the bride, and demand that he fulfill the terms of the contract and send his daughter to meet her groom. The groom's friends would accompany the bride in a procession to the groom's home.

The ceremony that followed was the "presentation." The bride's father would take the bride's hand and put it into the hand of the groom's father to signify that he had fulfilled his contract—he had delivered his daughter to the father of the groom. Then the father of the groom would place the bride's hand into the hand of his son to signify that he had fulfilled his part of the contract—he had delivered the bride to his son. At that point the couple was legally married. Immediately after the ceremony—which came months or even years after the betrothal—they began their life together as husband and wife.

The church, which is made perfect by the grace of God, will be delivered from the earthly scene and presented to the Bridegroom (the Lord Jesus Christ). We often refer to this event as the Rapture of the church—when believers are removed from this earth, when the graves of believers are opened, death is overcome, and we leave this mortal sphere to go into the presence of the Father. But when we speak of the presentation of the bride to the Bridegroom, we are speaking of the moment the saints enter the Father's house, where the Father presents them as His gift of love to the Son.

When the Father presents the bride to the Son she will not have a single blemish (Ephesians 5:27). This confirms the perfection of the work of Christ. If we look at ourselves, we know that not one of us would make an acceptable bride for the eternal and infinite Son of God. We all have moral blemishes and the marks of sin's decay. Yet the work of God is such that when the Father presents us to the Son, we will be perfect.

The third part in the Oriental marriage, like the other two, was frequently referred to as "the marriage." It was what we would call the marriage supper or marriage banquet or wedding reception. It is at this reception, or marriage supper, that the bridegroom would gather together all his friends and introduce his bride. The length of the marriage supper was determined by the financial and social status of the bridegroom. It might last one or two days or as long as a week.

God's Word includes many references to the marriage supper. In Matthew 22:1,2, "Jesus answered and spake unto them again by parables, and said, The kingdom of heaven is like unto a certain king, which made a marriage for his son." The word *marriage* here refers to the marriage feast. The king had prepared a banquet so his son could introduce the bride to his friends. However, not all who were invited chose to attend. So the invitation was extended in order that the banquet hall might be filled with guests.

We find a similar story in Matthew 25 in the parable of the wise and foolish virgins. "Then shall the kingdom of heaven be likened unto ten virgins, which took their lamps, and went forth to meet the bridegroom. And five of them were wise, and five were foolish" (verses 1,2).

Of the ten virgins only five had enough oil to keep their lamps burning until the groom came. The other five had to go buy more oil, and while they were gone the groom came and opened the door for the wise virgins to enter. Those who were unprepared were excluded. This illustration of the marriage feast speaks of the future consummation of Christ's program in the millennium. The purpose of the marriage feast is found in Revelation 19:7 which states, "Let us be glad and rejoice, and give honour to him: for the marriage of the Lamb is come, and his wife hath made herself ready." According to this passage, the purpose of this marriage feast is not to congratulate the bride nor to tell her how beautiful she looks. In the Oriental wedding the bride had little place. The bridegroom was in the place of prominence. They gathered, therefore, to honor him, not her. And the reason they honor Him is because "the marriage of the Lamb is come and his wife hath made herself ready."

John was speaking of an event that will take place at the Second Advent—the return of Christ to the earth. During the age in which we live, the Spirit has been calling out a bride; we have been betrothed to Him. In Revelation 19, the Rapture has already taken place and the bride has already been presented to the Bridegroom. But one important part of the marriage picture is still missing—the wedding feast, when the bride is introduced.

After speaking about the presentation of the bride, John moved to the subject of the marriage supper and said that "his wife hath made herself ready. And to her was granted that she should be arrayed in fine linen, clean and white: for the fine linen is the righteousness of saints" (19:7,8). We know that at the Judgment Seat of Christ the believer's works will be examined. After this examination the Lord will remove anything that would not bring glory to the Groom. Then the Bridegroom will tell His bride to put on the garment prepared for the occasion.

Revelation 19:8 calls this garment "the righteousness of saints." This is not speaking of the righteousness of Christ, in which we will always be clothed but of that which we will put on *after* the Judgment Seat of Christ, to bring honor and glory to Christ. Imagine how a bride would feel if she spent years planning and preparing her wedding garments and discovered on her wedding day that a mouse had gnawed everything to shreds. That scenario would be similar to what will happen at the Judgment Seat of Christ. We will appear there, thinking we have prepared many beautiful things to present to the Lord. But because we did them with our own energy or for our own glory, they will be unacceptable to Him. Much that we thought would bring glory to our Bridegroom will be destroyed.

"Blessed are they which are called unto the marriage supper of the Lamb" (Revelation 19:9). "The armies [of saints] which were in heaven followed him upon white horses, clothed in fine linen, white and clean" (Revelation 19:14). When we put these two verses together, we discover that the wedding supper will be served on earth following the Second Advent of Christ. The wedding supper is God's name, or picture of the millennial reign of Christ.

A wealthy man in Bible times might have a banquet lasting a week. God's feast will last 1,000 years. Christ will appear as a judge to separate the saved from the unsaved. He will appear as a king to reign. But to the bride for that thousand years He will be the Bridegroom. The Son of God will bring His bride, the church, back to earth when He comes so that He might be honored, adored, and glorified through her. The perfect bride will demonstrate what His grace does for sinners. And for the thousand years of the millennium the Son will do what any bridegroom does—adore His bride and be adored by her.

On almost every wedding invitation there is printed, RSVP. We are expected to respond to an invitation. The Bridegroom is inviting us to participate in that wedding in heaven. Whether we participate or not depends upon our response to Him. God invites us to come—not by paying a price, but by accepting His gift—His Son, the Bridegroom.

And every creature which is in heaven, and on the earth, and under the earth, and such as are in the sea, and all that are in them, heard I saying, Blessing, and honour, and glory, and power, be unto him that sitteth upon the throne, and unto the Lamb for ever and ever.

REVELATION 5:13

The most exciting evidence that the Lord's return may well be very close at hand is the activity surrounding preparations for the rebuilding of the temple on the Temple Mount in Jerusalem. Every project and personality involved in the preparations for the next temple has been documented. Ezekiel 40 to 46 gives detailed instructions for the temple that will stand on the Temple Mount during the millennium. However, Daniel 9:27 states that there will be a temple in Jerusalem during the tribulation period, when the sacrifices will be stopped. Preparations for this temple are already complete!

CHAPTER 9

Preparations for the Potentate

Jimmy DeYoung

The shrill sharp sound of the siren broke the silence of the still night air over Jerusalem, to warn of an incoming Iraqi scud. This sound, an air raid warning, would become very familiar over the next three months as we established ourselves as journalists in Israel. Abruptly awakened, we hurriedly made our way into our sealed room, a room set aside for the protection from incoming scuds—courtesy of the "madman of Baghdad," Saddam Hussein.

Entering the sealed room, we started to assemble our gas masks. As we ran into the room and I started to put the finishing touches on sealing the door, the phone rang. We had been in Jerusalem only four days and couldn't imagine who would have our phone number, let alone be calling us at 2 o'clock in the morning. I rushed to the phone to hear the voice of my daughter, Jodi, calling from Chattanooga, Tennessee.

She informed me that she had been watching CNN, which had announced that a scud missile was headed right for Jerusalem. As the sirens blared through the streets of

Israel, I quickly responded that I already knew this information and that I had to go. I slammed the phone down and ran for the sealed room.

I sealed the door behind us, and for the next five hours Judy and I sat wondering if a scud would indeed hit our apartment. In our opinion, our apartment was the closest point between Iraq's missile launchers and the city of Jerusalem.

This scud attack forced us to have several hours of down time before the potential big storm. These hours were anxiously spent trying to communicate through our gas masks. We also spent an extensive amount of time in prayer. We had a lot of time to meditate upon what was taking place.

My wife and I moved to Jerusalem to be in the city where we knew biblical prophecy is unfolding, almost every moment of every day. Biblical prophecy is unfolding in Israel as it has at no other time in history. As journalists and students of prophecy, it has been our distinct advantage to be on the front row, center stage, where the last act will be played out.

Since we've been living in Jerusalem we have been witnessing what we consider to be the four majors trends of prophecy that point to the imminent return of Jesus Christ: (a) a mass immigration, or aliya of the Jewish people to Israel; (b) an alignment of nations against Israel; (c) an anticipation for peace among the nations of the Middle East; and (d) the arrangements for the building of the next temple in Jerusalem.

Aliya of the Jewish People

Aliya ("to go up") is the Hebrew word Israelis use to describe Jewish immigration to Israel, their homeland. In the book of Deuteronomy, God spoke through Moses to warn the Jewish people that if they did not obey God's commands, He would disperse them to the four corners of the earth. In A.D. 70, General Titus and the Roman army conquered Jerusalem, destroying the temple, devastating the city, and dispersing the Jewish people into all the countries of the world. However, God also promised in Deuteronomy 30:1-10 that He would bring them back into their own land one day. Since January of 1989, more than 800,000 Jews have "made Aliya," immigrating from the former Soviet Union to Israel. This is the crowning touch to a number of immigrations over the last hundred years from countries such as Ethiopia, Iran, Iraq, the United States, and throughout Europe.

As a journalist living in Israel, I listen faithfully to the BBC (British Broadcasting Corporation) from London, England. On a certain Friday afternoon, I was listening to the newscast when the comment was made that "Operation Solomon" was underway. I had never heard of Operation Solomon before and immediately I was interested in finding out what it meant.

It had all started a few years back when Jewish agencies in the United States raised money for the starving Jews in Ethiopia. The other Ethiopians became jealous of these Jews and threatened to kill them. It became expedient to save them from murder, so Israel stepped in to help the Ethiopian Jews.

On Friday afternoon May 24, 1991, 42 aircraft took off from Ben Gurion Airport, just outside of Tel Aviv, Israel. These flights were unique in and of themselves, because on Fridays at sundown the Sabbath starts and all transportation is closed down until sundown on Saturday. On this particular Friday, however, these aircraft took off heading for Addis Ababa, Ethiopia; the planes made their way across Israel, the Red Sea, and then on to Addis Ababa.

As the 747s landed in Ethiopia, the people were quickly boarded onto the planes. One 747 had all of its seats taken out so it could hold as many passengers as possible. One thousand and eighty-seven people were able to fit on this plane, and while they were in the air on the way to Israel, seven babies were born in flight. The next day, Saturday, they arrived in Israel, where they were taken to different absorption centers in Jerusalem and Tel Aviv. These absorption centers were to help the new immigrants assimilate into Israeli society. When we arrived at the absorption center in Jerusalem, we saw many of the immigrants barefoot and dressed in their native attire. There were young mothers with their babies strapped to their backs. When it came time for lunch, we followed the immigrants into the cafeteria. A plate filled with Israeli cuisine was placed in front of the Ethiopians, consisting of yogurt, tomatoes, cucumbers, olives, a boiled egg, and pickles. These Ethiopians had been used to eating only "mush" with pita bread, so they didn't even know how to eat the food that was set before them.

I went up to an older man, cracked his boiled egg for him, and showed him how to eat it. I continued to another table where a woman sat with her baby. I opened up their container of yogurt and started to spoonfeed the baby. As I went from table to table, helping these starving people, tears ran down my face. These Ethiopian Jews had returned "home" after almost two thousand years.

The prophet Zephaniah said that in the time of the end, in conjunction with the return of Jesus Christ, there would be an *aliya* out of Ethiopia. "From beyond the rivers of Ethiopia my suppliants, even the daughter of my dispersed, shall bring mine offering" (Zephaniah 3:10).

The word *suppliant* is translated in Isaiah 18:7, as "a host of worshipers." The prophecy states that the children of those who had been dispersed will return to Israel as a multitude of worshipers. They will be brought back to Israel as an offering to God.

Isaiah 66:20 tells that the Ethiopians will return to Israel upon horses and a variety of other conveyances. It says the Ethiopians will be brought as an offering unto the Lord. The prophecies of Jewish immigration continue to unfold even unto this day in Israel.

Alignment of the Nations

Another trend of the end times, which we have noticed from our vantage point in Jerusalem, is an alignment of nations against Israel. During the Gulf War, in 1991, there were a number of nations that wanted to join forces with Iraq to destroy Israel but were kept at bay by the American-led coalition. The book of Jeremiah prophesies that throughout history, nations would come against the people of Israel. Ezekiel 38:1-12 and Daniel 11:40-45 both explain that in the end times, a major coalition of nations will arise and try to crush Israel. This partnership of states, according to the prophetic Scriptures, will consist of such countries as Egypt, Syria, Iraq, Ethiopia, Libya, Russia, Turkey, and Iran. Any observer of current events can testify to the forming of this "last days" coalition of nations eager for confrontation with Israel.

God brought the nations of the world into existence after the incident at the Tower of Babel, when Nimrod tried to build a great city that would show forth man's greatness. Many of the nations formed then live on today, still nursing a disdain for God's program, His Chosen People; they are thereby eager to rid the world of any Jewish presence.

It is interesting to watch the leaders of the countries of the world moving into position on the world "stage" for the curtain to open on the final act. Sometimes, it's like the leaders have read the "prewritten" history and are rushing to get in place for the show to begin.

Anticipation for Peace

In October 1994, we had the opportunity to gather with hundreds of international journalists near the Red Sea in southern Israel for the signing ceremony of the peace agreement between Israel and Jordan. This history-making event was witnessed by millions as the media giants of the world reported back to their homelands from this dry, hot desert site.

Gathered with the journalists were the political leaders of Israel, Jordan, and the United States, including then Secretary of State Warren Christopher and President Bill Clinton and his entourage. They were in this remote location for the signing of this peace agreement, which was one in the series of supposed "peace treaties" between Israel and her Arab neighbors.

There has been, in the Mideast region, talk about peace for many years. In fact, the anticipation for peace has spread from the Middle East to the entire world. It is a key plank in most western nations' foreign policy platforms—one of those major trends to keep under close scrutiny.

In 1979, President Jimmy Carter, President Anwar Sadat, and Prime Minister Menachem Begin met at the presidential retreat center in Maryland. Taking the name from the retreat center, they called this first peace agreement the "Camp David Accords." This was the first peace treaty signed between the Israelis and one of their Arab neighbors.

The Camp David Accords was followed in 1993 by the Oslo Accords, the peace agreement between the Israelis and the Palestinians. This agreement was only in outline form, which placed the two parties at odds with each other as they endeavored to hammer out the final details.

The fact is, none of these peace agreements are actually working as they were designed. There have actually been more Jewish people killed in Israel since the peace agreements were signed than since the founding of the nation in 1948, before these peace accords.

The failure of these treaties has set the scene for the need of someone to help bring these agreements into some kind of workable order. The interesting thing about these peace agreements, which are already on the table, not working, is that they fit the biblical scenario of Daniel 9:27.

The prophet Daniel wrote that the Antichrist, the "one-world ruler," will confirm a peace accord with the Jewish people, not sign a peace agreement. The Hebrew word for "confirm," *gabar,* which is used in the Bible, is not the same word as to "sign." *Gabar* also means to "strengthen" or "make stronger." In order to strengthen, make stronger, or confirm something, it must already be on the table, which is where these three "peace treaties" are now located.

Preparations for the Coming Temple

The most exciting evidence that the Lord's return may well be very close at hand is the activity surrounding preparations for the rebuilding of the temple on the Temple Mount in Jerusalem. Every project and personality involved in the preparations for the next temple has been documented in a video that I produced several years ago, *Ready to Rebuild.*

Ezekiel 40 to 46 gives detailed instructions for the temple that will stand on the Temple Mount during the millennium. However, Daniel 9:27 states that there will be a temple in Jerusalem during the tribulation period, when the sacrifices will be stopped. Preparations for this temple are already complete!

There is evidence that all of the items needed to build and operate a third temple, plus man this worship center for the sacrifices that are to be performed there, are already set in place. The men qualified to be priests in the coming temple are now in Jerusalem studying priestly duties. Even the priestly garments for these priests have been made and are in storage.

The implements for the sacrificial activities and the worship at the temple have been made. These implements would include the harps that are to be played at the temple when it is in full operation. A red heifer has been approved for the purification of these priests and all the implements needed to operate the temple.

There is one problem, however, the spot where the temple is to stand in Jerusalem. This piece of real estate is already occupied by the gold-domed shrine, the Dome of the Rock. Those preparing for the temple have said that the Lord will take care of the problem with the Dome of the Rock, in His time.

Trends to Watch

These four major trends were actually mentioned by the ancient Jewish prophets, up to 2,500 years ago. These are the signposts along the way that the prophets and Jesus alerted the Jewish people to look for at the time of the end, the time of the Second Coming of Jesus Christ.

When you speak of the "Preparations for the Potentate," these four trends mark this present world with evidence of His Second Coming. But remember, these trends are pointing to the "Second Coming," not the "Rapture," which takes place at least seven years before the Second Coming. Therefore, if these trends give evidence of the closeness of the Second Coming, how close must the Rapture be?

Aliya of the Jewish people, alignment of the nations, anticipation for peace, and arrangements for the temple—these are the four trends that we need to watch closely, especially in the exciting days in which we live.

And the LORD said unto Abram, after that Lot was separated from him, Lift up now thine eyes, and look from the place where thou art northward, and southward, and eastward, and westward: For all the land which thou seest, to thee will I give it, and to thy seed for ever.

GENESIS 13:14-15

Second Thessalonians 2 anticipates a Jewish temple over which the Antichrist and Christ will struggle. Most pointedly, in A.D. 95, after the first temple had lain in ruins for 25 years and Paul's revelation of the new aspect of God's program—the church—had been circulated via the epistle to the Ephesians for 34 years, John still anticipates a temple over which Satan and God will struggle and to which Christ will come in victory. If ever there was a time for an inspired author of Scripture to abandon the concept of a physical kingdom for Israel, it would have been John in the book of Revelation, but he did not. As the church was rapidly growing into a Gentile entity, John still promoted God's program for national Israel.

CHAPTER 10

Israel's Title Deed to Palestine

Thomas N. Davis

Overview of the Topic

In this chapter we want to consider the biblical, theological, legal, and practical claims Israel has to the geographic territory referred to as the land of Palestine. It is, no doubt, a controversial and complicated subject. It is controversial in that some individuals, such as liberal theologians, recognize Israel's ancient existence in the land but deny her current and even future right to that territory. Others, such as the Muslims, go so far as to deny any ancient existence in the land and are actively opposed to Israeli archaeology that might prove otherwise. A third group, which includes some ultra-orthodox Jews, cherishes the ancient heritage and longs for the future messianic era but labels the modern state of Israel illegitimate due to its secular carnality.

The subject is complicated by the various time-periods–past, present, or future. It is complicated by the triumphalism and replacement theology of some Christian groups, which views Christians as the new Chosen People, replacing unrepentant Israel and inheriting all of her blessings in spiritual form. This position suffers from the historic propensity to lend itself to anti-Semitism. Actually, the major divisions of evangelical theology that have developed since the Protestant Reformation are distinguished by their answers to two key questions: (a) Why did God choose the Jews? and (b) Why did God choose Saul of Tarsus?

The handling of the first question defines the past, present, and future roles of Israel in God's program for human history. The answer to the second question defines the nature of the church in relationship to Israel; namely, "Does the church incorporate Israel in the past and replace Israel in the present, or is there a separate past and future for national Israel?" The Apostle Paul's relationship to that theological point may not be immediately apparent, but consider the unusual transition from Christ's ministry with the 12 disciples to His ministry with Saul/Paul. If God had only one program—the church, then why spend three and one-half years with the 12 and then abruptly choose an outsider to become "the apostle to the Gentiles?" Answer: The 12 were primarily groomed for the messianic kingdom, and in its postponement they helped to found the church. The Apostle Paul was trained primarily as the theologian of the "new thing" ("mystery") and subsequently dominates the church epistles.

A final complication is the name "Palestine" itself. It is actually a poor term to use to label the real estate promised to Israel in that it is derived from the "Philistines" and was coined by Rome in A.D. 135 to de-Judaize the land of Israel. Hence the popularity among Muslims for the title, Palestine Liberation Organization (PLO) currently headed by the terrorist, Yasser Arafat. Arafat goes so far in his revision of history to proclaim that Jesus of Nazareth and Paul of Tarsus were "Palestinians." The term "Holy Land" is a term of endearment familiar to Christians, but not appreciated by modern Israelis because of that very association with Christendom. Actually, the term "Holy Land" occurs only once in Scripture (Zechariah 2:12). The pet name for the land in rabbinic literature is "The Land of the Gazelle" due to the small deer-like animals that grace the territory. Another designation in Hebrew is simply *Ha Aretz* ("The Land") or *Eretz Yisrael* ("Land of Israel"). In this discussion, "Israel" will be used to refer to both the Chosen People and the Promised Land.

The Biblical Claim to the Land

As early as Genesis 9:27, the scriptural record predicts the special place the Jews would have in God's program for human history. In the aftermath of the universal flood, God predicts through Noah that "He" (God, not the less logically probable antecedent in the sentence, "Japheth") would dwell in the tents of Shem.[1] It is from "Shem" that we obtain the word *Semites* of which the family of the Jews are one of the many branches. By Genesis 12 we have the famous Abrahamic Covenant, which promised a blessing (physical and spiritual), a seed (posterity in general and the Messiah in particular), and the land (the place that God would show Abraham, hence "The Promised Land"). This land-promise is repeated to Abraham in Genesis 13, 15, 17, and 22. It is confirmed with Isaac (Genesis 26), Jacob (Genesis 28), and assumed in the predictions to the 12 sons (tribes) in Genesis 49. One of these 12 sons, Joseph, is so taken with the promise that when anticipating his death in Egypt, he decrees that his body eventually be transported back to the land for burial.

The four hundred years that the Jews spent out of the land is considered a tragic exile from this land promised to Abraham, Isaac, and Jacob. Every year now for more than 3,400 years, the Jewish people have celebrated the deliverance from Egypt and the return to the land in their annual

Passover celebration, making it the longest-observed holiday in human history. Exodus, Leviticus, and Numbers recount the journey home and the re-establishment of the Jewish presence in that land. In Genesis 15, the northern and southern boundaries of the Promised Land are given. It is in Numbers 34 and Deuteronomy 28–30, as Moses passes the baton of leadership on to Joshua, that the boundaries of the land are described in great detail and formalized in what has been termed the "Palestinian Covenant" (Deuteronomy 30:1-10). Similar boundaries are also mentioned in Obadiah 19-21 and Ezekiel 47. In general, Israel has been promised from the Mediterranean on the west to the Jordan on the east; and from the "River of Egypt" in the south (not the same word for "Nile River" in Hebrew, so either the east branch in the Nile delta or the seasonal brook toward Egypt called Wadi el-Arish) to the Euphrates River in the north.

The Davidic Covenant (2 Samuel 7:4-17; 1 Chronicles 17:4-15) promises that a descendant of David will sit upon the throne forever. This certainly assumes that along with the physical king and his kingship (right to rule) there is a physical kingdom to rule over. The New Covenant (Jeremiah 31) does emphasize the spiritual blessings of the messianic age, but amazingly concludes with the physical evidence of ultimate fulfillment: As long as the sun comes up in the morning, the stars come out at night, and the earth rotates on its axis, God still intends to fulfill His promises to Abraham.

Even the spiritual setbacks of Israel do not interfere with God's unconditional promises. In Genesis 15, God anticipated and announced to Abraham the first failure that would result in Israel's enslavement in Egypt for four hundred years. In Deuteronomy 28–30, right in the midst of affirming the Abrahamic promise, Moses anticipates another exile (and subsequent return!), which occurred under the Assyrians (northern Israel, 720 B.C.) and the Babylonians (southern Israel, 586 B.C.). Jeremiah was assured that the

Babylonian exile would last for only 70 years (Jeremiah 25:11; 2 Chronicles 36:21). Daniel took note, counted off the years from his personal deportation in 605 B.C., and in 539 B.C. asked the Lord when the return would take place (Daniel 9). Daniel, the only Bible hero designated "greatly beloved" by God, was promised a future in the land for his people, the Jews.

Malachi, the last prophet to write before the birth of Christ, predicted the forerunners of Messiah to be Elijah (the great reforming prophet) and Moses (the great lawgiver). John the Baptist was enough of a fulfillment to hold that generation accountable for accepting Jesus of Nazareth as the promised Messiah. The actual appearance of Elijah and Moses on the Mount of Transfiguration confirms Malachi's prediction and points to the final fulfillment in the form of the two witnesses of Revelation 11, who represent the Messiah in His capital city, Jerusalem.

Finally, we cannot overlook some of the assumptions, especially in the New Testament, concerning the physical nature of the messianic era. In Matthew 24, Christ certainly envisioned a military event that would eventuate with His rule from a throne in Jerusalem. The 12 disciples were even promised that they would sit on 12 thrones ruling over the tribes of Israel. More pointedly, 2 Thessalonians 2 anticipates a Jewish temple over which the Antichrist and Christ will struggle. Most pointedly, in A.D. 95, after the temple had lain in ruins for 25 years and Paul's revelation of the new aspect of God's program—the church—had been circulated via the epistle to the Ephesians for 34 years, John still anticipates a temple over which Satan and God will struggle and to which Christ will come in victory. If ever there was a time for an inspired author of Scripture to abandon the concept of a physical kingdom for Israel it would have been John in the book of Revelation, but he did not. As the church was rapidly growing into a Gentile entity, he still promoted God's program for national Israel.

The Theological Claim to the Promised Land

It is obvious that Israel's claim to the territory under discussion, at least in the future, depends on the nature of the promise to Abraham, Isaac, Jacob, Moses, David, and Daniel. If the promise is unconditional, then there is no question. If, however, as those who hold to replacement theology would argue, the covenant is conditional, then at best, Jews will enjoy their land as members of the church only during the millennial reign of Christ. Of course, some propose no physical kingdom for anyone—all promises are translated into some sort of spiritual blessing or applied to the streets of gold in heaven.

We start the argument for the unconditional nature of the covenants by pointing out that when God ratified the covenant with Abraham in Genesis 15, Abraham did not physically participate because he had been placed in a deep sleep. It was God alone who performed the ritual binding His integrity to the final fulfillment. A second line of argumentation is the repetition of the key elements of the covenant throughout the Old Testament, despite continuous failure on Israel's part. A third, and especially strong argument, is Paul's teaching in Romans 9–11, wherein he concludes that the church has not replaced Israel in God's program "for the gifts and calling of God are without repentance" (Romans 11:29).

Further witness from the New Testament can be gleaned from the references to Israel as a people separate from "church saints." Galatians 6:16 says, "And as many as walk according to this rule, peace be on them, and mercy, and upon the Israel of God." *And* occurs three times in this one short verse. To argue that the third *and* should be translated *even,* thereby implying that all church saints are the "true Israel" flies in the face of contextual example, not to mention normal grammatical usage of the Greek word for *and.* Paul is not collapsing categories and announcing that the church is now Israel. Hebrews 12:23 likewise recognizes the difference between church saints and Old Testament saints: "To the general assembly and church of the firstborn, which are written in heaven, and to God the Judge of all, and to the spirits of just men made perfect." Revelation 22 ends the New Testament on the same note, teaching that even in the eternal state, the difference between Old Testament Israel (the names of the 12 tribes inscribed on the gates of the city) and the New Testament church (the names of the 12 apostles engraved on the foundations of the city) will be remembered.

Insisting on the unconditional nature of the promise to Israel does not contradict such dire warnings as found in Deuteronomy 28–30. There Moses warned the new generation that was ready to enter the Promised Land that they would be driven out by God if they disobeyed Him. There is a consistent interplay between the promise and this warning. Any individual or generation of Israel that expects to benefit from the promise must obey. The contingent nature of the fulfillment of the unconditional promise is best seen in Zechariah 6:15, written after the Babylonian captivity and five hundred years before the birth of Christ: "And they that are far off shall come and build in the temple of the LORD, and ye shall know that the LORD of hosts hath sent me unto you. And this shall come to pass, if ye will diligently obey the voice of the LORD your God."

It might be argued that God is not fair to the faithful if indeed He promised them a physical kingdom, but because of their neighbor's disobedience it doesn't come in their lifetime. It should be clear that God can rectify such "injustices" in the afterlife. What is undeniable, if somewhat obscure, is that in relationship to the fulfillment of this promise, God views the "Chosen People" as a whole. This can be called "corporate solidarity." It is immaterial if a godly Jew living in 783 B.C. has the privilege of experiencing the coming of Messiah. The point is, a godly generation one day will have that experience. Look at Zechariah 14:5, written around 500 B.C.: "And ye shall flee to the valley of the mountains; for the valley of the mountains shall reach unto Azal: yea, ye shall flee, like as ye fled from before the earthquake in the days of Uzziah, king of Judah: and the LORD my God shall come, and all the saints with thee." Not one of the people who heard Zechariah speak this prophecy was alive more than two hundred years earlier when this earthquake occurred during the reign of Uzziah, yet God speaks to them and treats them as the same people.

The descendants of Abraham were chosen by God for his purposes about four thousand years ago. Ogden Nash may puzzle, "How odd of God to choose the Jew." Jewish comedians may elicit a laugh by crying, "Please, choose someone else!" The fact of history remains—they were chosen. They were chosen to be representatives—priests—of God to the Gentile nations (Exodus 19:6, Deuteronomy 32:8, Ezekiel 5:5, Zechariah 8:23). They were chosen to be the biological line of the Messiah. They were chosen to be the bearers of His inspired revelation to mankind. With the debatable exception of Luke, every book of the Bible, Old and New Testaments, was penned by Jewish people (and Luke was probably a Jew raised in a Gentile culture). Despite these privileges, no generation of Israel ever came close to properly honoring God, hence, the land-promise to Abraham has not yet been fulfilled. There is coming a generation, however, that will be maneuvered by the elective grace of God into 100-percent compliance. During the seven-year tribulation period, God will see to it that every last descendant of Abraham either repents and believes in Jesus Christ (Zechariah 12:10) or is killed by the horrors of the tribulation period (Zechariah 13:8). That generation, the terminal generation, will therefore be worthy—and they will receive.

Legal Claims to the Land Today

A maelstrom of disagreement surrounds the existence of the modern state of Israel. The firestorm of controversy shows no signs of letting up. Literally hundreds of books and articles, by both Jewish and Christian authors, have documented the amazing return of the Jews to their ancient homeland over the last hundred years, the revival of their nation, and equally amazing, the revival of Hebrew as a spoken language (this last feat is unparalleled in human history). All such books document the various steps toward the statehood of Israel.[2] No matter what details are provided concerning due process (e.g., the purchase of unwanted swampland from Turkish officials, official decisions of governing bodies, international treaties, and so on), there will always be Arab sympathizers who will vehemently proclaim the "illegality" of the Jewish presence in Israel.[3] (It should be noted that in Israel and the countries immediately surrounding her, those opposed to the Jewish presence are primarily Arab of both the Islamic and Christian religions. Further afield, such as in Iran, the opponents are Islamic but ethnically they are not Arab. On the global scale, it is not an Arab/Israeli conflict, but rather an Islam/Israeli conflict).

Evangelical Christians have been great supporters of Israel. This is in stark contrast to liberal Christians who have sided with the Arab cause. Liberal Christians accuse Evangelicals of selfishness, implying that their support of Israel is an attempt to speed up the return of the Lord based on their understanding of prophecy. Some Jewish people are also skeptical of Evangelical support assuming that such "philo-Semitism" ("love of Semites") masks the ulterior motive of proselytizing. Other Israelis aren't concerned about religious issues but ponder the implications of "fair weather" support. As one Israeli soldier told me, "The last thing Israel needs is a group of Evangelical Christians willing to fight to the last drop of Israeli blood!"

A parallel problem is the failure of some Evangelicals, in their enthusiasm for Israel, to note unethical or immoral behavior when it occurs. It should be remembered that although, in general, we have a biblical mandate to support Israel, the Israeli leaders are not followers of Jesus of Nazareth and any tolerance of Evangelical activity in Israel is a tolerance of convenience, not necessarily conviction. Perhaps the most troubling problem and the most pertinent legal issue is the misapplication of the Abrahamic Covenant as a valid title deed to the land of Israel. In one sense, the Abrahamic Covenant is valid in that it is historically legitimate and, in fact, will one day be divinely applied. For the present, however, the curses of Deuteronomy 28–30 imply that Jewish people only "deserve" their land when they are in right relationship to their God. There is no contradicting the fact that it was the irreligious, socialistic segment of Jewish society that pioneered the modern state. Flight from racial persecution, socialistic theory, and nationalism drove the pioneers, not religious convictions. In fact, religious Jews condemned the attempt at statehood as a violation of the prerogative of Messiah. Gradually, over the years, the Israeli society has developed a growing religious segment.

In the secular legal sense, manifest Israel has the blessings of the international community to possess at least a portion of her ancient territory. It can be argued that the decision is flawed, but that has been the legal decision of world bodies dating from the 1922 British Mandate (which included the right of Jewish nationalism and was approved by the League of Nations) to the November 29, 1947, partition of Palestine by the United Nations.[4] Despite calls for the return of land captured in the 1967 and 1973 wars, the United Nations and even the recent agreement with the PLO calls for the recognition by all parties of the right for Israel to exist as a nation. However, in the biblical legal sense, the current state of Israel does not derive its divine mandate from the Abrahamic Covenant. We can safely argue that it is part of God's end-time plan to bring the Jewish people back to the land in unbelief, just as Ezekiel saw the bones in the valley form first into lifeless bodies, and only then did the wind of God breathe life into them so they arose and stood to their feet (Ezekiel 37). Israel today is analogous to Esther and Mordacai in the Persian court. There is little evidence of spiritual life but incredible evidence of God's hand working in her midst!

Practical Considerations

The plight of the Palestinian refugees has been kept before the unblinking eye of the camera ever since the War of Independence in 1948. Never mind that more Jews have been harassed and dispossessed of houses and lands in Arab countries in this century than any other. Overlook the fact that Israel quickly absorbed 600,000 disposed Jews in the years following 1948, while the Arab nations with billions in oil wealth have maintained the Palestinians in squalid refugee camps to this day.[5] It is still heart-wrenching to observe the humiliation of the Palestinian Arab. Sympathy, however, should not warp reality. Stark reality announces that (a) Israel is the only democracy in a sea of socialistic-leaning, despotic governments; (b) the very freedom of speech that allows reporters to enter and criticize Israel is forbidden in most of the surrounding countries and by the PLO itself; (c) Israel by far and away votes with the United States in the United Nations a greater percentage of the time than any Arab nation; and (d) if we demand that land taken as a spoil of war must be returned, then the United States will cease to exist as well.[6]

A Choice: Jerusalem and Antioch or Alexandria and Rome

C.S. Lewis's apologetic work popularized the pithy statement, "Lunatic, Liar, or Lord of all" as the only three options people have when confronted with the question of Jesus' identity. A similar reduction can be made in the question of Israel's title deed to Palestine. God's choice of Israel is either a fairy tale, a fabrication, or the final determiner of world destiny. Alexandria (where allegorical interpretation of Scripture developed) and Rome (where the temporal power of the church is championed) should not replace God's choice of Jerusalem (the spiritual and physical capital of the world) and Antioch (Paul's home church and champion of the literal interpretation of biblical teachings).

*And thine house and thy kingdom shall be estab-
lished for ever before thee: thy throne shall be
established for ever. . . . so did Nathan speak unto
David.*

2 SAMUEL 7:16-17

When our Lord taught His disciples to pray "Thy
kingdom come," He was not thinking that this world
was to get better and better until all would be a
kingdom of love and light; He was presenting Himself as
their King, who would establish His earthly kingdom,
prepared in the eternal purpose of God, promised in
the eternal Covenants of God, and proven in the eternal
Son of God.

CHAPTER 11

Thy Kingdom Come: Christ's Title Deed to the Throne

Thomas O. Figart

Many people think of the kingdom of God and the kingdom of heaven as strictly spiritual concepts, having their fulfillment in the Christian church. Part of the reason for this approach is in their theology, that the Jews rejected Christ as Messiah, therefore they are no longer God's Chosen People. All their promised blessings are incorporated into the lives of those who have accepted Christ, so that the kingdom of God is here now. Another part of the reason is in the hymnology of the church. One of the most beloved missionary hymns declares that the darkness shall turn to dawning, the dawning to noonday bright, and Christ's great kingdom will come on earth, the kingdom of love and light!

When our Lord taught His disciples to pray "Thy kingdom come," He was not thinking that this world was to get better and better until all would be a kingdom of love and light; He was presenting Himself as their King, who would establish His earthly kingdom, prepared in the eternal

143

purpose of God, promised in the eternal covenants of God, and proven in the eternal Son of God.

The Throne and Kingdom Prepared in the Eternal Purpose of God

It is evident from Isaiah 46:10 that Jehovah has declared "the end from the beginning," including the fact that He "will place salvation in Zion for Israel my glory" (verse 13); from Psalm 33:11 that "The counsel of the LORD standeth forever"; and from Ephesians 1:11 that He "worketh all things after the counsel of his own will." It is in Matthew 25:31,34 where Christ gave specific instructions as to when He would sit upon the throne: "When the Son of man shall come in his glory, and all the holy angels with him, then shall he sit upon the throne of his glory.... Then shall the King say unto them on his right hand, Come, ye blessed of my Father, inherit the kingdom prepared for you from the foundation of the world."

This promise was given to Gentiles in the context of the Olivet Discourse where Christ had already given similar assurance to the elect of Israel at His return to earth "with power and great glory" (Matthew 24:30). What this shows is that it will be no accident that Christ will establish a worldwide kingdom and a throne; they were *prepared* by the Father at the *beginning*, just as Christ the Lamb was "foreordained before the foundation of the world" (1 Peter 1:20) to accomplish our salvation, be glorified (1 Peter 1:21), and fulfill the purpose of God pertaining to the kingdom.

The Throne and Kingdom Promised in the Eternal Covenants of God

Curious as it may seem, the so-called covenant theologians never deal adequately with the scriptural covenants God made with Israel. Instead, they have formulated the "Covenant of Works" and the "Covenant of Grace," which are not part of the Word of God. In reality, the *true* covenant theologian is the dispensationalist who recognizes that four of the five covenants made with Israel are called *"eternal"* or *"everlasting"* including the Abrahamic Covenant, the Davidic Covenant, the Palestinian Covenant, and the New Covenant. Only the Mosaic Covenant, the Law, has been completely fulfilled in Christ (Matthew 5:17,18; John 1:17; Galatians 3:13,14). What, then, do those eternal covenants reveal concerning the throne and the kingdom?

The Abrahamic Covenant: Genesis 12:1-3

Basic to any kingdom is the land on which it exists, generations of *"seed"* (human beings) from which to form a nation, and *"kings"* (rulers) to administrate the government. All of these requirements are met in the provisions of the Abrahamic Covenant, originally given in Genesis 12:1-3 and reiterated and confirmed a number of times to Abraham and to his seed.

First, then, is the land: "Now the LORD had said unto Abram, Get thee out of thy country, and from thy kindred, and from thy father's house, unto a *land* that I will shew thee" (Genesis 12:1, emphasis added). This promise of the land was reiterated to Isaac in Genesis 26:3 and it was repeated to Jacob in Genesis 35:12.

A second promise was that generations of human *"seed"* be given to form the nation. This was mentioned specifically in five of the passages already quoted, in addition to the original grant in Genesis 12:2 that God would make of Abram "a great *nation*" (emphasis added). Twice in these passages, the land is designated to be theirs *forever*, as an *everlasting possession.*

A third part of these promises was that *"kings shall come out of thy loins"* (Genesis 35:11, emphasis added). Right before Jacob died, he gave the blessings on the 12 tribes of Israel. The line of kings was not to come from Reuben, the firstborn, as might have been expected, because Reuben defiled his father's bed "and lay with Bilhah his father's concubine" (Genesis 35:22). Even the beloved Joseph, who sustained them in Egypt, would not beget the kings of the southern kingdom; one of his sons, Ephraim, did become the progenitor of the kings of the northern kingdom. The *true* kings would originate from Judah (Genesis 49:8-12). In that passage, mention is made that "The *sceptre* shall not depart from Judah, nor a lawgiver from between his feet, until Shiloh come; and unto him shall the gathering of the people be" (verse 10).

Historically, the kings of the southern kingdom came from Judah through the family of David, the ancestor of Jesus Christ. The word *Shiloh* has been taken as a reference to the Messiah from two points of view. First, it may be grammatically related to *shalom* (peace), and thus to Messiah as "the Prince of Peace" (Isaiah 9:6), or it may mean *"the one whose right it is,"* being connected with Ezekiel 21:27, where the *crown* for the true prince of Israel will be given when "he come whose right it is; and I will give it him."[1]

In summary, the Abrahamic Covenant promised the land, the nation, and the throne, all of which would come together in the person of the Lord Jesus Christ, whose right it is to sit on the throne of His father, David, and rule over the house of Israel: "And the angel said unto her, Fear not, Mary: for thou hast found favour with God. And, behold, thou shalt conceive in thy womb, and bring forth a son, and shalt call his name JESUS. He shall be great, and shall be called the Son of the Highest: and the Lord God shall give unto him the throne of his father David: And he shall reign over the house of Jacob for ever; and of his kingdom there shall be no end" (Luke 1:30-33).

The Palestinian Covenant: Deuteronomy 28–30

This covenant was made by Jehovah with Israel as they were in the land of Moab, ready to possess the land of

Palestine: "These are the words of the covenant, which the LORD commanded Moses to make with the children of Israel in the land of Moab, beside the covenant which he made with them in Horeb" (Deuteronomy 29:1). This cannot be confused with the Mosaic Covenant (The Law), or with the Abrahamic Covenant, both of which were made earlier. In this Palestinian Covenant the lands of Heshbon and Bashan were taken from Sihon and Og "for an inheritance unto the Reubenites, and to the Gadites, and to the half tribe of Manasseh" (Deuteronomy 29:8). The LORD would then bring the ten remaining tribes "into *the land* which thy fathers possessed, and thou shalt possess it; and he will do thee good, and multiply thee above thy fathers" (Deuteronomy 30:5, emphasis added). This included "*all the land* of Canaan, for an *everlasting* possession" (Genesis 17:8, emphasis added).

How does the Palestinian Covenant concerning the eternal possession of the land help to prove Christ's title deed to the throne? Prophecies of three dispersions of Israel, first to Egypt (Genesis 15:13), then to Babylon (Jeremiah 25:11), then to all nations (Luke 21:20-34), have been fulfilled literally. Prophecies of the first two returns were fulfilled historically. Thus, prophecies of the third return will also be fulfilled literally. Ever since Israel was declared a nation in 1948, Jews from all over the world have been returning to Israel, and the full restoration will eventually fulfill such prophecies as Isaiah 11:1-12; Jeremiah 31:31-34 when the land will blossom and prosper under Messiah, the greater Son of David; and Amos 9:11,12,15, when God will "raise up the tabernacle of David that is fallen, and close up the breaches thereof; and I will raise up his ruins, and I will build it as in the days of old: That they may possess the remnant of Edom, and of all the heathen, which are called by my name, saith the LORD that doeth this. . . And I will plant them upon *their land,* and they shall no more be pulled up out of *their land* which I have given them, saith the

LORD thy God " (emphasis added). This will occur when "the children of Israel return, and seek the LORD, their God, and David, their king, and shall fear the LORD and his goodness in the latter days" (Hosea 3:5). In the context of Acts 15 when James shows that the salvation provided by Jesus Christ is not for Jews only, but also for Gentiles, he connects it with this very passage from Amos 9:11-15 as proof (Acts 15:15-18).

The Davidic Covenant: 2 Samuel 7:8-17

As is evident from the quotation from Luke 1:30-33, the Davidic Covenant is also involved in the establishing of proof for the claims of Christ as the coming king. In the Covenant with David, seven aspects are to be noted: "and have made thee a great *name*" (verse 9); "I will appoint a place for my people Israel, and will plant them, that they may dwell in *a place of their own*, and move no more" (verse 10); "Also the LORD telleth thee that he will make thee an *house*" (verse 11); "I will set up thy *seed* after thee" (verse 12); "and I will establish his *kingdom*" (verse 12); "I will establish the *throne* of his kingdom for ever" (verse 13); and in verse 16, "And thine house and thy kingdom shall be established *for ever* before thee: thy throne shall be established *for ever*" (2 Samuel 7:9,10,11,12,13,16, emphasis added).

Psalm 89 is the psalm of the Davidic Covenant, and it makes clear that though disobedience will bring chastening to David, or to his seed, the covenant will remain eternally intact: "I have made a covenant with my chosen, I have sworn unto David my servant, Thy *seed* will I establish *for ever*, and build up thy *throne* to all generations. Selah. . . . If his children forsake my law . . . If they break my statutes . . . Then I will visit their transgression with the rod, and their iniquity with stripes. Nevertheless my lovingkindness will I not utterly take from him, nor suffer my faithfulness to fail. My covenant will I not break, nor alter the thing that is gone out of my lips" (Psalm 89:3,4,30-34, emphasis added).

In summary, all the promises of the Abrahamic Covenant are duplicated in the Davidic Covenant, with the added assurance that human failure cannot cause Jehovah to change his mind *or* alter his promises made to David and his seed. The prophet Jeremiah lived at the time of the destruction of the Davidic kingdom by Babylon; yet, even in that day he prophesied of a restored Davidic kingdom and king: "Behold, the days come, saith the LORD, that I will raise unto David a righteous Branch, and *a King shall reign* and prosper, and shall execute judgment and justice *in the earth*. In his days Judah shall be saved, and Israel shall dwell safely: and this *is* his name whereby he shall be called, THE LORD OUR RIGHTEOUSNESS" (Jeremiah 23:5,6, emphasis added). Then Jeremiah added that people shall say "The LORD liveth, which brought up and which led the seed of the house of Israel out of the north country, and from *all countries* whither I had driven them; and they shall dwell in *their own land*" (23:8, emphasis added). This means that any attempt to transfer the blessings of Israel to the church because of the disobedience of the Jewish nation, or anyone in it, is unscriptural and should not be a part of Christian theology! Nor is the throne of David to be confused with the seat upon which Christ sat down on the right hand of the Father in heaven (Hebrews 1:3,13; 8:1; 10:12; 12:2). If the throne of David is to be forever, then the claims of Scripture that Christ will sit upon the throne of Israel in the place of their own and reign over the house of Israel must be fulfilled literally, or language means nothing.

The New Covenant: Jeremiah 31:31-34

In the same way that the prophet Jeremiah gave Jehovah's promise of a restored Davidic kingdom, he also recorded Jehovah's promise of the "new covenant with the house of

Israel, and with the house of Judah (Jeremiah 31:31). This covenant would be in contrast to the Mosaic Covenant (31:32). It will come in the future, "After those days" (verse 33) of tribulation when the nation as a whole will serve God and will know God, and when the LORD will "remember their sin no more" (verse 34). The *nation* is promised to be in existence "for ever" (verse 36) and the city of Jerusalem will be rebuilt, never to be "thrown down any more for ever" (verse 40)

How does Jesus Christ, the Messiah, relate to this new covenant? Basic to its formation, He is the "*mediator* of the new covenant" (Hebrews 12:24, emphasis added) because it was made in His blood: "For this is *my blood* of the new testament [covenant], which is shed for many for the remission of sins" (Matthew 26:28, emphasis added).

All of these promises in the eternal covenants will culminate in the declaration of "ten thousand times ten thousand, and thousands of thousands; Saying with a loud voice, Worthy is the Lamb that was slain to receive power, and riches, and wisdom, and strength, and honour, and glory, and blessing" (Revelation 5:11-12).

The Throne and Kingdom Proven in the Eternal Son of God

Proven by His Genealogies: Matthew 1:1-17; Luke 3:23-38

In the gospel of John the title "*Son of David*" does *not* occur *even* once, and the term "seed of David" referring to the Messiah, is used *only* once, in John 7:42 where the *people* reason: "Hath not the Scripture said, That Christ cometh of the seed of David, and out of the town of Bethlehem, where David was?" It is in Matthew where the title "*Son of David*" is given in reference to Christ nine times. This is not surprising, because Matthew's emphasis is on Christ as king. If Christ is the rightful heir to the throne of David, as the angel Gabriel revealed to Mary before she conceived Jesus (Luke 1:31-33), then it should be expected that His genealogies would reflect this directly; and they do!

Matthew 1:1 begins: "The book of the generation of Jesus Christ, the son of David, the son of Abraham," immediately relating Him to the Abrahamic and Davidic Covenants, David being mentioned first, because this is to be Matthew's thrust. Through David's son Solomon (verse 6) the ancestry of Christ is traced, which gives Him the *legal* claim to the throne of David. In verse 16 further proof is added by the specific wording "Jesus, who is called Christ." Jesus (Joshua) was a common name, so here, the participial phrase distinguishes Him as "Jesus, the one being called Messiah." He is therefore being presented as Joseph's *legal* son and heir to the throne of David. However, though this helps to solve one problem, it introduces another. According to Jeremiah 22:24-30, Coniah (Jeconiah) was cursed by God to the effect that none of his seed could sit upon the throne of David; therefore Messiah could not be born of the family of Solomon, through whom Jeconiah descended.

Thus, in Matthew 1:16 when the lineage is traced down through Joseph, he is called "the husband of Mary, of whom was born Jesus, who is called Christ." The phrase "*of whom*" is feminine, indicating that Mary is the antecedent of "*whom*" so it was through Mary that Jesus was born, and not by Joseph. McNeile clarified this when he wrote: "The nature of the genealogy shows that *egennesen* throughout denotes legal, not necessarily physical descent: Not till the Lord's mother is reached is the formula altered, and *egennethe* denotes physical birth."[2]

In other words, the entire listing uses "*begot*" (*egennesen*, aorist active), which simply means "to beget," not necessarily immediate parentage, but merely direct descent. However, when speaking of the birth of Christ through Mary, Matthew changed to the aorist *passive* form (*egennethe*) showing *direct, immediate* birth.

Luke's genealogy (Luke 3:23-38), begins with "Jesus himself" (verse 23) and traces the family line back to David through Nathan instead of Solomon (Luke 3:31). Nathan was also born of David and Bathsheba (1 Chronicles 3:5). This listing bypasses the curse on Jeconiah, and therefore must be the genealogy of Christ through His mother Mary. Godet has presented an excellent, extended discussion of this genealogy, making a number of pertinent points.[3]

The comments of Godet deal with Luke 3:23: "And Jesus himself began to be about thirty years of age, being (as was supposed) the son of Joseph, which was the son of Heli." The *transliterated* Greek text is: "*on (hos enomidzeto) huios Ioseph, tou Heli.*" Literally *translated* it is: "*being, (as was supposed) son of Joseph, of the Heli.*" Godet observed that the definite article "*the*" (*tou*) was omitted "... before the name Joseph. This word is found before all the names belonging to the genealogical series.... This want of the article puts the name Joseph outside the genealogical series properly so called.... If the name Joseph had been intended by Luke to be the basis of the entire genealogical series, it would have been fixed and determined by the article with much greater reason certainly than the names that follow. The genitive *tou Heli* (*of Heli*) depends therefore not on Joseph, but rather on the word *son*. . . . With this reading, the only thing left to us is to make *tou Heli* depend on the participle *on*: 'Jesus . . . being . . . [born] of Heli.' An antithesis might be found between the real fact (*on, being*) and the apparent (*enomidzeto, as was thought*): 'being, as was thought, a son of Joseph, [in reality] born of Heli'"[4]

From all this, Godet drew two conclusions. First that the genealogy in Luke is that of Heli, the father of Mary and the *grandfather* of Jesus, and second that this is opposed to His affiliation by Joseph but can be nothing else than the genealogy of Jesus through Mary. Because mothers were not normally listed in the genealogical records: "There was only one way of filling up the hiatus, resulting from the absence of the father between the grandfather and his grandson—namely, to introduce the name of the *presumed* father, noting at the same time the falseness of this opinion."[5]

In his extended work on the gospel of Luke, Darrell Bock lists six theories concerning the genealogies, but finds discrepancies in each one. He concludes: "Nevertheless, the genealogy's point is obvious. Jesus has a claim to the throne through David and is related to all of humanity through Adam."[6] The view presented by Godet, however, solves many of the difficulties and satisfies the major requirements, namely, that Matthew's gospel gives the genealogy through Joseph, maintaining Christ's *legal* right to the throne of David. And Luke's gospel presents the genealogy of Christ through Mary's father, Heli, affirming Christ's *natural* right to the throne of David.

Proven by His Four Witnesses: John 5:33-39

In the first part of John 5, Jesus healed an impotent man at the pool of Bethesda in Jerusalem. Soon after, the Jews accused Jesus of breaking the sabbath. When He replied, "My Father worketh hitherto, and I work," (John 5:17) the Jews sought the more to kill Him, because He not only had broken the sabbath, but said that God was His father, making Himself equal with God. These Jews actually perceived correctly the two things Jesus had claimed: that God was His *own* Father (*idios*, His own specifically, in a way no one else could claim), and that He was *equal* (*isos*, equal in person) with God. Immediately after this, Jesus gave an extended testimony of His relationship with the Father (John 5:19-31) and followed this with a list of four witnesses to His Person and work. Each of the first three witnesses can be traced to the fourth witness, the Scriptures. John the Baptist is first, then the works of Jesus, third is the Father, and finally the Scriptures.

The Witness of John the Baptist: John 1:15-34; cf. Isaiah 40:1-5. Four times in this passage John the Baptist is specified as a "*witness*" of Jesus, and the purpose of John's ministry is "that he should be made manifest to Israel" (John 1:31). John claims that he is the forerunner prophesied in Isaiah 40:3, which he quotes as proof. Had he quoted verse 5, it would have extended to the time when "the glory of the Lord shall be revealed, and all flesh shall see it together." John therefore not only bore witness to Jesus as the Lamb of God and the only begotten of the Father, but as the One who would some day make all the crooked places straight and the rough places plain, when He revealed the glory of Jehovah to all the earth! Only in an earthly, Messianic kingdom could this be possible!

The Witness of His Miraculous Works: John 7:31; cf. Isaiah 35:5-6.

"Many of the people believed on him, and said, When Christ cometh, will he do more miracles than these which this man hath done?" (John 7:31). Apparently the Jews were expecting a miracle-working Messiah from such prophecies as Isaiah 35:5,6 which specify that "then the eyes of the blind shall be opened, and the ears of the deaf shall be unstopped. Then shall the lame man leap as an hart, and the tongue of the dumb sing." Yet, Christ had performed much *more* than this; He had multiplied the loaves and fishes, had walked on water, had calmed the stormy sea of Galilee, and had restored life to the dead! This prompted the Apostle John to record: "And many other signs truly did Jesus in the presence of his disciples, which are not written in this book: But these are written, that ye might believe that Jesus is the Christ, the Son of God; and that believing ye might have life through his name" (John 20:30,31). What further witness is needed that Jesus has proven (by His works) His right to reign as the Son of David, the Messiah, the Son of God?

The Witness of His Father: Psalms 2,45,102,110.

When Jesus said, "And the Father himself, which hath sent me, hath borne witness of me" (John 5:37), He may have had reference to the Father's *voice* from heaven at His baptism (Matthew 3:17), at His Transfiguration (Matthew 17:5), and at His approaching death (John 12:28), or He may also have included in this statement the Old Testament witness of His Father, as exemplified in Psalms 2,45,102,110.

1. Psalm 2:6-9; cf. Acts 13:33; Hebrews 1:5. The second psalm contains prophecies of both advents of Messiah. With regard to the first advent, Psalm 2:1-4 predicts the antagonism of the kings and rulers against the LORD and His Messiah. The fulfillment of this occurred at the crucifixion of Christ, as noted by Peter in Acts 4:25-27. In Psalm 2:6-9 the Second Advent of Messiah is in view, when, as Jehovah witnesses, "I have set my king upon my holy hill of Zion" (verse 6). In verse 8 Jehovah declares, "Ask of me, and I shall give thee the heathen for thine inheritance, and the uttermost parts of the earth for thy possession." In Acts 13:33 Paul quoted Psalm 2:7 as referring to the resurrection of Christ, thus showing that the crucifixion at the First Advent was overcome by His victorious resurrection, enabling Him to fulfill the prophecies of the Second Advent when He will return and rule as king over the uttermost parts of the earth. Hebrews 1:5 uses Psalm 2:7 to prove that Jesus is better than the angels because God never said to an angel, "Thou art my Son, This day have I begotten thee." Jesus was not only the eternally begotten Son of God, but was begotten again from the dead as well!

2. Psalm 45:6,7; cf. Hebrews 1:8,9. This psalm speaks of Messiah's throne, of the scepter of His kingdom, of His righteousness, and of the fact that *"God hath anointed"* Him above His fellows. In Hebrews 1:8,9 this is prophesied to be fulfilled by the Son of God. Significantly, the Greek text is very strong, for it reads: "But unto the Son he saith [that is, in

contrast to the angels, who are merely ministers of God],
"thy throne, *the* God [*Ho thronos sou, Ho Theos*] is forever and
ever" (verse 8, emphasis added). Thus, another direct witness from the Father, includes two facts: that Christ will have
His own throne, and that He is proclaimed as "*the God*" by
none other than God the Father!

3. Psalm 102:25-27; cf. Hebrews 1:10-12. Here the Father assures
the dying Messiah, who says: "O my God, take me not away
in the midst of my days," that Messiah's "years are
throughout all generations," and that Messiah, who created
the earth and the heavens, will outlast the old creation and
will change heaven and earth! How do we know that this is
referring to Messiah? Again, the book of Hebrews (1:10-12)
has made it clear by quoting these verses, which are a direct
vocal witness of the Father, as a proof of the superiority of
the Son of God over the angels.

4. Psalm 110:1,2, cf. Hebrews 1:13. This fourth prophecy giving
the witness of the Father is quoted a number of times in the
New Testament. For example, in Matthew 22:15-40, Christ
patiently answered all the questions of the Herodians, Sad-
ducees, Pharisees, and scribes. After this, He asked them,
"What think ye of Christ [Messiah]? whose son is he?...
They say unto him, The son of David. He saith unto them,
How then doth David in spirit [by the Holy Spirit—cf. Mark
12:36] call him Lord, saying, The LORD said unto my Lord,
Sit thou on my right hand, till I make thine enemies thy foot-
stool? If David then called him Lord; how is he his son?"
(Matthew 22:42-45).

There was no answer to His question. In bringing this
psalm to their attention, Jesus proved three things: first, that
Christ the Messiah is the Son of David; second, that Christ
the Messiah is the Son of God; third, that Christ the Messiah
will sit on Jehovah's right hand until God sends Him to rule
His enemies. The book of Hebrews also used this passage to

prove that Christ the Messiah is superior to the angels (Hebrews 1:13), and further, to prove that "after he had offered one sacrifice for sins for ever, sat down on the right hand of God; From henceforth expecting till his enemies be made his footstool" (Hebrews 10:12-13).

In summary, all four of these psalms, which are all quoted in Hebrews as well as in other passages, clearly present the Father as speaking these words of witness to the title deed of Christ to the throne.

The Witness of the Scriptures: John 5:39. It has already been shown that the Scriptures have verified the witness of John the Baptist, the witness of Christ's miraculous works, and the witness of His Father. There are many other prophecies in the Old Testament concerning His birth (Isaiah 7:14; 9:6; Micah 5:2; cf. Matthew 1–2), His death (Psalm 22:1-21; cf. Matthew 27), His resurrection (Psalm 16:10; Isaiah 53:10b), His ascension (Isaiah 52:13), His return (Psalm 24:7-10), and His earthly reign on the throne of David (Psalm 72:2-8; 89:3,4,29-37).

Conclusion

No more fitting summary to this subject of Christ's title deed to the throne can be found than His own response to the question of the two disciples on the road to Emmaus, after they said, "But we trusted that it had been he which should have redeemed Israel: and beside all this, to day is the third day since these things were done."…Then he said unto them, "O fools, and slow of heart to believe all that the prophets have spoken: Ought not Christ to have suffered these things, and to enter into his glory? *And beginning at Moses and all the prophets, he expounded unto them in all the Scriptures the things concerning himself* " (Luke 24:21,25-27 emphasis added).

And I saw the woman drunken with the blood of the saints, and with the blood of the martyrs of Jesus: and when I saw her, I wondered with great admiration.

An increasing number of "rational" people, including psychiatrists at noted universities, have documented alien abductions. UFO sightings are regularly reported. Millions of dollars are spent every year to search for intelligent life in the universe. New Age believers proclaim that earthlings must open up their hearts and minds to these highly evolved extraterrestrials so they can provide maximum help when they arrive. Is it too outlandish to suggest that this could be Satan's way of preparing mankind for the unleashing of demonic hordes in the planet's final conflict?

CHAPTER 12

The Coming World Religion

David Breese and Thomas N. Davis

A dominant theme throughout Scripture is Satan's rebellion against God. God plans to rule over mankind in a "theocracy" ("God's rule"). Satan has been trying to establish his "Satanocracy" ("Satan's rule") ever since the beginning of terrestrial history. Isaiah 14:12-14 and Ezekiel 28:1-19 critique the kings of Babylon and Tyre, respectively, but clearly have in view the evil spirit that energized them in their wickedness, thereby providing hints at Satan's origination and fall from grace.[1] Pride is identified as the sin that caused Satan's fall, and ever since he has been a deceiver and a murderer in his attempts to overthrow God's program for human history (John 8:44).

Because deceit is clearly his primary *modus operandi*, it should not surprise us that Paul, Peter, John, and Jude all provide warnings, even at the start of the church age, of the dangers of false teachers and apostasy. Matthew and Revelation indicate that the hallmark of tribulational religious observance will be demon-influenced Judaism and Christendom

(Matthew 12,24; Revelation 9,13,16). A subtle, but equally significant warning is that false teachers boast of their power over Satan, claiming to be able to manipulate him and his demonic henchmen (Jude 8-23; 2 Peter 2:10-22). First Timothy 4:1 provides the succinct warning: "Now the Spirit speaketh expressly, that in the latter times some shall depart from the faith, giving heed to seducing spirits, and doctrines of devils."

Apostasy

The word *apostasy* is a compound of two Greek words *apo* ("away from") and *istimi* ("to stand"). It means to stand away from where one used to stand. In scriptural usage, this refers to a doctrinal shifting from formerly held biblical teachings. It is clear from Colossians and Galatians that the two key doctrines subject to erosion are the person of Jesus Christ and the work of Jesus Christ (His deity and His substitutionary blood atonement). It is significant that all the major deviations from biblical Christianity err in one or both of these doctrines. This would include Roman Catholicism, which teaches a works-oriented plan of salvation; cults, such as the Jehovah Witnesses and Mormons, who deny both the deity of Christ and salvation by faith alone; and also classic liberalism, which finds both the deity of Jesus and His blood atonement intellectually untenable.

In recent church history (A.D. 1870–1900) the philosophies of Europe, and especially Germany, crept into the universities and seminaries of the western world, undermining belief in the supernatural. As man's confidence in his ability to understand science increased, so did the tendency to explain all phenomena by merely natural processes. These philosophies are characterized by the words *naturalism, materialism, evolution,* and *humanism.* Their application to theology was devastating to traditional Christianity.

Orthodox Versus Liberal Theology

Supernaturalism (God-Centered):	Naturalism (Man-Centered):
Virgin Birth	Human Christ Indwelt by God
Vicarious Atonement	His Death Was an Example
Bodily Resurrection	No Resurrection
Inerrant Scripture	Human Book with Errors
Divine Creation	Evolution
Depraved Humanity	Man Is Perfectible

These "liberated" thinkers wanted to modernize Christian theology by appealing to the intellect and intuition. They wanted to replace the authority of the Bible with man's intellect. They argued that "man's mind is capable of thinking God's thoughts after Him" and "all truth is God's truth." They wanted to apply the theory of evolution to religion, implying that "man is getting better." In regards to man's obvious sinful tendencies, they argued that before a child can run, he must first crawl, toddle, fall, and walk. Eventually man will learn to overcome his meanness through a social and psychological evolution.

As a result, the "theology" of liberal Christianity has apostatized into the following form.

1. Bibliology: The Bible is not inspired by God but rather the product of man's flashes of insight into the spiritual realm ("exalted thinking" such as Shakespeare evidenced).

2. Sin: There is no original sin. Man is not totally depraved. Man will evolve into perfection. Sin is relative, therefore we have to consider Joseph Fletcher's "situation ethics." We must emphasize the "dignity and

worth of man," consider the "ascent of man," and comfort those who seem to fall short with the sentiment, "good football players don't lose games—they just run out of time."

3. Christ: He was not divine. His death was an example of love, not an atonement (the "big hero concept").

4. Salvation: Christians should follow Christ's example of good works and strive for social reform. Christians are challenged to "fix the open sores of society [the slums]" and "society must be Christianized" because "environment controls character."[2] The famous "Social Gospel" is predicated on the mistaken idea that nurture is stronger than nature. Take the man out of the ghetto, and he will become a productive member of society, pulling himself up by his own boot straps.[3]

5. Future things (eschatology): Liberal theologians provide few details. They postulate that eventually "good" will banish "evil." Universalism is very appealing with the hope that eventually even Judas Iscariot and Lucifer will be reconciled to God.

6. Evangelism (missions): Missionaries should try to educate, not convert. People merely need to be informed that they are already acceptable to the creator. All religions are beneficial. Ecumenical harmony should be sought among all persons of faith.

7. Conclusion: In the sentiments of liberal theologian H. Richard Niebuhr, "A God without wrath brought men without sin into a kingdom without judgment through the ministrations of a Christ without a Cross."

The New Testament also uses the word *apostasy* in a technical sense. In 2 Thessalonians 2:3 Paul says, "Let no man deceive you by any means: for that day shall not come, except there come a falling away first, and that man of sin be revealed, the son of perdition." Here the King James Version translates the Greek phrase "the apostasy" as "a falling away." This is not any old apostasy but rather *the* [ultimate] apostasy when the world abandons its native religions, opening the way for the new religion of the Antichrist, which will eventuate in the earthdwellers worshiping his image (2 Thessalonians 2:4) and receiving his mark "by faith" believing *the* [ultimate] lie (Greek text of 2 Thessalonians 2:11). The goal is to unite the whole world into a common religious system. Initially, this will be headed by an already-established ecumenical organization—the "Harlot" of Revelation 17 ("Ecclesiastical Babylon"). Eventually the harlot will be destroyed and the Antichrist will demand direct worship. The calls and movements toward ecclesiastical unity, therefore, are of great import as we see the stage being set for Satan's end game on planet earth.

Obviously, in order to achieve a consensus, the lowest common denominator must be reached. Currently, the theme of that ecumenical body, the World Council of Churches, is: "The fatherhood of God and the brotherhood of man." Of course, with the powerful movement toward gender-neutral language, this may have to be altered to: "The parenthood of God and the siblinghood of persons." Since the 1950s, barely a year goes by without a dramatic announcement of ecumenical talks and compromises between the various denominations and divisions within Christianity. Even the current pope has made favorable statements concerning the eternal salvation and worthiness of other religions, despite the rather exclusive dogmas of Roman Catholicism. It should be noted that in all of these ecumenical discussions, the trend is "back to Rome" as usually all the compromises are being made by the protestant denominations in the ecumenical process. It is also stunningly significant that in the current controversy over the legal status of Jerusalem, the pope has offered, and the Israelis have entertained, the suggestion that Jerusalem become an international city under the care of Rome. It is hard to imagine Israel parting with their capital, but it would appear that, for at least some, Israel's internationalization would be preferable to division (East Jerusalem being given back to the Palestinians).

The So-called New Age Movement

Another recent wrinkle in religious development is the New Age Movement. Practitioners claim to be in contact with "highly evolved extra-terrestrials"—"ascended masters" who will lead mankind out of the wilderness of despair into the age of Aquarius. Actress Shirley MacLaine and her book *Out on a Limb* dramatically illustrates the unusual popularity of this bizarre belief. As is usually the case, many of the New Age channelers of these so-called highly evolved life forms (read "demons") are making a financial fortune as they manipulate the gullible and desperate. They claim that the climax of human history is near. They even have a ready-made excuse for the Rapture of the church saying that those with "bad karma" will have to be removed for the golden age to descend! In fact, some frankly admit that this "removal" might involve bloodshed, but this would be acceptable because those poor, blighted souls would be reincarnated and have another chance to join the "enlightened ones" in this great evolutionary leap upward to the age of Aquarius.

The New Age Movement does not have an authoritative center, spokesperson, or Scriptures. Therefore, it is best viewed as a loose association of mystical beliefs that borrow heavily on the metaphysical teachings of Oriental religions. It is reminiscent of the "flower-child philosophies" of the '60s. The general characteristics of this philosophy can be recognized in a variety of new belief systems such as New Orientalism, Cosmic Humanism, Cosmic Consciousness, and the Human Potential Movement.

Buzz words and phrases associated with the New Age teachings would include "awakening," "centering," "cosmic energy," "the force," "the global village," "planetary vision," "yoga," "transcendental meditation," "inner space," "the third eye," "harmonic convergence," "consciousness altering," and "channeling." Some of the symbols favored by New Age practitioners include the rainbow, pyramids, an eye in a triangle, the unicorn, Pegasus, the yin-yang circle, and a goat head on a pentagram. They are fascinated by ancient cultures and customs, seeking to rediscover the herbal remedies, spirituality, and harmony with nature supposedly enjoyed by aboriginal Indians on the various continents. The supposed power of crystals and even investigation of "white magic" are powerful draws as they seek to "draw down the moon" and harness the energy that permeates the universe. Perhaps the latest development in this evolving system is the "Gaia Hypothesis" (Gaia was the Greek goddess of the earth–Mother Earth). The Gaia Hypothesis claims that earth is a rational entity and will purposely retaliate on those who dare defile her environmentally.

While the New Age Movement is just a reformulation of old age satanic paganism, we can mark the modern rise of its current permutation to the writings of Helena Petrova Blavatsky. She was a Russian mystic and the cofounder of theosophy. She wrote *Isis Unveiled* in 1877 and *The Secret Doctrines* in 1888. Other influential thinkers include Alice A. Bailey (who died in 1949), David Spangler, and Benjamin Creme. David Spangler claims that his revelations are as important as Jesus Christ's. In 1976 he published *Revelation: The Birth of a New Age*. His publisher is the Lucis Publishing Company (an abbreviation for Lucifer!). Benjamin Creme is the self-appointed John the Baptist of the New Age Christ. He claims to receive telepathic messages from this "Christ," coming to international attention by placing full-page ads in key newspapers announcing the soon appearance of this exalted individual.⁴ In 1980 he published *Messages from Maitreya the Christ.*

The teachings of the New Age priests and priestesses are eclectic and broad. Most argue that revelation is on-going and supercedes the Bible. God is considered to be an impersonal pantheistic force. Jesus was a great man upon whom the spirit of "the Christ" descended, as it has on other great men throughout human history, such as Hercules, Krishna, Buddha, and Mohammed. Man is primarily a spirit being ("subatomic energy force"). Matter is not important. Man is basically good, in fact, man is a divine being. The goal of religious expression (worship) is to get in touch with yourself and thereby be "at-one-ment" with God (a perversion of what "atonement" means scripturally). "Evil" is just an imbalance, a lack of harmony in life, therefore there is no need for salvation in a theological sense. Meditation brings tranquility and tranquility opens the way for harmony. Reincarnation is the purifying process that leads to Nirvana ("blowing out," the Hindu and Buddhist idea of ultimate peace by being absorbed into the All-Soul). Lucifer brings wholeness to the receptive life. He is not to be viewed as an enemy of Christ but rather the necessary opposite, just as electricity requires both a negative and a positive pole to circulate.⁵

> Lucifer, like Christ, stands at the door of man's consciousness and knocks. If man says, "Go away because I do not like what you represent, I am afraid of you," Lucifer will play tricks on that fellow. If mans says, "Come in, and I will give you the treat of my love and understanding and I will uplift you in the light and presence of the Christ my outflow," then Lucifer becomes something else again. He becomes the being who carries that great treat, the ultimate treat, the light of wisdom.⁶

Maitreya ("the Christ") will come to inaugurate a new age of peace, untold prosperity, and happiness. Maitreya is in the world today waiting for the opportune time to reveal himself and his program. According to Benjamin Creme, Maitreya descended in July 1977 from his ancient retreat in the Himalayas and took up residence in the Indian-Pakistani community of London. He has been living and working there, seemingly as an ordinary man. Among other things, this new world order will need a world government led by Maitreya. Of him it is said:

> He has been expected for generations by all of the major religions. Christians know Him as the Christ, and expect His imminent return. Jews await Him as the Messiah; Hindus look for the coming of Krishna; Buddhists expect Him as Maitreya Buddha; and Muslims anticipate the Imam Mahdi or Messiah. Preferring to be known simply as the Teacher, Maitreya has not come as a religious leader, or to found a new religion, but as a teacher and guide for people of every religion and those of no religion. At this time of great political, economic and social crisis Maitreya will inspire humanity to see itself as one family, and create a civilization based on sharing, economic and social justice, and global cooperation. He will launch a call to action to save the millions of people who starve to death every year in a world of plenty. Among Maitreya's recommendations will be a shift in social priorities so that adequate food, housing, clothing, education, and medical care become universal rights.... From behind the scenes, the outpouring of His extraordinary energy has been the stimulus for dramatic changes on many fronts, including the fall of communism in the Soviet Union, the collapse of apartheid in South Africa, the rapprochement between East and West, the growing power of the people's voice, and a worldwide focus on preserving the environment.... On the Day of Declaration, the international television networks will be linked together, and

Maitreya will be invited to speak to the world. We will see His face on television, but each of us will hear His words telepathically in our own language as Maitreya simultaneously impresses the minds of all humanity. Even those who are not watching Him on television will have this experience. At the same time, hundreds of thousands of spontaneous healings will take place throughout the world. In this way we will know that this man is truly the World Teacher for all humanity.[7]

Evaluation of the New Age Movement

Some may ask what happens when a channeler receives a message from the unseen world. It is rather clear, in many cases, that the channeler is a fraud. Linguists have done studies on a number of these modern-day medicine men. Their "entities" claim to have lived in a particular period of human history, however, their accents, vocabulary, and practical knowledge of that time period is terribly inaccurate.[8] If they were "real" or even a demon, then the language and knowledge would be accurate.

Scriptures indicate that demons are capable of impersonating humans. In fact, the Old Testament phrase "familiar spirit" is based on the idea that demons are assigned to become "familiar" with a person to then impersonate that individual after his death in order to deceive the living. This was the practice of the witch of Endor in 1 Samuel 28. Looking at what these different entities teach, their demonic origination should be apparent. One reporter writes: "The entities endlessly repeat the primal lie, the three-fold creed of error: 'There is no death; man is God; knowledge of self is salvation and power.' "[9]

It is interesting to note the impact of the theory of evolution on twentieth-century thought. It has destroyed supernaturalism, sending man alone into the cosmos with no creator to guide him. Now that man has been without God for more than half a century, and the world has gotten very dangerous (via man's scientific endeavors!), there is suddenly a strong yearning for a touch from the spirit world. God has been defined out of existence, so what can evolution provide? It can suggest that there are other worlds where beings have evolved further than us. They have overcome their problems and are on their way to our planet to help us avoid the devastation of a nuclear holocaust. Some, in fact, have already visited—scouting parties to survey the layout of the land. An increasing number of "rational" people, including psychiatrists at noted universities, have documented alien abductions;[10] UFO sightings are regularly reported;[11] and millions of dollars are spent every year to search for intelligent life in the universe. New Age believers proclaim that all earthlings must open up their hearts and minds to these highly evolved extraterrestrials so that we can provide maximum help when the aliens arrive. Is it too outlandish to suggest that this could be Satan's way of preparing mankind for the unleashing of demonic hordes in the planet's final conflict?

Lest it be argued that "kooks" have always been among us, let us be reminded of the great popularity of the New Age teachings as evidenced by the recurrence of these themes in TV and Hollywood productions, video games, and the printed page. Walk into any bookstore chain and note the size of the New Age section. Most chillingly, note the number of books published for public school use that promote these beliefs. In one school library catalog, a mystery series of books averaging 100 pages each was offered. Of the 42 titles in the series, at least 15 discussed popular New Age topics, including: *Reincarnation, Shamans, Stonehenge, Unicorns, Alternative Healing, Astrology, ESP,* and *Poltergeists.*[12] Some school teachers encourage students to meditate, visualize, invite spirit guides, contemplate alternate lifestyles, and commune with the life force present in animals and nature. How very *special* that the Bible is banished from our public schools but non-Christian belief systems are openly investigated and sometimes even encouraged!

The Antichrist's Ecumenical Religion

Revelation 13:1-18 contains the gripping discussion of the religious system which will emerge at the end of time. It identifies seven characteristics of this global world religion. First, the religion is satanic: "And they worshipped the dragon…" (Revelation 13:4). The dragon is Satan. We can be both sad and amazed that he is able, by perverse spiritual magnetism and external coercion, to cause all the world to worship him. Satan is already the god of this world (2 Corinthians 4:4), so it is but a small step for people, by the millions, to fall in obeisance to him. Second, the satanic religion will be humanistic: "…and they worshipped the beast, saying, Who is like unto the beast? who is able to make war with him?" (Revelation 13:4). Who is the beast? The beast is a man of great, but perverse capabilities. He is known by many names, but his most common name is the Antichrist.

Third, the satanic religion will be universal. It will not allow for any other: "And all that dwell upon the earth shall worship him, whose names are not written in the book of life of the Lamb slain from the foundation of the world" (Revelation 13:8). Fourth, this satanic religion will be ecumenical. The organizers of this global religion will invent a minimal doctrinal statement to which people can easily subscribe: "And I beheld another beast coming up out of the earth; and he had two horns like a lamb, and he spake as a dragon. And he exerciseth all the power of the first beast before him, and causeth the earth and them which dwell therein to worship the first beast, whose deadly wound was healed" (Revelation 13:11-12). Worship implies a worship methodology, and we can be sure that the Antichrist will have a most beguiling one.

Fifth, the satanic religion will be phenomenal: "And he doeth great wonders, so that he maketh fire come down from heaven on the earth in the sight of men" (Revelation 13:13). We can be sure that anyone with this capability would instantly gather great attention. Many will believe in him as God because of what they see him do. Sixth, this devilish religion will be essentially pagan. The beast authorizes the construction of an image of himself and requires the world to worship that image: "And deceiveth them that dwell on the earth by the means of those miracles which he had power to do in the sight of the beast; saying to them that dwell on the earth, that they should make an image to the beast, which had the wound by a sword, and did live" (Revelation 13:14). Seventh, the Antichrist's religion will be exceedingly cruel: "And he had power to give life unto the image of the beast, that the image of the beast should both speak, and cause that as many as would not worship the image of the beast should be killed" (Revelation 13:15).

Rather than providing the peace, love, and security the religions of the world proclaim today, this ultimate form of religious expression will be the most oppressive system in all of human history. No wonder Satan is called the master deceiver!

. . . hide us from the face of him that sitteth on the throne, and from the wrath of the Lamb: For the great day of his wrath is come; and who shall be able to stand?

REVELATION 6:16,17

If the population of the world at the time of the Rapture is about five billion, and if 10 percent are believers and thus are raptured (that percentage may be too large or too small, I do not know), the Rapture will remove 500 million people and leave 4.5 billion. If half of that number are killed by two judgments that would leave 2.25 billion. But from that number many more who will die from other judgments must be subtracted.

One would think that in the face of all these judgments people would cry out to God for mercy, but not so. Instead they continue to worship demons and idols and refuse to repent of their acts of murder, misuse of drugs, fornications, and thievery (Revelation 9:20,21). The terrible judgments seem only to increase the hardness of men's hearts.

CHAPTER 13

The Tribulation

Charles C. Ryrie

The Uniqueness of the Tribulation

Unique.

That's the way our Lord described the coming tribulation period.

Even though we often modify *unique* by saying "almost unique" or "very unique," such is really unnecessary, because the word unique means "being the only one, unequaled."

"For then there shall be great tribulation, such as was not since the beginning of the world to this time, no, nor ever shall be" (Matthew 24:21).

Unique.

What will make this coming period unique? Two things at least.

First, the tribulation will be worldwide, not localized. It will "come upon all the world" (Revelation 3:10). There have been and are today areas of the world where God's people suffer terrible persecution. There have been and are today areas of the world where famines and wars are rampant. But the tribulation as described by the Lord will be worldwide.

Second, when the tribulation arrives people will act like the world is coming to an end (Revelation 6:15-17). "Acting like" is different from "talking like." Off and on throughout history people talk about Armageddon and the end of the world, especially when there is an outbreak of war somewhere or a new deadly weapon is invented and threatened to be used—but they do not act as if they really believe Armageddon is at hand. They still buy and sell real estate, accumulate savings and retirement plans, and plan for the future. But when the tribulation comes, all classes of society will act like the end is at hand and will prefer death to survival during those awful days. The future then, will hold no attraction for people. The uniqueness of the tribulation lies in its being worldwide and in its terror, which will cause people to want to die rather than continue living.

The Beginning of the Tribulation

The tribulation does not necessarily have to begin the day the church is taken to meet the Lord at the Rapture. The Scriptures do not say whether or not some time or how much time might elapse between the Rapture and the beginning of the tribulation. I personally think it will be very little time. But the tribulation actually begins with the signing of a covenant or treaty between the western leader, the Antichrist, and the Jewish people. This will signal the beginning of the events of the seventieth week predicted by Daniel (Daniel 9:27). "And he [the prince that shall come (verse 26)] shall confirm the covenant with many [of the people] for one week." This treaty will guarantee protection to Israel so that her people can safely reestablish the worship of Judaism and build a temple in Jerusalem. We know this because Daniel 9:27 goes on to relate that in the middle of that seventieth week Antichrist will break his covenant or treaty and sit himself up in the temple demanding to be worshiped (2 Thessalonians 2:4). Obviously then, some sort of temple will have been built in Jerusalem during the first half of the tribulation.

The Judgments of the Tribulation

Revelation 6–19 describes the tribulation period in detail and climaxes with the Second Coming of Christ (19:11-16). Within this section are three series of judgments: judgments described as seals of a scroll are broken open (chapter 6), judgments announced by blowing of trumpets (chapter 8,9), and judgments poured out of little bowls (chapter 16).

Interpreters differ as to the relationship of these three series of judgments. Some teach that they are a recapitulation of the same events.[1] That is, the trumpets review what the seals previously described but with greater intensity, and the bowls review the same events with even more severity. Others, including myself, see these three series following consecutively and doing so distinctly and in chronological sequence. That is, the trumpets come out of the seventh seal and follow that first series. For instance there are no explicit corresponding judgments for seals numbers one (false peace), three (famine), and five (martyrs) in the other two series. Further, there are no similar judgments to bowls number one (sores) and six (drying up of the Euphrates River). Even though these judgments occur in sequence, this does not mean that these judgments are evenly spaced throughout the seven years, for the bowl judgments apparently occur rapidly one after the other near the very end of the tribulation. These three series form a chronological structure of the seventieth week of Daniel's prophecy, the tribulation period.

The Seal Judgments

The seal judgments will happen during the first part of the tribulation. Two other passages support this conclusion. In 1 Thessalonians 5:2,3 Paul wrote that the day of the Lord (the time of judgment) "cometh as a thief in the night.... when they shall say, Peace and safety...." The first seal will bring conquest without war, for peace is not taken from the earth until the second seal is broken (Revelation 6:2,4).

There is also a chronological sequence in our Lord's conversation on the Mount of Olives (Matthew 24,25). This sequence hinges on Matthew 24:15, which describes Antichrist's placing himself in the temple and demanding to be worshiped. This we know will occur at the mid-point of the tribulation. The verses that follow verse 15 describe events in the second half of the tribulation and climax with the Second Coming of Christ (Matthew 24:16-31). Thus the verses that precede must be describing the first half of the tribulation. Indeed, the results of the six seal judgments find correspondence in Matthew 24:6-11, which specifically mention wars, famines, earthquakes, martyrs, and false religion, all of which correspond to the seal judgments.

The first seal reveals a white horse and a rider (Revelation 6:1,2). This is Antichrist, not Christ. He will conquer some unspecified nations and/or territory, but he does not remove peace from the earth. That happens under the second seal. Today we would call this "cold war."

The second seal reveals a rider on a red horse, which suggests bloodshed, and he does not bring war on the earth (Revelation 6:3,4). The fact that a great sword "was given" to him suggests that God is controlling all these events.

The third seal will bring severe famine to the inhabitants of the world (Revelation 6:5,6). The pair of scales suggests rationing of food. Normally one "penny" or denarius was a day's wage for a rural worker in Jesus' day (Matthew 20:2) and would buy ten quarts of wheat and thirty quarts of barley. At this point in the tribulation the food supply will be reduced by 90 percent. Because one quart of wheat was the daily ration for one soldier, that is, one person, what will families with only one wage earner do?

The judgments of the fourth seal will kill one-fourth of the people on the earth (Revelation 6:7,8) The means will be sword (war), hunger, death (fatal plagues that often accompany wars), and wild beasts who apparently will be unrestrained to roam the earth killing people.

The fifth seal reveals a heavenly scene in which martyrs are asking the Lord for revenge on those who killed them (Revelation 6:9-11). Obviously, before this time they were living on earth, having been saved after the Rapture. They were killed because of their testimony or witness (verse 9). As soon as they died they were taken to heaven and told to wait until, in the Lord's best timing, they would be avenged.

The sixth seal will bring widespread havoc on the earth (Revelation 6:12-17). There will be a great earthquake (other earthquakes during the tribulation are predicted in Revelation 8:5; 11:13; 16:18,19); the sun and the moon will be affected; there will be a great meteor shower pummeling the earth; and mountains and islands will be moved. The reaction of people will be to seek death by calling on rocks and mountains to kill them. The great day of God's wrath "is come" (Revelation 6:17). The tense of that verb indicates that His wrath will have begun to be poured out after it is opened. The Greek scholar, Henry Alford, affirms that the "virtually *perfect* sense of the aorist *eithen* [has come] here can hardly be questioned."[2]

In addition to these judgments, two powerful witnesses will be active during the first part of the tribulation (Revelation 11:3-12). They will have power to kill their enemies by fire coming out of their mouths. They will be able to turn water into blood and bring plagues "as often as they will" (verse 6). When Antichrist finally kills them at the mid-point of the tribulation, their corpses will lie in a street in

Jerusalem for all to see, but three and one-half days after they are killed, God will raise them from the dead and take them to heaven. Jerusalem will then suffer an earthquake, which will destroy one-tenth of the city and kill 7,000 people (Revelation 11:13).

Additionally, at the beginning of the tribulation, 144,000 Jewish people will be sealed to do some service for God (Revelation 7:1-8). What their service will be is not specifically stated, though their descriptions are immediately followed by showing us a great multitude in heaven who have been saved during the tribulation (7:9-17). Likely the salvation of some in that group will be as a result of the witnessing efforts of the 144,000.

The Mid-point of the Tribulation

Several very significant events will happen at the middle of the tribulation.

1. Antichrist will break his covenant with the Jewish people, stopping their worship and sitting himself in the temple to be worshiped (Daniel 9:27b).

2. Antichrist will kill the two witnesses (Revelation 11:7).

3. Antichrist will destroy the worldwide counterfeit religious system that has flourished during the first part of the tribulation (Revelation 17:16). These three events alone will remove all religious opposition to Antichrist.

4. Satan and his angels will be cast out of heaven (Revelation 12:7,8), and Satan will seek to destroy the Jews. Those who flee to a place of asylum, however, will be protected by God (12:13-16), but those who do not will suffer (12:14-17).

5. Antichrist will begin to force people to receive his mark either on their foreheads or right hands in order to buy or sell (Revelation 13:16,17). He will also kill as many

as he can who refuse to worship him or his image (13:15).

6. Although there is debate about the time of the battle of Gog and Magog (Ezekiel 38,39), many believe it will begin near the mid-point of the tribulation.

7. The trumpet judgments will likely begin then and continue for a time during the second half of the tribulation.

The Trumpet Judgments

When the seventh seal is opened (Revelation 8:1) seven trumpets prepare to announce further judgments on the world.

The first trumpet brings hail and fire mingled with blood on the earth so that a third part of the earth (a phrase not in the King James Version but in other translations) and a third part of the trees are burned plus all the grass (8:7).

The second trumpet results in a third part of the sea becoming blood, one-third of the creatures in the sea dying, and one-third of the ships destroyed (8:8,9). The ramifications for shipping, trade, and food supply from this judgment are staggering.

The third trumpet smites one-third of the fresh water supply, so that the water becomes bitter and apparently lethal because many die as a result (8:10,11).

The fourth judgment will affect one-third of the sun, moon, stars, and the uniformity of the day-night cycle. This may mean that the 24-hour cycle will be reduced to 16 hours or that the output of the power of these heavenly bodies will be reduced by one-third. In either case this would seem to result in a drastic reduction in temperature (though the opposite happens under the fourth bowl judgment in Revelation 16:8,9).

The fifth trumpet or first woe judgment releases demon-locusts on the earth (Revelation 9:1-11). No ordinary locusts, they come from the bottomless pit (or literally, the shaft of the abyss, verse 2). They have a tormenting scorpion-like bite, and unlike normal locusts they will not feed on vegetation but on people—except the 144,000 who will be exempt from their torment (verses 3, 4; compare 7:3,4). For five months they torture people who will attempt suicide without success (verses 5,6). How people will be kept from killing themselves is beyond our imagination, but that's the way it will be. Poisons, pills, bullets, knives, and all other means which people ordinarily use to kill themselves will not work. In describing these locusts John has to resort to using the words *like* and *as* frequently because they are so horrible (verses 7-10).

The sixth trumpet or second woe apparently also involves demonic activity (Revelation 9:13-21). John saw an army of two hundred million out of whose mouths came fire, smoke, and brimstone (verses 16,17). Some equate this army with the coalition of the kings of the east mentioned in Revelation 16:12. Others see them as demons or demon-possessed people. That demons are apparently involved seems reinforced by their weapons of fire, smoke, and brimstone—the elements of hell. Their killing a third of the world's population means that this judgment along with those who have been killed under the fourth seal judgment (6:8) will reduce the total population on the earth by one-half. Add to this the many who will be killed by famines, plagues, wars, and natural disasters, and the world by the latter part of the seven years will be inundated in corpses.

If the population of the world at the time of the Rapture is about five billion, and if 10 percent are believers and thus are raptured (that percentage may be too large or too small, I do not know), the Rapture will remove 500 million people and leave 4.5 billion.

If half of that number are killed by two judgments, that would leave 2.25 billion. But from that number many more who will die from other judgments must be subtracted. Let's say that at the time of the sixth trumpet there are 2 billion people on the earth and two hundred million demons are let loose. That means one demon for each ten human beings!

One would think that in the face of all these judgments people would cry out to God for mercy, but not so. Instead they continue to worship demons and idols and refuse to repent of their acts of murder, misuse of drugs (sorceries, literally pharmacies), fornications, and thievery (verses 20,21). The terrible judgments seem only to increase the hardness of men's hearts.

With the sounding of the seventh trumpet (the third woe) comes the announcement that the end is at hand, even though the bowl judgments must yet be poured out on the earth. But this last series happens one right after another and so near the end of the tribulation that the announcement of the end can be made with the sounding of the seventh trumpet.

The Vial or Bowl Judgments

The seven angels who have these bowls are given orders simultaneously to pour out these judgments, which they do in quick succession during the final months of the tribulation. At this same time Antichrist will still be forcing people to receive his mark, and many will.

The first bowl results in a "loathsome and malignant" sore on people who have the mark of the beast (Revelation 16:2), and Antichrist whom they worship will be unable to help them because they continue to curse God for these sores even after the fifth bowl has been poured out (verse 11).

The second bowl will result in turning water into blood so that every living thing in the sea will die (16:3). The seas will literally wallow in their own blood. After the second trumpet, one-third of the sea will be affected (8:9); but the destruction is not total. Imagine the stench and disease this will bring, especially to seashore areas of the world.

The third bowl, like the third trumpet, will turn the fresh water supply into blood (16:4-7). Apparently this blood-water will not be toxic because people will drink it without dying. This is severe and appropriate retribution because those who shed the blood of saints and prophets will have to drink blood.

The fourth bowl will increase the power of the sun to scorch people with fierce heat (16:8,9). The fallout from this single judgment staggers the imagination. Henry Morris details some of those effects.

> The intense solar radiation will again evaporate great quantities of water from the oceans and other water surfaces, lowering sea level and water tables.... Thus more and more water vapor will remain aloft.... Rain and hail as do reach the surface [of the earth] will probably be in the form of violent thunderstorms and tornado cells, adding yet more to earth's misery.... [To compensate] the great ice sheets on Greenland and the continent of Antarctica will melt [from the intense heat]. There is enough ice stored in these great reservoirs, it is estimated, to raise the world's sea levels about 200 feet if it were all melted...[3]

The fifth bowl will pitch the capital and kingdom of Antichrist into darkness (16:10,11). This will likely slow his efforts to force people to worship him.

The sixth bowl will dry up the Euphrates River, which forms the northeastern boundary of the promised land (Genesis 15:18) and which will have previously been turned into blood (Revelation 16:12-16). This will facilitate the crossing of that river by the armies of the kings of the east as they march toward Armageddon (see Daniel 11:44).

The seventh and final bowl brings widespread destruction on an already battered earth (Revelation 16:17-21). A great earthquake unlike all previous ones will divide Jerusalem into three parts and cause other cities to fall; islands and mountains will disappear; and a great hailstorm, each stone weighing about one hundred pounds, will pummel the world. The reaction of people? Blaspheming rather than bowing.

Babylon

Babylon, which has consistently had a long and dishonorable history, will be destroyed during the tribulation period. The religious/political facets of Babylon, the ecumenical religious system that will arise and be very powerful politically in the first half of the tribulation, will be destroyed by the Antichrist at the mid-point (Revelation 17:16). The commercial aspects of Babylon (18:3,7,9,11-13,19) will be destroyed by God in a single day at the end of the tribulation (18:8). In spite of the difficulties of carrying on normal commercial activities during the tribulation because of shipping and land transportation destroyed by the judgments, trade will continue until the end (18:11-19). Joyless, dark, and silent, Babylon's destruction will be a vivid reminder of the righteous vengeance of God.

The Campaign of Armageddon

In the latter part of the tribulation, a series of wars that will culminate at Armageddon will also be fought. These, too, will kill many and will end with the glorious Second Coming of our Lord Jesus Christ (Revelation 19:11-16). Details of these battles are found in chapters 15 and 16 of this book. When Christ returns, the terrible tribulation will finally come to an end.

"Come quickly Lord Jesus."

Who opposeth and exalteth himself above all that is called God, or that is worshipped; so that he as God sitteth in the temple of God, shewing himself that he is God.

2 Thessalonians 2:4

The Antichrist will strive for unity with a one-world religion, one-world economic system, and one-world government. In an effort to bring the whole world under satanic domination, the Antichrist will manipulate men through religion, economics, and government. The goal will be "peace at any price" (1 Thessalonians 5:3: "For when they shall say, Peace and safety. . ."). It is fascinating to note the desperation of twentieth-century man as far back as the 1950s: In October 1957, Paul Henri Spaak, Secretary General of NATO, said in Paris: "We do not need another committee; we have too many already—what we want is a man of sufficient stature to hold the allegiance of all people, and to lift us out of the economic morass into which we are sinking. Send us such a man, and be he god or devil, we will receive him."

CHAPTER 14

The Abominable Antichrist

Thomas N. Davis

His Names in Scripture

"Antichrist" is a familiar designation for the individual who will seek to control the world and oppose Christ during the tribulation period. John refers to "antichrists" in the plural referring to any opposer to God's program, but he is also aware of the ultimate embodiment of satanic rebellion, the "Antichrist." "Little children, it is the last time: and as ye have heard that antichrist shall come, even now are there many antichrists; whereby we know that it is the last time" (1 John 2:18). The word *antichrist* means either "opposed to Christ" or "substitute Christ." This allows for the possibility that not only will this individual oppose God's program, but he might also offer himself as the long-awaited Messiah for the nation Israel. The phrase "Abomination of Desolation" (or "abomination that makes desolate") is actually a reference to the image of the Antichrist placed in the temple by his right-hand man, the False Prophet, which is designed to be worshiped by the world (Daniel 9; Matthew 24; Revelation 13).

The name "Little Horn" (Daniel 7:7,8) is a symbol of Antichrist's insignificant beginning, but rapid rise to power: "After this I saw in the night visions, and behold a fourth beast, dreadful and terrible, and strong exceedingly; and it had great iron teeth: it devoured and brake in pieces, and stamped the residue with the feet of it: and it was diverse from all the beasts that were before it; and it had ten horns. I considered the horns, and, behold, there came up among them another little horn, before whom there were three of the first horns plucked up by the roots: and, behold, in this horn were eyes like the eyes of man, and a mouth speaking great things." It should be noted that the Greek king ruling over the territory of Syria around 170 B.C., a man by the name of Antiochus Epiphanes, also persecuted the Jews and desecrated the temple in Jerusalem (as Antichrist will do again someday). Some of the prophetic titles of Antiochus in Daniel 7 are applied by extension to the Antichrist (such as the "king of fierce countenance" in Daniel 8:23). It should also be noted that the parallel phrases from other translations (e.g., the New American Standard Bible) have been added to our theological vocabulary, such as "that lawless one" for "wicked one" (2 Thessalonians 2:8 NASB).

The descriptive phrase "the prince that shall come" (Daniel 9:26) refers to the Antichrist's nationality (Roman): "and the people of the prince that shall come shall destroy the city and the sanctuary." The title "Willful King" speaks of his strong headedness: "And the king shall do according to his will; and he shall exalt himself, and magnify himself above every god, and shall speak marvellous things against the God of gods, and shall prosper till the indignation be accomplished: for all that is determined shall be done" (Daniel 11:36). In 2 Thessalonians 2, Paul refers to him as "that man of sin," "the son of perdition," and "that Wicked [one]."

In Revelation 13 we have the famous symbol of his personal nature, "the beast" and his number, "six hundred threescore and six," the "mark or the name, of the beast." Much speculation has surrounded the significance of the number 666. It is clear from the book of Revelation that those alive during the tribulation will understand the significance of the number. For now, we can only safely observe that the number 6 is one less than the number of God, the number of perfection–the number 7. The Trinity could be designated 777. Satan (the "Father"), Antichrist (the "son") and the False Prophet (the "unholy spirit") would be 666. This number (or a numbering system based on 6) will be branded in the hand or forehead of people to control mankind financially.

Names for the Antichrist

Passage	King James Version	New American Standard Bible
Daniel 7:8	Little Horn	"another horn, a little one"
Daniel 8:23	King of Fierce Countenance	"Insolent and skilled in intrigue."
Daniel 11:36	Willful King	Will Do as He Pleases
2 Thessalonians 2:3	Man of Sin	Man of Lawlessness
2 Thessalonians 2:3	Son of Perdition	Son of Destruction
2 Thessalonians 2:8	Wicked	Lawless One
Revelation 13	Beast	Beast

His Historic Counterpart

On many occasions in Jewish history, Gentile persecutors have arisen to afflict God's Chosen People. There is an apocryphal story of a Jewish man caught laughing at Hitler as he was rising to power in Germany. Asked why he was so happy in the face of the growing Nazi anti-Semitism, the old Jewish man purportedly said, "When Pharaoh opposed us in Moses' day, God delivered us and gave us the marvelous feast of Passover. When Haman opposed us in Esther's day, God delivered us and gave us the delicious desserts of the Purim celebration. When Antiochus Epiphanes opposed us in Judah Maccabaeus' day, God delivered us and gave us the sweet treats of Hanukkah. I'm just wondering, Herr Hitler, what wonderful food we will eat when God delivers us from your hands as well."

Hanukkah ("Dedication") or "The Feast of Lights" is not mentioned in the Old Testament, although it is a bonafide Jewish holiday. It is not mentioned because it came into existence after the completion of the Old Testament. It is mentioned in John 10:22, "And it was at Jerusalem the feast of dedication, and it was winter." It is an eight-day celebration of the Jewish victory over Antiochus Epiphanes, the Syrian King (of Greek heritage) who defiled the temple in Jerusalem in 167 B.C. by sacrificing a pig on the altar and erecting an idol with his own facial image to be worshiped by the Jews. This sparked a revolt, which in 164 B.C. led to the first independence the Jews had enjoyed since the Babylonian captivity in 605 B.C. There was a cleansing and "dedication" (Hanukkah) of the temple. Due to the legendary story of the miraculous provision of consecrated olive oil to light the lampstand (Menorah) for the eight days needed to make more consecrated oil, the holiday is celebrated for eight days and features the lighting of candles every day.

Daniel 11 predicts many of the events of this period, and Antiochus Epiphanes becomes the ultimate "type" (example) of what the Antichrist will be like. Key similarities include: (a) anger, (b) violence, (c) disregard for Jehovah, (d) desecration of the temple, (e) an image in the temple, (f) severe persecution of the Jews, (g) claims of deity, and (h) ultimate defeat by the saints.[1]

His Character and Mission

The Antichrist will be like Satan incarnate. He will be the "second member" of the "unholy trinity." He will be a "Satan indwelt" man like the King of Babylon in Isaiah 14 and the King of Tyre in Ezekiel 28. In both of these passages, the human king is in view initially, but the view eventually shifts to a description of the malevolent force energizing the human king, namely, Satan. Satan is not omniscient, but he is certainly more aware of God's plans than we are. Looking at the sweep of human history, most likely, Satan has always had a man "in training" for the role of Antichrist: "For the mystery of iniquity doth already work" (2 Thessalonians 2:7). This would be why such men as Hitler and Mussolini certainly behaved as the Scriptures indicate the Antichrist will behave. Hitler even dabbled in the occult and hijacked the biblical concept of the millennium for his Third Reich. John warns us that "many antichrists" have gone out into the world, referring primarily to the false belief system of Satan.

The Antichrist will strive for unity with a one-world religion, one-world economic system, and one-world government. In an effort to bring the whole world under satanic domination, the Antichrist will manipulate men through religion, economics, and government. The goal will be "peace at any price": "For when they shall say, Peace and safety..." (1 Thessalonians 5:3). It is fascinating to note the desperation of twentieth-century man as far back as the 1950s: In October 1957, Paul Henri Spaak, Secretary General of NATO, said in Paris: "We do not need another committee; we have too many already—what we want is a man of sufficient stature to hold the allegiance of all people, and to lift us out of the economic morass into which we are sinking. Send us such a man, and be he god or devil, we will receive him."[2]

It is also interesting to note the role of Babylon in biblical history and prophecy. Herodotus, the Greek historian who wrote around 450 B.C., claimed that Babylon was the source of all the religions of the world. Babylon was founded by Nimrod, whose name means "Rebel" and whose designation in Genesis 10:9 as "a mighty hunter before the LORD" can also be translated, "a mighty hunter against the Lord." Perhaps he was a mighty hunter of human souls. Jewish tradition says he used tyranny to force men to accept a new religion and that he led people to rebel against God. Supposedly, his wife was Semiramis and his son, Tammuz. Semiramis proclaimed Nimrod a "god" after his death (the sun god, who eventually became "Baal" in the Canaanite culture). She bore a son, Tammuz, who she claimed was conceived by Nimrod after his death and was his re-incarnation! The family promoted idol worship and in particular the mother-goddess cult, which eventually molded the Roman church's theology of Mary and the Christ child. In the Roman pantheon, this was Venus and her son, Jupiter. Significantly, it was an image of Jupiter that Antiochus IV (who called himself "Epiphanes"–"the Manifest God") placed in the temple in Jerusalem (167 B.C.) as the first "Abomination of Desolation." In the city of Ephesus, the mother-goddess was Diana. Significantly, it was in the same city in A.D. 431 that the church council of Ephesus approved the veneration of Mary, the mother of Jesus. In fact, "Madonna" comes from the Latin phrase, "Mea Domina" ("My Lady"), which was also the title for Baal's wife ("Baalti") in the Phoenician culture. Our word *Easter* is a derivative of the Babylonian goddess "Ishtar," the "goddess of sun and spring." In the Babylonian culture, the egg was a symbol of fertility. The Babylonians pled with Ishtar for 40 days, crying for the resurrection of Tammuz, the god of agriculture. This practice is mentioned in Ezekiel 8:14.[3]

Babylon was also the first city to rebel against God (Genesis 11, the Tower of Babel). It was the only government in

Old Testament times to destroy the temple in Jerusalem and overthrow the Davidic kingdom (under Nebuchadnezzar). It reemerges in Revelation as the epitome of man's institutions in revolt against God in the one-world church (Revelation 17) and one-world economic system (Revelation 18). Currently, Saddam Hussein of Iraq proudly proclaims his "Babylonian" heritage. He has even imitated Nebuchadnezzar by rebuilding part of the ancient city of Babylon using bricks with his name stamped on them.

His Identity

Geographically and politically, Daniel 9 indicates that he will rise to power from the ashes of the ancient Roman Empire, meaning that he will come from the Mediterranean basin, dominating Europe and probably those countries that have descended from Europe, such as the entire western hemisphere. Socially, he will be received by the Jews as a savior. He will be like Saul, a man after the people's hearts, who fortunately was followed by David, the man after God's own heart. Or, like Herod the Great: the king who binds versus Jesus, the King who frees; Herod, the king by might–Jesus the King by right; Herod, the king who took–Jesus, the King who gave; Herod, the king who came to make all men slaves–Jesus, the king who came to open every grave![4]

Spiritually, the Antichrist will be known for bringing peace to Israel, the Middle East, and the world. This is the definitive event that "reveals" ("apocalypse," 2 Thessalonians 2:4) who he is and starts the seven-year countdown to Armageddon (Daniel 9). In fact, the Antichrist also has a "coming" (2 Thessalonians 2:9) mimicking Christ's "Coming." He is predicted to be anti-religious, only worshiping the god of war (Daniel 11).

His Career

The Antichrist rises to some position of governmental authority in the area of the ancient Roman Empire. He signs a protection treaty with Israel, probably also allowing the Jewish people to rebuild their temple (even a church epistle, 2 Thessalonians, predicts his desecration of a tribulational temple). The first three and one-half years of this seven-year treaty period is relatively peaceful as he consolidates his power in the West, using religion, political intrigue, and warfare. In quick succession he has a string of victories at the mid-point of the tribulation period, giving him extraordinary confidence. These would include: (a) the defeat of Gog and Magog (Ezekiel 38; Daniel 11:40-45); (b) recovery from a severe setback, either on the battlefield or from a literal death-blow to his person (Revelation 13); (c) the murder of the two witnesses and the "satanic gift exchange" of Revelation 11; (d) the satanic indwelling as Satan is cast from heaven and limited to this earth (Revelation 12); (e) the destruction of the one-world church (Revelation 17); (f) the construction of the image in the temple to be worshiped by the world; and (g) the severe persecution of true believers and all Jews, leading to a second holocaust (Zechariah 13:8). His career comes to a sudden and abrupt end in the Valley of Megiddo as Christ returns and casts him alive into the Lake of Fire (Revelation 19).

Cautions

Speculation has been a downfall of Christendom for most of its 20 centuries. Let's not forget that at least two recent perversions of orthodox Christianity began with setting dates for the return of Jesus: (a) the Jehovah Witnesses and (b) the Seventh Day Adventists. Speculation on the identity and behavior of the Antichrist has also produced a number of troubling "teachings." One is the suggestion that he has to be Jewish because he does not "regard the God of his fathers" but worships "a god whom his fathers knew not," "the God of forces" and does not long for "the desire of women" (Daniel 11:37-39). To this argument is added the note that Dan is missing from the list of the 12 tribes in Revelation 7 with the intimation that the Antichrist must have come from that tribe. Although it is appealing to think that in every way the Antichrist apes the real Messiah, none of these arguments are conclusive. Dan could be missing because that tribe was absorbed into paganism even before the captivities in Old Testament history (Dan was the northernmost tribe). The phrases from Daniel 11 could equally apply to a Gentile, and in fact, because Antiochus was a Gentile and the Roman Empire is part of the "Times of the Gentiles," this final expression of Gentile oppression will probably also be Gentile (unless God arranges a mixture such as existed in Herod the Great who was a Gentile proselyte to Judaism but represented the Roman government and did not favor his "fellow" Jews).

A second area of fruitless speculation involves the number 666. Using Gematria (deriving mystical meaning by assigning letters numerical values) almost any combination of letters in any language can produce 666. "R" is the eighteenth letter in the English alphabet ($6 \times 3 = 18$!). Do we really need a theory suggesting that a world figure with a name that begins with "R" is a prime candidate for the Antichrist?! Only those alive when the Antichrist is active will understand the significance of 666, and it will be crystal-clear to everyone.

A third area of useless speculation concerns the "head wound" mentioned in Revelation 13. Because many people have died and will die from a blow to the head, it becomes pointless to suggest their resurrection as the Antichrist. Judas, Nero, Adolf Hitler—they'd all make "good" Antichrists, but it is much more reasonable to think that the wound occurs during the events of the tribulation period. It doesn't necessarily have to be a personal blow, but could refer to a dramatic military or political fall from which the Antichrist recovers and thereby is catapulted to world dominance as seemingly invincible.

A fourth suggestion, hardly worth refuting, is that the Antichrist must be a "soulless man" who then can be indwelt by Satan. The modern concept of cloning is put forth as the vehicle for creating such a man. This theory overlooks the fact that identical twins are basically a prototype and its clone with each obviously containing a human "soul."

Finally, while obviously a perverse man by any measuring rod, it is not appropriate to suggest that the Antichrist must be homosexual because he does not long for the "desire of women." This awkward phrase in Daniel 11:37 has nothing to do with romantic preferences, but is referring to the longing of Jewish women for the coming Messiah, a longing this man will not possess.

Conclusion

2 Thessalonians 2:11 implies that "them that dwell upon the earth" (Revelation 3:10) who receive the mark of the beast will, in effect, be receiving Antichrist as their savior "by faith" just as believers receive Christ by faith. "And for this cause God shall send them strong delusion, that they should believe [the] lie." This is reminiscent of William Cowpers's powerful observation: "Hear the Just Law, the Judgment of the Skies: He that hates truth must be the dupe of lies. And he who *will* be cheated, to the last, delusions strong as hell must bind him fast."[5] The study of the Antichrist can be depressing, but because it is taught in inspired Scripture, it cannot be ignored. Most importantly, we need to remember that church saints are told to look for the "revelation" and "Coming" of Jesus Christ, not the Antichrist!

And he gathered them together into a place called in the Hebrew tongue Armageddon.

REVELATION 16:16

John describes Armageddon as "the battle of that great day of God Almighty" (Revelation 16:14). Instead of translating *polemos* as "battle," some translations use the word *war*. "Battle" focuses on a single engagement while "war" includes several battles, a campaign. But, the final military battle will be mainly between West (under Antichrist) and East (under the kings of the east) and will engulf the entire Holy Land. It will also involve other nations that have not been destroyed (e.g., nearby African ones?) because the three demons will incite the kings of the whole world to join the war (verse 14). Satan knows the Bible, so he knows that Christ's Second Coming is near and that He will return to the earth, at the same place from which He ascended. So Satan, the prince of this world, will make one last and unsuccessful attempt to thwart God's plan to glorify His Son and establish Him as the rightful ruler of this world.

CHAPTER 15

The Campaign of Armageddon

Charles C. Ryrie

What is Armageddon?

The very word evokes different images in people's minds. When nuclear weapons were first discovered, many military and political leaders announced that Armageddon was at hand. This meant that the end of the world was near because of the terrible destructive power of those weapons. Whenever a war breaks out somewhere in the world, we are warned that if it cannot be contained or stopped it might lead to Armageddon. Many understand Armageddon as having "no specific geographical reference in the designation and take it to be a symbol of the final overthrow of evil by God."[1] But Armageddon, however conceived, conveys something to be greatly feared and, hopefully, something that will never happen in our lifetime.[2]

Nevertheless, Armageddon will happen someday, and it will not be a battle between certain nations on this earth or a general conflict between good and evil, but the decisive battle between our Lord Jesus Christ with His heavenly armies and armies of this earth.

The Campaign of Armageddon

John describes Armageddon as "the battle of that great day of God Almighty" (Revelation 16:14). Instead of translating *polemos* as "battle," some translations use the word *war.* "Battle" focuses on a single engagement while "war" includes several battles, a campaign. Probably both emphases are valid, for there will be several battles encompassing more than just the local area of Megiddo that precede the final and climactic battle at Megiddo. The concept of a single battle is found in Revelation 12:7 (Satan and Michael and their respective angels: see Luke 14:31), though the idea of a campaign or war is in Revelation 12:17 where Satan will mount a sustained campaign against Israel.

The Various Battles in the War of Armageddon

Not all agree as to the time of the battle of Gog and Magog prophesied in Ezekiel 38,39. I incline to the view that it will take place after the middle of the tribulation, in the last half of that seven-year period. At the mid-point of the tribulation, Antichrist will break his treaty with the Jewish people, which, among other features, will guarantee protection for their worship in a temple in Jerusalem during the first part of the tribulation, and he will place himself in the temple demanding to be worshiped (Daniel 9:27; Matthew 24:15; 2 Thessalonians 2:4). The battle of Gog and Magog will involve Antichrist pitted against a coalition of nations from northern Israel. Egypt, the king of the South, will also join the attack against Israel in a kind of pincer movement, which will require Antichrist either to divide his forces and take on both attackers at the same time or to try to defeat the weaker enemy first. He apparently will decide to do the latter and turn his attention first to defeating Egypt.

He will conquer Egypt and apparently at the same time subdue Libya and northern Sudan, which are part of the northern coalition (Daniel 11:42,43; Ezekiel 38:5). But while in Egypt, Antichrist will be troubled by threats from the east and north (Daniel 11:44). So he will apparently turn his attention to the coalition from northern Israel, which by this time will have entered Israel. If this northern coalition is the king of the North of Daniel 11:40 (which is likely), then those nations may start moving toward Israel shortly after the mid-point of the tribulation. But they will not arrive in the land in full force until months later because of greater distances and more difficult terrain involved. The king of the South will have to cross in order to attack Israel.

The countries of that northern coalition are listed in Ezekiel 38:2-6; they include the territory of Magog, which will be ruled by Gog and was identified by Josephus as the land of the Scythians, the region north and northeast of the Black Sea and east of the Caspian Sea. Today these are the countries of the Commonwealth of Independent States including Russia, Ukraine, and Kazakhstan and perhaps some of the smaller states of the commonwealth. Meshech and Tubal includes the area of modern Turkey. Persia is modern Iran; Ethiopia, northern Sudan; Put, Libya; Gomer, probably the eastern part of Turkey and Ukraine; Beth-togarmah, the part of Turkey near the Syrian border. Many, but not all of these nations, now have large Muslim populations.

When Antichrist returns from Egypt into Israel he finds no living opposing army. God will destroy that northern army by sending "pestilence and ... blood ... and overflowing rain, and great hailstones, fire, and brimstone" (Ezekiel 38:22). As a result, this mighty army "shalt fall upon the mountains of Israel, thou, and all thy bands, and the peoples that is with thee: I will give thee unto the ravenous birds of every sort, and to the beasts of the field to be devoured.... And I will send a fire on Magog.... I will give unto Gog a place there of graves in Israel . . . and there shall they bury Gog and all his multitude" (Ezekiel 39:4,6,11).

With Egypt subdued and Gog, Magog, and their allies destroyed by God, the only enemy remaining for the Antichrist (who is the western leader of the revived Roman Empire countries) comes from the east. This coalition of the "kings of the east" (Revelation 16:12) will discover to its great surprise that the Euphrates River, which it must cross in order to enter the Holy Land, will have been dried up, making it easy to cross. The Euphrates River is the longest river of western Asia originating in the mountains of Armenia in modern Turkey and emptying into the Persian Gulf 1,780 miles downstream. It is at its lowest in September but rises eight feet by May with the melting of winter snows.

Are the kings of the East the same as the two hundred million hoard that kill one-third of mankind in the sixth trumpet judgment (Revelation 9:13-21)? They will be released by four angels who until that time are bound in the Euphrates River. Some interpreters equate the two groups; others do not. The time between the sixth trumpet and the sixth bowl will be short, which may support identifying them as the same group. On the other hand, the kings of the East seem to be completely human, while the two hundred million are more likely either demons or demon-possessed humans. This may indicate that they are not the same group.

The final military battle will be mainly between West (under Antichrist) and East (under the kings of the East) and will engulf the entire Holy Land. It will also involve other nations that have not been destroyed (e.g., nearby African ones?) because the three demons will incite the kings of the whole world to join the war (Revelation 16:13,14). Satan knows the Bible, so he knows that Christ's Second Coming is near and that He will return to the earth, at the same place from which He ascended. So Satan, the prince of this world, will make one last and unsuccessful attempt to thwart God's plan to glorify His Son and establish Him as the rightful ruler of this world.

The Defeat and Destruction of the World's Armies

The Scriptures seem to indicate three foci of the destruction of the armies of the world at the Second Coming of Christ. One relates to Jerusalem, another to Megiddo in the north of Israel, and the third to Edom to the South and east of Israel (in present-day Jordan).

Jerusalem

> For I will gather all nations against Jerusalem to battle; and the city shall be taken, and the houses rifled, and the women ravished; and half of the city shall go forth into captivity, and the residue of the people shall not be cut off from the city.... And his feet shall stand in that day upon the mount of Olives, which is before Jerusalem on the east ... and toward the west, and there shall be a very great valley; and half of the mountain shall remove toward the north, and half of it toward the south. And ye shall flee to the valley of the mountains ... and the LORD my God shall come, and all the saints with thee (Zechariah 14:2-5).

According to this passage, at the end of the tribulation the armies opposing the Lord will attempt to capture Jerusalem with house-to-house fighting and will be temporarily successful. But the Lord will empower the inhabitants of Jerusalem to fight like the mighty King of David (Zechariah 12:8). Too, He will send "the plague wherewith the LORD will smite all the people that have fought against Jerusalem; Their flesh shall consume away while they stand upon their feet, and their eyes shall consume away in their holes, and their tongue shall consume away in their mouth" (Zechariah 14:12). And the Lord will come and stand on the Mount of Olives from which He ascended (Acts 1:11,12). The Mount of Olives will split, providing a valley through which survivors may flee, and He "will seek to destroy all the nations that come against Jerusalem" (Zechariah 12:9). At His Second Coming Israel will recognize Jesus as her Messiah, acknowledging with deep contrition that He was the One whom their forefathers pierced (Zechariah 12:10). The land will be healed and changed, and the Lord will be king over all the earth (Zechariah 14:9,10).

Jerusalem will be a center of tremendous fighting just before and at the Second Coming of Christ.

Megiddo

As we have noted, God will send an angel to pour out His wrath by drying up the eastern boundary of the Holy Land, the Euphrates River, to facilitate the crossing of the kings of the East. Satan, the Antichrist, and his false prophet will send three demons to convince world leaders to send their troops to Megiddo. To authenticate their message, these demons will be able to work miracles, which will convince the nations to mobilize for the battle of Armageddon. God is involved, Satan is involved, Antichrist is involved, and doubtless governmental bodies will be involved by ratifying the actions of their leaders—all are involved to bring the climactic battle at Megiddo.

The outcome of the conflict at Megiddo is certain—Christ and His heavenly armies will win and win decisively.

Will the conflict that centers in Jerusalem precede or follow that which centers in Megiddo? It is hard to tell. If Megiddo follows Jerusalem, perhaps it will be because having been routed from Jerusalem, the armies retreat north to Megiddo to regroup, bivouac, and prepare for what they assume will be the next attack on them. Then the coming of Christ will utterly destroy those armies. So extensive will be the slaughter that an angel will call birds to eat the flesh from the corpses of those who have been killed (Revelation

19:17,18). Then Antichrist, his false prophet, and his followers, those who received his mark and worshiped him, will be cast alive into the lake of fire and brimstone forever.

If the conflict in Jerusalem follows that at Megiddo, it would mean that some troops would be in Jerusalem fighting at the same time as others are gathered at Megiddo. In other words, warfare would be happening at Jerusalem and Megiddo simultaneously. If the war in Jerusalem follows that in Megiddo, then our Lord apparently will first destroy those armies gathered at Megiddo (though not necessarily setting foot on the earth), and then He will move to Jerusalem, stand on the Mount of Olives, and put down the conflict there.

By either scenario, the entire land will be engulfed in wars, which will only be stopped by the victorious coming of our Lord Jesus Christ.

Edom

Isaiah foresaw this center of conflict as recorded in Isaiah 63:1-6. The Lord is portrayed as coming from Edom (a nation that often opposed Israel and was therefore under God's wrath, Malachi 1:4) and from Bozrah in Edom, which is about 20 miles southeast of the southern tip of the Dead Sea. There He will tread the winepress of His wrath and destroy His enemies (see Revelation 14:17-20).

Rather than thinking of these centers—Jerusalem, Megiddo, and Edom—in some sort of sequence with regard to battles, we should perhaps think of them as giving us the total picture of the nearly simultaneous battles or the war of the great day of God Almighty (Revelation 16:14). In other words, the war will encompass the whole land from Megiddo in the north, Jerusalem in the center, and Edom in the southeast. That distance is about 140 miles. The clue that this might be the best way to view the war and these three centers is found in Revelation 14:20, which describes a river of blood 180 miles long and up to four and one-half feet deep. That would include the area from Megiddo to Edom with some miles to spare on both ends.

The Identification of Armageddon

To identify Armageddon with Megiddo is the most probable and usual interpretation. However, throughout history the site has been debated. The oldest identification was put forth by Hippolytus (died around A.D. 236) who understood it to be the valley of Jehoshaphat, mentioned in Joel 3:2 as the place of judgment of the nations.

It has also been connected with the area west of the Euphrates River across which the kings of the East will come. However, it is argued that because the Tell of Megiddo was probably only 70 feet high in John's day, it is not tall enough to designate it as a mountain (the meaning of *Har* in Harmagedon). In response, it is pointed out that Megiddo is near the Carmel range of mountains, which justifies the use of the word *mount.*

Another complicating factor is the fact that the spelling of Megiddo is different from Harmagedon. The Greek of Revelation 16:16 (Harmagedon) has only one "d" while some manuscripts spell Megiddo with two (including the Septuagint). The final "n" on Armageddon but not on Megiddo also presents a problem.[3]

On the other hand, the valley of Megiddo has been an important center as well as the site of various battles throughout history. About 1482 B.C. Thutmose III, one of the greatest Egyptian conquerors, launched a successful campaign to subdue his vassals in Palestine among whom was the king of Megiddo. In the days of Deborah and Barak (1195–1155 B.C.) a battle against the Canaanites under Jabin took place at Taanach "by the waters of Megiddo" (Judges 5:19). Solomon made Megiddo one of the locations for his standing army. After his anointing as king of Israel in

841 B.C., Jehu went to Jezreel and killed Jehoram, the reigning king of Israel. Ahaziah, king of Judah, fled from Jehu to Megiddo where he died (2 Kings 9:27). King Josiah, trying to intercept Pharaoh-necho at Megiddo in 609 B.C., was killed at Megiddo (2 Kings 23:29). However, none of these events can compare with the climactic battle at the Second Coming of Christ, and there is no compelling reason not to locate it at Megiddo at the head of the Jezreel (or Esdraelon) valley.

Why Will Armageddon Be Necessary?

Living as we are in the day of God's longsuffering, patience, and grace, it is sometimes difficult for believers to even think that God might act otherwise. And when you add the many displays of His grace during hundreds of years past, it tends to become even more difficult. Even with the judgments with which He afflicted Israel, and judgments that the world has seen since the First Coming of Christ, these pale beside the terrible judgments of the tribulation, the wars of that time, and especially the slaughter that leads to Armageddon.

Why will God do this? For one reason He must protect His people Israel. He made promises to them beginning with Abraham, some of which have not been fulfilled. If the Gentiles, who will hate Israel in the tribulation, would be able to exterminate them (Matthew 24:9), or if Satan, who will vent his fierce anger against Israel in the tribulation would be able to succeed in wiping Israel out (Revelation 12:13-17), then there would be no Jewish people left to fulfill the yet unfulfilled promises of God to them. The land from the river of Egypt to the Euphrates River was promised to Abraham's physical descendants (Genesis 15:18-21). That has never been literally fulfilled. One of the promises made to King David could not be fulfilled if Israel were not protected and preserved: "...I will appoint a place for my people Israel, and will plant them, that they may dwell in a place of their own, and move no more" (2 Samuel 7:10). Or: "...Judah shall dwell for ever, and Jerusalem from genera- tion to generation" (Joel 3:20). Or another: "... I will bring again the captivity of my people of Israel ... And I will plant them upon their land, and they shall no more be pulled up out of their land which I have given them, saith the LORD thy God" (Amos 9:14,15). Or another: "... ye also shall sit upon twelve thrones, judging the twelve tribes of Israel" (Matthew 19:28). Or another: "... This generation [the Jewish race] shall not pass, till all these things [the judgments of the tribulation described in the preceding verses] be ful- filled" (Matthew 24:34). If God does not prevent the Jewish people from being annihilated during the tribulation (or any other time) then these promises either have to be left unful- filled or fulfilled by Gentiles or the church, totally contra- dicting the words of these texts, which clearly and specifically say that Israel will fulfill them. But He will pro- tect Israel, and many who survive the tribulation will turn to Him in repentance and salvation (Zechariah 12:10).

For another reason, the Almighty must punish the wicked- ness of the nations of the world and put down all rebellion against Him, the living and true God. Since Adam and Eve first sinned, much of mankind has exhibited an unbroken record of rebellion against God. This in spite of all evidences He has given in the world around us, in His dealings with Israel in the Old Testament, and most vividly in the Coming of Jesus Christ and the worldwide proclamation of the good news that anyone who believes can be reconciled to God and possess eternal life. But people have rejected His advances and turned to their own wicked ways. In the tribu- lation, wickedness and rebellion will be unmasked to reveal the hardness of the human heart (Revelation 9:20,21; 16:9,11). God's patience has been for the purpose of giving people time to come to Him (2 Peter 3:9). But that will come to an end at His Second Coming. At Armageddon He will "smite the nations: and he shall rule them with a rod of iron" (Revelation 19:15). At Armageddon He will "destroy all the nations that come against Jerusalem" (Zechariah 12:9). And at Armageddon He says He will "tread down the people in [His] anger, and make them drunk in [His] fury, and [He] will bring down their strength to the earth" (Isaiah 63:6).

Enemies subdued, Israel exalted, the earth renovated, the King of kings and Lord of lords reigning in absolute righteousness, and, grace upon grace, we believers reigning with Him—all will usher in the glorious millennial reign of our Lord Jesus Christ.

And before him shall be gathered all nations: and he shall separate them one from another, as a shepherd divideth his sheep from the goats.

MATTHEW 25:32

The judgment of the nations takes place prior to the start of the millennial kingdom. This must be so because the results of the judgment of the nations determines participation in the millennial kingdom. As a result of this judgment, some will get to participate in the kingdom while others are excluded from it. Daniel 12:11,12 suggests that there will be a period of 75 days between the Second Coming and the actual start of the millennial kingdom. In these verses, Daniel declared that the one who makes it to the 1,335th day would be wonderfully blessed. This blessing, we would understand, is a reference to the privilege of entrance into Messiah's kingdom, which begins at that point.

CHAPTER 16

The Judgment of the Nations

Paul N. Benware

Like death, judgment is not a favorite subject for discussion. It is rarely the hot topic at parties and gatherings, unless of course it has something to do with a recent Hollywood movie. The subject of judgment makes many people feel uncomfortable because they instinctively sense that if there is such a thing as judgment, it may not go well for them on that occasion. So why talk about it? But like death, judgment is one of those ultimate realities that every created being will face someday. All creatures, whether angels or men, are accountable to the One who created them. As the writer of Hebrews succinctly puts it, "it is appointed unto men once to die, but after this the judgment" (Hebrews 9:27). The Bible forcefully declares that judgment is coming. However, it does not speak in terms of one great judgment but rather of a number of different judgments, which take place at different times and involve different people. The subject of this particular study is "the judgment of the nations." This is not some general judgment but involves a special group of people at a particular time in God's prophetic calendar. Joel 3:1-3 and Matthew 25:31-46 are the two primary sources of information about this coming judgment of the nations.

The Time of the Judgment

The two Scripture portions mentioned previously, along with Daniel 12, assist us in pinpointing the time when this judgment will take place. The judgment of the nations takes place in the same timeframe as several other judgments discussed in this book.

In Relationship to the Second Coming

According to the prophet Joel, this judgment of the nations takes place in connection with the "great and terrible day of the LORD," which makes it clear that Joel places this judgment in the end times of the tribulation and kingdom (Joel 2:31). But more specifically, Joel says that this judgment will take place when Judah and Jerusalem have their "fortunes restored" (Joel 3:1,2). The restoring of the fortunes of Israel is used often in reference to the millennial kingdom, which is established after the Lord Jesus Christ returns to this present earth in power and great glory (e.g., Ezekiel 39:25 and Amos 9:14,15).[1] This places the judgment after the Second Coming because it is only after that event that Israel will receive the blessings spoken of here.

In His prophetic Olivet Discourse, the Lord Jesus also placed this event in connection with His Second Coming. He said that the gathering of the nations for judgment would take place after He comes in His glory with the holy angels and is seated on His throne (Matthew 25:31,32). It is after His Second Coming, therefore, that He judges the nations.

In Relationship to the Millennial Kingdom

The judgment of the nations takes place prior to the start of the millennial kingdom. This must be so because the results of the judgment of the nations determines participation in the millennial kingdom. As a result of this judgment, some will get to participate in the kingdom while others are excluded from it. Daniel 12:11,12 suggests that there will be a period of 75 days between the Second Coming and the actual start of the millennial kingdom. In these verses, Daniel declared that the one who makes it to the 1,335th day would be wonderfully blessed. This blessing, we would understand, is a reference to the privilege of entrance into Messiah's kingdom, which begins at that point. To make it to the 1,335th day means that one will enter into the Messiah's kingdom. The starting point of the 1,335 days is at the mid-point of the tribulation period with 1,260 of those days covering the last half of the tribulation. The tribulation, of course, ends with Christ's return to earth. The remaining 75-day period appears to be an interval that exists between the end of the tribulation (the Second Coming) and the actual start of the 1,000-year reign of Jesus Messiah. It is during this interval that the judgment of the nations apparently takes place.

Because the judgment of the nations occurs before the millennial reign, it is not to be confused with the "Great White Throne" judgment, which takes place after the 1,000-year reign of Christ is completed (Revelation 20:11-15). Unfortunately these two judgments are sometimes equated. It must be remembered that there are 1,000 years between them, and there are some significant differences in the judgments themselves.

The Place of the Judgment

It may be assumed that because the judgment of the nations takes place after the Second Coming it will take place on the earth, because that is where Christ will have come. And the Lord Jesus did place the judgment after His return to the earth (Matthew 24:27-31; 25:31,32). The prophet Joel specifically stated that the nations would be gathered for judgment into the "valley of Jehoshaphat" (Joel 3:2,12). Some have identified this with the Kidron Valley next to Jerusalem while others see it as the location where God brought deliverance to King Jehoshaphat by defeating a coalition of enemies (cf. 2 Chronicles 20). But the exact geographic location is difficult to determine because this name historically is not attached to any specific place. Most likely the name (which means "Jehovah judges") is intended to be symbolic. This will be the place in Israel where the recently returned Lord Jesus will gather the nations in order to judge them. It probably refers to a future site, which will come into existence in connection with the topographical changes that will take place in Israel at the Second Coming (Zechariah 14:4). It is most likely that it will be near to the city of Jerusalem, the city of King Jesus.[2]

The Participants in the Judgment

The One Who Judges

The judge who carries out all judgments in the end times is the Lord Jesus Christ. According to the Lord Jesus Himself, the Father has committed all judgment to the Son. He will judge fairly and according to the will of the Father (cf. John 5:21-23,27). During His earthly ministry, Jesus was not impressed nor was He influenced by the wealth, power, or status of anyone. And this will be true of His judgments in the future (cf. Isaiah 11:4,5). When the nations gather before Him they can be sure that they come before One who sees all and knows all and cannot be fooled, deceived, or bribed (Revelation 1:14; 2:18; 3:7). He will make no mistakes, and there will be no miscarriage of justice when He invites some to enter His kingdom and prohibits others from doing so.

The Ones Being Judged

Both of the primary passages of Scripture concerning this judgment state that the "nations" are gathered before the Lord. The word translated "nations" also means "Gentiles" and is translated that way the majority of times in the New Testament.[3] It is used mainly regarding a category of people who do not belong to the chosen nation of Israel. So it would probably be clearer to speak of this as the "judgment of Gentiles" because these are set in contrast to the covenant people of Israel in both of the primary texts.

This judgment does not, however, include all Gentiles who have ever lived, but rather only those who are living when Christ returns at the Second Coming. The word *Gentile* is not used of those who are dead but rather of living, existing people. There is no mention of the dead or of a resurrection in the passages that discuss this judgment. Those being brought before the Lord for judgment are seen as those gathered from the various parts of the earth, the same nations out of which Israel has been regathered (Joel 3:2). And furthermore, the Gentiles will be judged for their deeds performed immediately before Christ's return (cf. Joel 3:2,3; Matthew 25:35-40). This judgment, then, is of Gentiles who are physically alive at the Second Coming.

A careful investigation of the Scriptures reveals that literally billions of Gentiles will perish during the horrible days of the tribulation (cf. Revelation 6,8,9,16). Many will die as a result of God's wrath being poured out on the earth (in the three series of judgments and in the campaign of Armageddon), and many others will perish because of the activities of Satan and the Antichrist. In fact, it is probably safe to say that the vast majority of Gentiles who enter the time of tribulation will not live through the entire seven-year period. But when Jesus Christ returns, millions will still be alive and these are the ones who will stand before Him at the "judgment of the nations (Gentiles)."

It should also be observed that this is a judgment of individual Gentiles. Because this judgment has been referred to as the judgment of "nations," some have thought that national groups will be judged at this time. But that would not be accurate. This is a judgment of individual Gentiles who are alive at the Second Coming.

> If this were a judgment of national entities, it is obvious that some unsaved would be included in an accepted nation; on the other hand, some saved would be excluded because they were in a rejected nation. Therefore, it must be concluded that this will be a judgment of individuals, not of nations.[4]

The Basis of the Judgment

When a person stands before the Lord Jesus, it is not to determine that person's eternal destiny. The determination of one's presence in or absence from the kingdom of God is settled during that person's earthly life and not at the time of judgment before the Lord Jesus Christ. Jesus clearly communicated to Nicodemus that entrance into the kingdom comes by the new birth (John 3:5). Entering the kingdom (salvation) is never by means of good works (Titus 3:5; Ephesians 2:8,9) but is always by faith alone in Christ (Romans 3:20-30; John 3:16; Galatians 2:16). Salvation is always seen as a gift from God which is received by trusting in Christ.

During the seven years of tribulation, everyone on this earth will hear the truth of the gospel of Christ (Matthew 24:14). Although the 144,000 will probably be the main proclaimers of the gospel message, millions of believers will give testimony of their faith in Jesus Christ (Revelation 7:4-17). So when the living Gentiles appear before the Lord Jesus at the time of this judgment, we can confidently conclude that they have already heard and have either received or rejected the offer of salvation.

If this is so, then why is there such an emphasis on the deeds that these Gentiles have done as an apparent prerequisite for entering Messiah's kingdom (Matthew 25:35 ff.; Joel 3:2,3)? The setting of the terrible days of the Great Tribulation is the key to understanding this judgment. During the last three and one-half years of the period of tribulation there will be an active, satanically energized anti-Semitism over the entire earth (Revelation 12:13-16). The Antichrist, empowered by the devil, will attempt to thwart the plan and purposes of God by annihilating the covenant people of Israel. "During the tribulation the Jews will become the dividing line for those who are believers and for those who are not."[5] The internal, spiritual condition of the Gentiles is revealed externally by the way in which they treat Israel during the Great Tribulation. This is the valid proof of true righteousness because of the intense persecution that Israel will endure during the second half of the tribulation period. Jews forced to flee death and destruction will have no means of caring for themselves. The righteous Gentiles (the sheep), at great risk to themselves, will provide food and shelter for the covenant people and will show many other acts of kindness.

> Under the widespread anti-Semitism that will prevail in the Great Tribulation, anyone who befriends a Jew in trouble will be distinguished as a person who has trust in the Bible and trust in Jesus Christ. Accordingly, while their works do not save them, their works are the basis of distinguishing them from the unsaved....[6]

Judge Jesus refers to these Gentiles as righteous (Matthew 25:37). The good deeds done to Jesus validate that designation of "righteous." However, these righteous Gentiles (the "sheep") were confused because they did not recall doing any good deeds to Jesus. But the Lord instructs them that when they did good deeds to "these my brethren" they did them to Jesus Himself (Matthew 25:40). Jesus' "brothers" is not a reference to mankind in general, but rather to the Jews who are true believers and the subjects of the satanically inspired persecution. Jesus referred to His followers in this way during His earthly ministry (cf. Matthew 12:46-50). He is speaking about the believing Jews who lived during the time of persecution in the Great Tribulation. It could be that He is specifically referring to the 144,000 evangelists of the Tribulation, who are the special targets of the Antichrist and Satan. These righteous Gentiles will be welcomed into the millennial kingdom by the King. They are righteous because they were saved by grace, but the manifestation of their righteousness was seen in their care for Jesus' "brothers" during those terrible days.

In like manner, the deeds of the unrighteous ("goats") reveal their true spiritual condition. Their unbelief of the gospel message is seen by their anti-Semitism.

> The sins committed against Israel listed in this indict-
> ment (Joel 3:2b,3) are: first, scattering the Jews (in the
> middle of the tribulation); secondly, parting the land...;
> and thirdly, selling the Jews into slavery.... Each Gentile
> living at that time will be judged on the basis of his par-
> ticipation or his refusal to participate in these deeds.[7]

Jesus also will indict them on their refusal to give aid and assistance to His "brothers" during the Great Tribulation (Matthew 25:45). Their negative treatment of Jesus' "brothers" is proof positive that they are not righteous and, therefore, are to be excluded from entrance into the millennial kingdom.

The Purposes for the Judgment

To Demonstrate the Character of God

It is essential for man to see and acknowledge that God is God. The judgments recorded in Scripture reveal that all creatures eventually will bow the knee and accept their rightful place of submission to their Creator God (Philippians 2:9-11; John 5:22,23). When the judgments are completed, no creature will challenge or speak against the character of the one and only God. The judgment of the Gentiles will contribute to that significant end.

It is also important for man to see that what God has said is true and that He will always do what He says He will do. The judgment of the Gentiles, with its focus on how they treat Israel, brings to light the ancient but still relevant word from God to Abraham in Genesis 12:3. In that initial giving of the Abrahamic covenant, God said that He would bless those who bless Abraham's descendants but would curse those who cursed his descendants. This has held true through the millenniums since God spoke to Abraham some 2,000 years before Christ. And the judgment of the Gentiles is as clear and immediate an application of this truth as one can find in the Bible or history. The Word of God is true and trustworthy.

To Grant Entrance to the Righteous

The righteous Gentiles will be welcomed into the kingdom of Jesus the Messiah when He tells them to "inherit the kingdom" (Matthew 25:34). These saved Gentiles are received with joy into Messiah's kingdom. Some have pointed out that this "inheriting the kingdom" is not a reference to mere entrance into the millennial kingdom that is being granted but to the giving of rewards to these faithful Gentiles.[8] It is argued that "inheriting the kingdom" in the Scriptures is conditioned upon some good works being done by the individual. In other words, "inheriting the kingdom" is always conditioned upon good works after one's salvation and is focusing on the matter of rewards. "Entering the kingdom" is referring to our justification by faith, is unrelated to works, and is, therefore, not an equivalent term to "inheriting the kingdom." So when King Jesus speaks to the righteous Gentiles of their "inheriting the kingdom" He is speaking of their rewards and blessedness in the kingdom.

That these righteous Gentiles are being honored (rewarded) by the King is undoubtedly going to be true. The emphasis on their good works to Jesus' "brothers" would probably point to something other than "justification by faith" though the presence of good works can validate a faith that is genuine. It is also said that these regenerated Gentiles are going to enter eternal life at this time (Matthew 25:46). But how can saved people who already possess eternal life at the moment of faith in Christ now enter eternal life? Part of the answer is to remember that there is a future aspect of eternal life. Whenever eternal life is seen as being obtained by a work, it is always something that is described as a future acquisition (e.g., Matthew 19:28-30; Galatians 6:8; Romans 2:5-13). "The Christian who perseveres in doing good works can obtain the reward of eternal life, an enriched experience of that life given to him freely at justification through faith alone."[9] So then, this entering into eternal life is looking at the rich rewards granted to the faithful justified Gentiles.

However, while rewards indeed can be found here, the emphasis of the Lord's teaching in this passage seems to be on entering the millennial kingdom. The focus of the passage is on the sheep who enter the millennial kingdom and the goats who are not allowed entrance into the kingdom. There is no mention of any degrees of rewarding among the "sheep," characteristic of reward passages, and there is no reference to the degree of punishment that would be true of the "goats." Also, there is no discussion of sheep who may be unfaithful, which would be expected if the emphasis of the passage was on the rewarding of the righteous. But, we must say that the passage does seem to become clearer when we allow the rewarding element to be included even if it is not the focus of the Lord's discussion.

The Judging of the Unrighteous

As with the righteous "sheep," the deeds of the unrighteous "goats" reveal their true spiritual condition (Matthew

25:41-46; Joel 3:2,3). They are refused entrance into the Messiah's glorious kingdom and sent away to eternal punishment. These will enter into a punishment of unending duration, which is said to be the eternal fire that has been made for Satan and his angels (Matthew 25:41). It should be noted that the same word that is used for "eternal life" in this passage is used for "eternal punishment." If "eternal life" applies to the never-ending future of blessedness for the believer, it must follow that the wicked face future punishment that is equal in duration.

The "goats" reveal their rejection of the gospel message by their refusal to give aid and comfort to Jesus' "brothers" during the Great Tribulation. Joel emphasizes the fact that they were not passive in their dealings with the people of Israel (Joel 3:2,3). They were responsible for bringing great distress to the Jews as they drove them out of their land, divided up the land, and enslaved the people. These unrighteous Gentiles committed the terrible crime of taking the Lord's portion for themselves. "The nations will have to answer directly to God for having treated His own personal possession, the 'apple of His eye' so lightly."[10] These unrighteous Gentiles will have to bow the knee to the One they have rejected and treated with contempt.

Final Thoughts

Men are accountable to the Lord God for what they do with His truth and His people. And while some might think that God is not watching, the Scriptures reveal that everything man does and says is known to Him. Man will be rewarded or punished in accordance with the standard of God's truth. This holds true with the Gentiles who live in the times of the Great Tribulation. They will stand before the King at His Second Coming, where they will enter into or be excluded from the Messianic kingdom.

They shall not hurt nor destroy in all my holy mountain: for the earth shall be full of the knowledge of the LORD, as the waters cover the sea.

ISAIAH 11:9

The entire Old Testament expectation is involved with an earthly kingdom, the glory of Israel, and the promised Messiah seated on David's throne in Jerusalem. When these are applied to the church, as too often they are, there is not so much as an accidental similarity on which to base that application. The premillennial position is not only supported by a literal interpretation of Scripture and abundant Old Testament prophecies, but it was also the dominant position of the early church. The central focus of the millennium, though, is not Satan; it is the Savior, the Lord Jesus Christ. It is His time of manifestation, His time of revelation. There Christ in all of His glory will institute His reign of righteousness and peace. In the millennium, the unveiled glory of Christ will shine forth in all of its fullness.

Chapter 17

The Marvelous Millennium

Joe Jordan

Countdown to Armageddon now brings us to our subject of "The Marvelous Millennium." The concept of the millennium is for some a point of great controversy; for others a problem of confusion. But, for those who look for our Lord's soon return, it is a peaceful conviction that the millennium plays a vital part in the unfolding of God's drama of the ages. The word *millennium* comes from the Latin word, *mille*, meaning a thousand and *annum* meaning year. The Greek word, *chilias,* also meaning a thousand, appears six times in the Greek text in the twentieth chapter of the book of Revelation, defining the duration of Christ's kingdom before the destruction of the old heaven and the old earth.

Concerning this future time, Charles Ryrie states:

> The millennium is the period of a thousand years of the
> visible, earthly reign of the Lord Jesus Christ who after
> His return from heaven will fulfill during that period
> the promises contained in the Abrahamic, Davidic and

New Covenants to Israel, will bring the whole world to
a knowledge of God, and will lift the curse from the
whole creation.[1]

Therefore, the millennium refers to a thousand years of
Christ's future reign on earth, which will precede eternity. It
is important to note that the millennium deals with a time-
space order as it relates to the reign of Christ.

Positions on the Millennium

The interpretation of this doctrine has been expressed by
three different schools of thought—amillennialism, postmillennialism, and premillennialism. Amillennialism means no
millennium; that is, there will be no literal kingdom. The
proponents of this school of thought argue that millennial
prophecies cannot be considered literal and, thus, would
need to be fulfilled in nonliteral ways. Postmillennialism
states that the return of Christ will come after the millennium. This position became popular in the nineteenth century, suggesting that the millennium would occur during the
last 1,000 years of the present age with the whole world
being won to Christ. Thus, the millennium would be that
golden age lasting for 1,000 years. With the coming of the
great world wars, the postmillennial interpretation met its
"Waterloo." Today this position is being revived through a
movement called Christian Reconstructionism (also
"Dominion Theology" or "Theonomy").

The premillennial interpretation is that the kingdom will
follow the Second Coming of Christ and will be a literal
1,000-year reign of Christ on earth. This position is not only
based on the literal fulfillment of the prophecies of the book
of Revelation but also on abundant Messianic prophecies
from the Old Testament. Some opponents of premillennialism contend that the entire system is based on a few verses
in Revelation 20, but this is not so. In reference to this crit-
icism, Lewis Sperry Chafer states:

It has been the practice of the opponents of chiliasm (premillennialism) to contend that chiliasm is based on Revelation 20:4-6 and that if this passage can be so interpreted as to assign it to the past or as now fulfilled, the entire structure of chiliasm is dissolved.[2]

Chafer goes on to say:

The entire Old Testament expectation is involved with its earthly kingdom, the glory of Israel and the promised Messiah seated on David's throne in Jerusalem. When these are applied to the church, as too often they are, there is not so much as an accidental similarity on which to base that application.[3]

The premillennial position not only is supported by a literal interpretation of Scripture and abundant Old Testament prophecies, but was also the dominant position of the early church. To this end, David Larsen writes:

Beyond any question, the premillennial or chiliastic understanding of the end of history was dominant in the early church in contrast to amillennialism that spiritualizes the one-thousand-year reign of Christ, making it the present experience of the church or postmillennialism that over-optimistically sees the church as triumphing in history and ushering in the kingdom....[4]

A champion of premillennial thought, Ryrie, states:

Premillennialists believe that theirs is the historic faith of the church. Holding to a literal interpretation of the Scriptures, they believe that the promises made to Abraham and David are unconditional and have had or will have a literal fulfillment. In no sense have these promises made to Israel been abrogated or fulfilled by the church, which is a distinct body in this age having promises and a destiny different from Israel's. At the close of this age, premillennialists believe that Christ will return for His church, meeting her in the air, which event, called the Rapture or translation, will usher in a seven-year period of tribulation on earth. After this, the Lord will return to the earth to establish His kingdom on the earth for a thousand years, during which time the promises to Israel will be fulfilled.[5]

God's promises in the fulfillment of His covenants to Israel will come to pass when Jesus Christ, a Son of David, will come and sit on the throne of David, rule over the house of David, from the city of David, Jerusalem. At that time, the Abrahamic Covenant with its promises of the land and the seed (Genesis 13:14-17, 15:5,18-21; Isaiah 10:21,22; Jeremiah 30:22; Ezekiel 34:24; Micah 7:19,20), the Davidic Covenant, with its promises concerning David's house or seed, throne, and kingdom (2 Samuel 7:16-19; Isaiah 11:1,2; Jeremiah 23:5-8; Hosea 3:5) and the New Covenant with its promises of a new heart for God's law, the forgiveness of sins, and the indwelling of the Spirit for a converted nation (Jeremiah 31:31-34, Ezekiel 11:18-20, 36:24-28; Romans 11:26-29) will all be literally fulfilled. Fulfillment of these promises and covenants in the millennial reign of Christ will bring about God's purpose on earth for man. This is clearly stated by J. Dwight Pentecost:

> God's purpose for this earth is to subject all things to man (Genesis 1:26,27) and to bring all things into subjection to Himself through man. This ultimately will be realized as the Son of man subjects all things to Himself and through Him to the authority of His Father. Establishing the rule of David's Son as Sovereign over the earth demonstrates that Satan's kingdom is a false kingdom. Satan is a false king—God alone is God, and He alone has a right to rule. He has the authority and the power to bring all things into subjection to Himself. Apart from the reign of Christ in a Davidic kingdom here on earth, God's promises and God's covenants would have failed and apart from this rule, God's purpose for man would never be brought to conclusion. God's purpose for the earth would be unrealized and

the problem generated by Satan's rebellion would never be resolved. Thus the physical, literal reign of Christ on the earth is a theological and biblical necessity—unless Satan is victorious over God.[6]

Without the millennial reign of Christ, there is no ultimate and complete fulfillment of these covenants.

Another evidence that the millennial reign of Christ is yet a future event is the binding of Satan. Revelation 20:2 says: "And he laid hold on the dragon, that old serpent, which is the Devil, and Satan, and bound him a thousand years."

As we consider the truth of this text, it becomes almost impossible to think that someone can say that we are now in the millennium.

A look at Revelation 20:1-3 shows that the purpose of binding Satan was to prevent him from deceiving the nations. This passage teaches that Satan is not simply restricted but is totally inactive in the millennium. This stands in stark contrast to his activity in the present age as we are reminded by the Apostle Peter: "Be sober, be vigilant; because your adversary the devil, as a roaring lion, walketh about, seeking whom he may devour" (1 Peter 5:8).

Though Satan is not bound in this present age, he is under the sovereign restraints of God. This is evidenced by Satan's dealings with God concerning Job (Job 1:6-22). The binding of Satan during the millennial age does have a divine purpose. The purpose Godward is to manifest His perfect righteousness and toward man is to give him an ideal state in which to live and worship Messiah. This is well expressed by Pentecost:

> The millennial age is to be the age in which divine righteousness is to be displayed (Isaiah 11:5; 32:1; Jeremiah 23:6; Daniel 9:24). It is also to be God's final test of fallen humanity under the most ideal circumstances. All outward sources of temptation must be removed so that man will demonstrate what he is apart from Satanic influence. So that there can be the full manifestation of

righteousness and a test of humanity apart from external temptations, Satan must be removed from the sphere.[7]

The Personage of the Millennium

The central focus of the millennium, though, is not Satan; it is the Savior, the Lord Jesus Christ. It is His time of manifestation, His time of revelation. There Christ in all of His glory will institute His reign of righteousness and peace. In the millennium the unveiled glory of Christ will shine forth in all of its fullness. Pentecost states:

> There will be the manifestation of the glory associated with the humanity of Christ. There will be the glory of a glorious dominion in which Christ by virtue of His obedience unto death is given universal dominion to replace that dominion which Adam lost. There will be the glory of a glorious government in which Christ as David's Son is given absolute power to govern (Isaiah 9:6; Psalm 45:4; Isaiah 11:4; Psalm 72:4; Psalm 2:9).[8]

A look into the Second Psalm manifests God's purpose that Jesus Christ, His Son, will reign over the earth in spite of the rage of nations and their rebellion against God. His sovereign purpose will be realized. Psalm 2:6-9:

> Yet have I set my king upon my holy hill of Zion. I will declare the decree: the LORD hath said unto me, Thou art my Son; this day have I begotten thee. Ask of me, and I shall give thee the heathen for thine inheritance, and the uttermost parts of the earth for thy possession. Thou shalt break them with a rod of iron; thou shalt dash them in pieces like a potter's vessel.

Daniel, the Prophet, also spoke of this event when he stated in Daniel 7:13,14:

> I saw in the night visions, and, behold, one like the Son of man came with the clouds of heaven, and came to

the Ancient of days, and they brought him near before
him. And there was given him dominion, and glory,
and a kingdom, that all people, nations, and languages,
should serve him: his dominion is an everlasting
dominion, which shall not pass away, and his kingdom
that which shall not be destroyed.

Principal Characteristics and Conditions of the Millennium

Much has been written concerning the characteristics and
conditions of the millennium. It is important to note that the
Bible teaches it will be a time of both political and spiritual
rule. From the political side, it will be universal (Daniel
2:35), authoritative (Isaiah 11:4), characterized by righteousness and justice with assurances for the poor (Isaiah
11:3-5) and admonition and judgment for the violators of
Messiah's rule (Psalm 2:10-12).

This literal earthly reign of Christ will also have spiritual
characteristics. Some think that the kingdom cannot be spiritual in character and an earthly kingdom at the same time,
but the two are compatible and there is no contradiction.
First and foremost it will be a reign of righteousness where
Christ will be the King reigning in absolute righteousness
(Isaiah 32:1). It will also be a period of time where the fullness of the Spirit and also the holiness of God will be manifested (Isaiah 11:2-5). "In that day shall there be upon the
bells of the horses, HOLINESS UNTO THE LORD;...Yea,
every pot in Jerusalem and in Judah shall be holiness unto
the LORD of hosts" (Zechariah 14:20,21).

How wonderful it will be to live in an age where everything from work to worship will be holy. Sin will be punished (Psalm 72:1-4; Zechariah 14:16-21), ultimately, in an
open, just way. The golden age will also be characterized by
a reign of peace (Isaiah 2:4; 11:5-9; 65:25; Micah 4:3). Messiah's reign of righteousness and peace will display many

blessed conditions. A study of Christ's future reign in Isaiah's prophecy reveals many of these conditions. They include but are not limited to:

- Joy–Isaiah 9:3,4

- Glory–Isaiah 24:23

- Justice–Isaiah 9:7

- Full knowledge–Isaiah 11:1,2

- Instruction and learning–Isaiah 2:2,3

- The removal of the curse on the earth and also the elimination of sickness–Isaiah 11:6-9, 33:24

- Longevity of life–Isaiah 65:20

- Prosperity in work–Isaiah 4:1; 35:1,2; 62:8,9

- Animal natures will be changed–Isaiah 11:6-9, 65:25

We also see from Zephaniah 3:9 and Isaiah 45:13 that there will be a pure language and pure worship. The concept of pure worship is possible because of the awesome presence of God (Ezekiel 37:27,28). The physical presence of Messiah guarantees these blessings. Commenting on the presence of God in the millennium, Walvoord states: "The glorious presence of Christ in the millennial scene is, of course, the center of worship and spirituality."[9]

It will be marvelous to live under a government of perfect righteousness and absolute peace!

The Place of Jerusalem in the Millennium

Although the reign of Messiah will be universal, the center of His government will be in Jerusalem, for we read "...out of Zion shall go forth the law, and the word of the LORD from Jerusalem" (Isaiah 2:3). As we look into Isaiah 2:2,3, without a doubt, Jerusalem will be the center of the millennial government. Isaiah states:

And it shall come to pass in the last days, that the mountain of the LORD's house shall be established in the top
of the mountains, and shall be exalted above the hills;
and all nations shall flow unto it. And many people
shall go and say, Come ye, and let us go up to the
mountain of the LORD, to the house of the God of
Jacob; and he will teach us of his ways, and we will walk
in his paths: for out of Zion shall go forth the law, and
the word of the LORD from Jerusalem.

It is interesting to note that Jerusalem, the city of David,
will again witness the presence of David, this time in his resurrected body, serving as a prince or regent under Christ
and administering the millennial kingdom as it relates to
Israel. According to Ezekiel, David will act as a shepherd
over the people. Ezekiel 34:23,24: "And I will set up one
shepherd over them, and he shall feed them ... and he shall
be their shepherd. And I the LORD will be their God, and
my servant David a prince among them; I the LORD have
spoken it."

How glorious it will be when Christ, a son of David, will
give to David himself a responsible place in His capital government as it relates to the people of Israel. This concept of
David ruling under Christ is also found in Jeremiah 30:9;
33:15-17; Ezekiel 37:24,25; Hosea 3:5.

As we think of Jerusalem being the center of Messiah's
government and consider the size of the millennial temple,
it is evident that there must be topographical changes. This
will happen as Christ comes to set His feet on the Mount of
Olives.

And his feet shall stand in that day upon the mount of
Olives, which is before Jerusalem on the east, and the
mount of Olives shall cleave in the midst thereof toward
the east and toward the west, and there shall be a very
great valley; and half of the mountain shall remove
toward the north, and half of it toward the south
(Zechariah 14:4).

Concerning these physical changes around Jerusalem, Larsen states:

> Some very striking geographical and topographical changes will take place when Christ returns in glory to set up His kingdom. A great earthquake will rend the Mount of Olives (Zechariah 14:3,4) and the mount of the Lord will be sufficient size for the building of the millennial temple described in Ezekiel 40-48. From its summit will flow the life-giving stream depicted in Ezekiel 47:1-12 which will reach to the Dead Sea with its rejuvenating qualities. Then, indeed, Jerusalem will be raised up and remain in its place and the promise will be kept. It will be inhabited. Never again will it be destroyed. Jerusalem will be secure (Zechariah 14:10,11).[10]

The Participants of the Millennium

From the personage, the Lord Jesus Christ Himself, and the place, Jerusalem, we now turn to the participants of the kingdom. The people related to the millennial reign of Christ will be Old Testament saints (Daniel 12:1,2,6,13), tribulation saints (Jews and Gentiles, both living and resurrected ones), and the church of the Lord Jesus Christ. Ryrie says:

> Three groups of people will be related to the millennial government. Israel, regathered and turned to the Lord in salvation, will be exalted, blessed and favored throughout the period. The nations will be subject to the King during the millennium. "Yea, all kings shall fall down before him: all nations shall serve him" (Psalm 72:11; Daniel 7:13,14; Micah 4:2; Zechariah 8:22). In addition, the church will reign with Christ, not as a subject of the King but as one who rightfully shares the rule (2 Timothy 2:12; Revelation 1:6; 5:10; 20:6).[11]

So the participants of Messiah's kingdom will be Old Testament saints, the tribulation saints, both Jew and Gentile, and the church of our Lord Jesus Christ. The tribulation saints will be made up not only of those who are living at the time of our Lord's return but also the resurrected tribulation saints as is evidenced by Revelation 20:4:

> And I saw thrones, and they sat upon them, and judgment was given unto them: and I saw the souls of them that were beheaded for the witness of Jesus, and for the word of God, and which had not worshipped the beast, neither his image, neither had received his mark upon their foreheads, or in their hands; and they lived and reigned with Christ a thousand years.

The Priesthood, the Passover Lamb, and Worship in the Millennium

Although only the redeemed will go into Messiah's kingdom, the living saints from the tribulation will enter into that kingdom in their natural bodies with the power of procreation. Those born to them during the millennium will be in need of salvation, and this salvation will be brought to them through Israel. Speaking of salvation during this period, Pentecost says:

> During the millennial reign of Christ, Israel as a nation will fulfill the function for which they were originally set apart by God. They will become a kingdom of priests (Exodus 19:6) who are intermediaries between those who need to be saved and the King who provides salvation. They will become as they were originally appointed to be God's lights to the world. Those born in the millennium who need salvation will approach the Savior through Israel (Zechariah 8:20-23). Salvation during that period will be provided through the benefits of the death of the passover Lamb. That is why the passover will be observed throughout the millennial age

as a memorial of the death of Christ (Ezekiel 45:21) and why blood sacrifices will be offered in the millennial temple as memorials of the death of Christ (Ezekiel 43:19-27).[12]

Some have objected to animal sacrifices in the temple during the millennium saying it is a regression in the program of God. They base their arguments on Hebrews 9 and 10, which teach that sacrifices have come to an end with the death of Christ. Addressing this problem, Ralph Alexander says:

> Everything in the temple passages in Ezekiel hinge on a restoration of Israel in the end time. But is not a return to literal animal sacrifice retrogression and, indeed, contrary to the message of the book of Hebrews in the New Testament? (Hebrews 10:1-8,14,18). That the finished work of Jesus Christ for the sins of the world on the cross is completed and that no more sacrifice for sin is necessary or possible does not rule out the perpetuation of symbolism or sacramental witness.[13]

Also supporting the view of animal sacrifices in the millennium, Horatius Bonar writes:

> The temple, the worship, the rites, the sacrifices have all their centre in the Lamb that was slain. To Him they point, and of Him they speak. Why should they not be allowed to do so in the millennial age, if such be the purpose of the Father? They are commemorative, not typical. They are retrospective then, not prospective as of old.[14]

As far as the emotional response of the believing Jews to that symbolism, John Mitchell states:

> It is true that these sacrifices will be types and symbols of their faith in Christ's death but that does not make them nonetheless real. There will probably be mingled sorrow and joy in these sacrifices as they recall how their fathers refused to accept this Christ as their Messiah and how now they have the privilege of seeing it all so clearly.[15]

We also observe that the millennial sacrifices will be more than a memorial. In a theocracy (where the government law is God's law—such as Israel had under the Mosaic law), the breaking of the theocratic law brings temporal judgment (Zechariah 14:16-19)—no rain, famine, illness, or death. In order to escape the temporal judgment, an animal sacrifice is offered to atone for the breaking of the theocratic law. This will be the case during the millennium where the whole world will be under a theocracy.

The Problem of Satan and His Last Revolt

As Messiah's 1,000-year reign of righteousness and peace comes to an end, Satan will be loosed for a season. As Revelation 20:3 says: "...till the thousand years should be fulfilled: and after that he must be loosed a little season."

The question arises, why is Satan loosed? Why did he not remain in that bottomless pit forever? Concerning this, Larsen comments:

> The successive periods of God's dealing with human-kind all but put certain hypotheses and theories to a test. Human conscience or government cannot fully answer our problems; the law cannot provide salvation and the hardened human heart often resists the gospel of the grace of God. But lurking down in human hearts and expressed in many a treatise on the human condition is the notion that were only human beings economically self-sufficient, if only we were spared the graft, crookedness and prejudiceness of public officials, if only we did not have to face the insecurity of hostile threat and war, we would do well.[16]

The end of the millennium will reveal how unregenerate hearts will still be open to believe the lie of the devil and follow him in his final revolt against God. Again it will be evident that without redemption through God's saving grace there is no answer for sin. For a thousand years there will be no satanic or demonic activity, no corrupt government, no war, no sickness, no bad weather, yet people will rebel. So we learn that all rebellion during the millennium will find its cause not in man's external circumstances but in his own internal corrupt nature. The loosing of Satan will demonstrate that no type of social order or environment in the world can possibly change the sinfulness of man's degenerate heart.

Thus, only by a personal relationship with Messiah through redemption can one not only resist his own evil human heart but Satan himself.

After this final rebellion, Satan and his followers will be cast into the Lake of Fire (Revelation 20:10), and then will come the resurrection and judgment at the Great White Throne of all unsaved dead of all ages of history with the result of them being cast into the Lake of Fire (Revelation 20:12-15). After that will come the ushering in of new heavens and a new earth with its eternal state (Revelation 21:1). What a glorious moment that will be!

Passing from the Millennium to the Eternal State

As we come to a close, we must consider a very important Scripture as it relates to the millenium and the eternal state. The passage is 1 Corinthians 15:24-28:

> Then cometh the end, when he shall have delivered up the kingdom to God, even the Father; when he shall have put down all rule and all authority and power. For he must reign, till he hath put all enemies under his feet. The last enemy that shall be destroyed is death. For he hath put all things under his feet. But when he saith all things are put under him, it is manifest that he is excepted, which did put all things under him. And when all things shall be subdued unto him, then shall the Son also himself be subject unto him that put all things under him, that God may be all in all.

Does this passage teach that Christ at the end of His 1,000-year reign has no future reign or that the eternal state or reign of God should be equated with the millennium? Pentecost comments:

> God's original purpose was to manifest His absolute authority and this purpose is realized when Christ unites the earthly theocracy with the eternal kingdom of God. Thus, while Christ's earthly theocratic rule is limited to 1,000 years, which is sufficient time to manifest God's perfect theocracy on the earth, His reign is eternal.[17]

Concerning the question of the surrender of authority of the Son to the Father, Chafer writes:

> The delivery to God of a now unmarred kingdom does not imply the release of authority on the part of the Son. The truth asserted in 1 Corinthians 15:27,28 is that at last the kingdom is fully restored, the kingdom of God to God. The distinction to be noted lies between the presentation to the Father of a restored authority and the supposed abrogation of a throne on the part of the Son. The latter is neither required in the text nor even intimated. The picture presented in Revelation 22:3 is of the New Jerusalem in the eternal state and it is declared that "the throne of God and of the Lamb shall be in it."[18]

The millennial kingdom of Christ will usher in the eternal manifestation of the glory of the Lamb of God. Without the scriptural doctrine of the millennium, we would have no bridge between history and God's eternal order. This golden age will not only be God's way of linking history but also giving to man through the God-man, Jesus Christ, the dominion lost by the fall.

Yes, the millennium is marvelous because Messiah will be magnified as the Son of David coming to sit on the throne of David and reigning over the house of David, from the city of David, Jerusalem.

And shall go out to deceive the nations which are in the four quarters of the earth, Gog and Magog, to gather them together to battle: the number of whom is as the sand of the sea.

REVELATION 20:8

A few decades ago, liberal theologians were enamored with the concept touting the inherent goodness of mankind. To be sure, their views were more Freudian than theological. Nonetheless, they were convinced that, given a proper environment, the natural goodness of mankind would bring forth a kind of utopian revolution that would hold out the possibility of transporting the planet into an Edenic era. It would be a time when no one would be held responsible for iniquitous conduct—all would merely be victims of their environment. That the final revolt will become a historic reality forever puts this deception to rest.

CHAPTER 18

The Final Revolt

Elwood McQuaid

The climactic battle of Armageddon, which will occur at the end of the tribulation period, is often mistakenly referred to as the "last battle" between God and His archenemy, Satan. It is not. There is yet another engagement that, in many respects, surpasses the battle of Armageddon. It does so in the scope of the contest, in the total finality of the result, and certainly in what it reveals about mankind and the human condition.

That conflict is described in Revelation 20:7-9:

> And when the thousand years are expired, Satan shall be loosed out of his prison, and shall go out to deceive the nations which are in the four quarters of the earth, Gog and Magog, to gather them together to battle: the number of whom is as the sand of the sea. And they went up on the breadth of the earth, and compassed the camp of the saints about, and the beloved city: and fire came down from God out of heaven, and devoured them.

The Background and Timing of This Battle

It is important to understand the prophetic setting for this conflict in order to fully understand the monument of the issues set forth in the passage under consideration. The confrontation between human elements identified as "Gog and Magog" and the Lord will take place at the close of the millennium. During the millennial age, Christ will have returned, put down Satan, and judged the nations. His 1,000-year reign on the throne of David in Jerusalem will have been established over those survivors of the tribulation period who are believers. It is critical to note that only saved people will enter the kingdom age. Believers who were raptured at least seven years prior to that time will return to the earth with Christ and, according to Scripture, "shall reign with him a thousand years" (Revelation 20:6). Therefore, believers who are reigning with Christ will not be susceptible to the lie that will cause millions of unbelievers to participate in the last revolt.

Some have also mistakenly equated the last great battle with Gog and Magog referred to in Ezekiel 38. This cannot be the case for a number of reasons.

1. The invasion described in Ezekiel 38 will come from the north. Russia and its Islamic allies are described as principal participants in the conflict. In the final revolt, Satan will "deceive the nations which are in the four quarters of the earth" (Revelation 20:8).

2. A limited number of nations are identified as consorts with the invaders from the "north quarters" (Ezekiel 38:4-6). In Revelation 20, a host of nations from those existing during the era of millennial bliss is identified.

3. The invading hosts of Ezekiel 38 will be decimated upon the hills to the north of Israel, largely by elements found in nature (Ezekiel 38:22; 39:4). In Revelation 20, the entire host will be consumed by "fire [that]

came down from God out of heaven" (Revelation 20:9).

4. After the invasion from the north, it will take seven full years to bury the dead and clean up the debris from the battle (Ezekiel 39:9-11). Revelation 20 describes fire from heaven that "devoured them" (verse 9).

The Central Lesson to Be Drawn from the Conflict

J. Dwight Pentecost, in his book *Things to Come,* makes a telling point:

> It [the final revolt] is necessary in order to provide a final test of fallen humanity. Man will be placed under the most ideal circumstances. With all outward source of temptation removed, in that Satan is bound, and every want supplied, so that there is nothing to covet, it will be demonstrated through those who are born in the millennium with a fallen, sinful nature that man is corrupt and worthy of judgment. In spite of the visible presence of the King and all the blessings that come from Him, by rebellion at the termination of the millennium (Revelation 20:7-9), men will prove that the heart is corrupt.[1]

Identity of Gog and Magog

As indicated previously, the identity of Gog and Magog in Revelation 20 is obscure. We simply are not given details as to who these people are, except to say that they will be gathered from "the four quarters of the earth" (Revelation 20:8). Perhaps there are similarities related to past occurrences in God's judgment on humanity at given junctures in history. For example, His judgment on Russia and the nations coming against Israel certainly comes to mind. In this confrontation, the Lord Himself will take the initiative to reap vengeance on those who move against His Chosen People and the city of Jerusalem.

We can also compare His actions to those taken against the wicked Sodomites in Genesis 19, when He rained "brimstone and fire" on a city and people wholly given over to licentious perversion (Genesis 19:15-29).

Another example is God's wrath poured out upon the prophets of Baal in the storied contest with Elijah on Mount Carmel (1 Kings 18:20-40). The issue on that occasion was not perversion, but idolatry. Fire from the Lord fell upon the altar erected by Elijah to demonstrate God's wrath on the emissaries of idol worship and the propriety of serving the invisible but sovereign God of Israel (1 Kings 18:38,39). The objective was to turn the hearts of the people of Israel back to God.

Addressing the final annihilation of the Babylonish system that will be destroyed in the conflagration of the great tribulation, we are told that "she shall be utterly burned with fire: for strong is the Lord God who judgeth her" (Revelation 18:8). Perhaps the implication we can draw from these events is that the Gog and Magog of Revelation 20 are a composite representation of the wrath of God poured out upon mankind's debauchery in its entirety.

The Depravity of Mankind

A few decades ago, liberal theologians were enamored with the concept touting the inherent goodness of mankind. To be sure, their views were more Freudian than theological. Nonetheless, they were convinced that, given a proper environment, the natural goodness of mankind would bring forth a kind of utopian revolution that would hold out the possibility of transporting the planet into an Edenic era. It would be a time when no one would be held responsible for iniquitous conduct—all would merely be victims of their environment. That the final revolt will become a historic reality forever puts this deception to rest.

In the final scenario, Satan will be removed from the scene:

> And I saw an angel come down from heaven, having the key of the bottomless pit and a great chain in his hand. And he laid hold on the dragon, that old serpent, which is the Devil, and Satan, and bound him a thousand years (Revelation 20:1,2).

Thus, Satan will be incarcerated throughout the millennium. Therefore, people will be relieved of "the devil made me do it" justification for wrongdoing. Whatever evil emanates from any human being will spring from his or her own fallen nature, not from outside influences—such as the voice of the devil. This extremely important truth emphatically illustrates, once and for all, that every person born on this planet—except one, the Lord Jesus—is born with a sinning nature inherited through Adam. In the final analysis, people do what they do because they are what they are—in this case, sinners by nature. David expressed it succinctly: "Behold, I was shapen in iniquity; and in sin did my mother conceive me" (Psalm 51:5).

Consider also that during the millennium, the curse will be lifted; the King will execute perfect justice. There will be the peace that people have longed for across the centuries and millennia. People will have what they want, when they want it, free of deprivation or the fear of repression. In other words, everything that mankind has said will satisfy and fulfill them will be theirs to enjoy. Will it be enough?

The answer is a resounding *No.*

Opportunities to See the Light

The rebels of the last revolt will be privileged above any generation of human beings since the fall of Adam and Eve in the Garden of Eden. Of no little consequence will be the testimony of God's grace emanating from the city of Jerusalem. Not only will the Holy City be the place of the Messiah's throne, it will also be the center of worship for no less than a thousand years.

Zechariah 14 provides a magnificent sketch of the fusion of Israel's ancient feasts with the worship of the millennial age.

> And it shall come to pass, that every one that is left of all the nations which came against Jerusalem shall even go up from year to year to worship the King, the LORD of hosts, and to keep the feast of tabernacles. And it shall be, that whosoever will not come up of all the families of the earth unto Jerusalem to worship the King, the LORD of hosts, even upon them shall be no rain (Zechariah 14:16,17).

It is my belief that the much-debated sacrificial system at the millennial temple, described in Ezekiel 40–44, will have two essential aspects. The first will be memorial, much as we come today to the communion table to look back on our Lord's sacrifice for us. But we must remember that millions of the people who will come to Jerusalem to worship during the millennium will be unsaved. For this reason, there is sound basis to assume that temple worship will be testimonial, as well as an occasion to worship the King, remembering all aspects of His person and work. For those who are lost, the temple and its sacrifices may provide a great testimonial object lesson on the work of the Savior in redemption.

Embracing Darkness

Inexplicably, when living in the light of all that people could ask or think, millions of earth dwellers will join the final revolt.

"And when the thousand years are expired, Satan shall be loosed out of his prison" (Revelation 20:7).

Astonishingly, he will receive a tumultuous welcome from millions of people across the face of the earth. Scripture tells us that he will gather them "to battle: the number of whom is as the sand of the sea" (Revelation 20:8).

All of these people will be descendants of those who entered the millennium as saved individuals. Yet, under perfect conditions provided by the Creator and Sustainer of all the earth, they will choose to join Satan in his last grand push to depose God and His Christ. Can we adequately answer the inevitable question, Why? No, we cannot.

We can, however, make observations based on historical evidence. First, and in a sense foremost, is the observation that affluence has seldom contributed to mankind's drawing closer to God. To the contrary, it seems that under the best of conditions, people turn inward rather than to Him. This has been eloquently illustrated throughout the history of the nation of Israel. In the best of times, they seemed to drift further from the Lord. It does seem that the majority of people cannot abide sustained prosperity.

Therefore, when Satan arrives on the scene after a thousand years in the "bottomless pit," he will be received with open arms and hailed as a deliverer—so much so that he will successfully marshal a global military aggregation, "the number of whom is as the sand of the sea" (Revelation 20:8).

Calling It Like It Is

We frequently hear the phrase, "the rest of the story." In Revelation 20, the Lord sets before us the astonishing "rest of the story." It is indeed an old story. As Satan and his minions rebelled against a benevolent God in the past, humanity will fall into the same iniquitous pit during the millennial kingdom. It seems incomprehensible. In actuality, our being exposed to it is a consummating necessity. It is a story that must be fully told. Without Revelation 20, there is no last chapter to the drama. What will happen, we might ask, if mankind is not given the opportunity they asked for: a society with justice, peace, prosperity, and the visible evidence of the existence of God? Will they remain rebellious? Or will they embrace and rejoice in the light of God? In short, are people, in essence, naturally good?

That notion is forever dispelled when we are exposed to the somewhat grim realities of Revelation 20. People are not naturally good. They are inherently inclined toward evil. When given a choice, the majority—as in the case of "the sand of the sea" contingent—choose to do evil rather than good.

Instead of being depressed over these somber facts, we should embrace a confirmation. With this final act of rebellion against God, there is a concluding exclamation point. With the millennium will come the last great act in the drama of redemption. Humanity will have been tested under every conceivable condition—innocence, human government, law, grace, and finally the Messianic kingdom, to name a few. Under the test of every conceivable dispensation, mankind has failed. Therefore, it can never be said that under the right conditions, mankind's goodness, like cream in a bottle, will rise to the top. No. God was right. Mankind is totally and wholly depraved.

And so, the book on the story of the nature of man closes on this dour note:

"And they went up on the breadth of the earth, and compassed the camp of the saints about, and the beloved city: and fire came down from God out of heaven, and devoured them" (Revelation 20:9).

The Good News

Although this may be the closing chapter on the story of mankind's rebellion against Christ, it is not the final chapter in the Book. In staccato-like fashion, the Scriptures chronicle the final demise of Satan (Revelation 20:10), the Great

White Throne judgment (Revelation 20:11-15), and the entry of a new heaven and a new earth (Revelation 21–22).

Above all of these monumental events rings the great sounding bell of redemption. The case has been emphatically made for the necessity of the new birth. If there are elements in the story of the total depravity of mankind that seem somewhat obscure, this can never be said of God's plan of redemption. Reading the entire account, from Eden to the last revolt of Revelation, only creates a conclusion: We desperately need a Savior—and, thankfully, He has come.

> If thou shalt confess with thy mouth the Lord Jesus, and shalt believe in thine heart that God hath raised him from the dead, thou shalt be saved. For with the heart man believeth unto righteousness; and with the mouth confession is made unto salvation (Romans 10:9,10).

And I saw a great white throne, and him that sat on it, from whose face the earth and the heaven fled away; and there was found no place for them.

In other words, the principle that the greater the light rejected, the more severe the judgment anticipated would apply at the Great White Throne as well. Because the eternal destiny of all of those who have rejected God's gift of grace in Christ is eternal separation from Him, then the judgment at the Great White Throne according to their deeds is simply the time at which the actual degrees of judgment are finally announced. The expression "the punishment fits the crime" is an apt description of what will take place as the dead stand before the throne to receive judgment on the basis of what they have done.

CHAPTER 19

The Great White Throne Judgment

John R. Master

Pattern for Judgment

"In the beginning God created the heaven and the earth" (Genesis 1:1). The first two chapters of the book of Genesis record God's great creative activity, which climaxed with the creation of Adam and Eve and their placement in the Garden of Eden. God had created a paradise state in which He placed humankind. However, despite the perfection of God's creation, Adam and Eve fell to the temptation of the serpent. They sinned and disobeyed God's Word and, as a consequence of their sin, they suffered the judgment that God had pronounced would come if man sinned against God (Genesis 2:17). They died, just as God had said.

Death involves separation. Adam and Eve, through their sin, separated themselves from God as evidenced by the fact that they were hiding from God in the Garden when God came to walk in the cool of the day and to fellowship with them (Genesis 3:8). This spiritual separation from God is illustrated by physical death, which itself is a separation from our present state of existence. Death does not mean annihilation or the cessation of all things. In the spiritual area, death involves separation from God and, in the physical arena, separation from our present earthly existence. That one does not cease to exist after death is well illustrated in Luke 16. There both the righteous and the wicked are seen to continue to exist as genuine human individuals. In death they were separated from earthly existence, but they did not cease to exist.

The book of Revelation records God's final acts in human history to bring about a restoration of humankind to a state even greater than that experienced by Adam and Eve in the Garden. In Revelation 21 and 22, John describes the new Jerusalem in which there is perfect fellowship with God. Humankind is restored to its original place of preeminence to rule over creation on God's behalf (Genesis 1:26; Revelation 22:5), and the possibility of sin, which unfortunately became a reality for Adam and Eve, no longer exists. By His grace, God so transforms the human race that, unlike Adam and Eve, those who belong to God will perfectly obey Him and will enjoy intimate fellowship with Him forever.

In the Garden, when Adam and Eve sinned, God placed a curse on the serpent, on Eve, and on the land. From the very outset, the Bible emphasizes the reality that sin must and will be judged by God. This principle is stated in Genesis 2:17 and sadly realized in Genesis 3. The entire history of the Old Testament is a record of this reality; sin leads to judgment. For sin to go unpunished would violate the character of God and what His righteousness and holiness demand.

The Bible begins with the first sin, which was related to Satan's deception of Eve (1 Timothy 2:14) and which brought about the judgment of death. The Bible ends with the final sin of humankind, once again brought about by Satan's deceptions (Revelation 20:8), and with the final judgment of sin (Revelation 20:11-15). At the end of the millennium, Satan will gather together anyone who will join him in one last attempt to destroy the plan and purposes of God. Instead of achieving his objective of destroying the people of God and the beloved city of God, Satan will be defeated. God will send fire from heaven to devour all of those involved in this final act of rebellion. This sin will then become the background for God's final judgment at the Great White Throne. Just as humankind's first sin brought the first judgment, so also will this final rebellion bring final judgment.

Setting for Judgment

"And I saw a great white throne and Him who sat upon it, from whose presence earth and heaven fled away, and no place was found for them" (Revelation 20:11 NASB). The image of a "white" throne probably relates to the descriptions of the judge found in Daniel 7:9,10, the Ancient of Days, whose "vesture was like white snow, and the hair of His head like pure wool...and the books were opened" (NASB). This same imagery is associated with Jesus in Revelation 1:14, where He is described as having a head and hair "white like white wool" (NASB). Throughout the book of Revelation, the word *white* is associated with deity and with those rightly related to God. In the one exception, Revelation 6:2, the white horse suggests the deceptive nature of the horse and rider who come proclaiming themselves to be of God when, in fact, they are agents of the devil (cf. 2 Corinthians 11:14). The description of the throne as "white," therefore, points to the holiness and purity of the One who sits on it to judge.

This vision of the Great White Throne follows immediately upon the statement, "And the devil who deceived them was thrown into the lake of fire and brimstone, where the beast and the false prophet are also; and they will be tormented day and night forever and ever" (Revelation 20:10 NASB). Those who had been leaders in the opposition against our Lord will finally have been judged. Their judgment is to be "tormented day and night forever and ever," one of the strongest statements that could be made in pointing to the eternal suffering of Satan, the Antichrist, and the false prophet. The judgment of the leaders of those who reject God establishes a pattern for the judgment of all those members of the human race that have sinned against God and followed after the deceptive lies of the devil. This pattern of first judging those most responsible follows that of Genesis 3, where Satan is the first to be cursed by God.

In this final judgment of humankind, it is difficult to be absolutely certain concerning the identity of the One sitting upon this Great White Throne to judge. Is it God the Father or God the Son? Many would argue, based on passages such as John 5:22,23, that the Son, our Lord Jesus Christ, will be the judge. Because the text does not specifically identify the One sitting on the throne as the Lord Jesus Christ, however, it may be better not to be dogmatic or to say more than the text itself explicitly states. In either case, it is divine judgment.

So awesome is the presence of God sitting on His Great White Throne of judgment, that the earth and heavens flee away. Whenever this word *flee* is used in the New Testament, it carries with it the idea of one fleeing from something that is perceived to bring harm or danger. Even the heavens and the earth, that is, God's creation, contaminated by sin, recognizes that it cannot be in the presence of a holy and righteous God. Other passages such as Isaiah 51:6 and 2 Peter 3:10-12 teach that the present heavens and earth will be destroyed by fire. They will be judged because of the effects of sin on the creation itself. The One who sits on the throne is One whose holiness and righteousness will not allow anything or anyone contaminated by sin to be in His presence.

The creation must be restored to a "very good" state (cf. Genesis 1:31).

People Under Judgment

Their Position

After John saw this Great White Throne and was given a revelation of the holiness of God, he saw all the dead, "the great and the small," standing before the throne. The expression "the great and the small" is used as a figure of speech to make it clear that all of the dead are involved. This is an indication that the Great White Throne is to be God's final judgment against human sin. No loose ends remain.

The fact that all were standing before the throne may paint the picture of these masses of people coming as criminals before the judge. On the other hand, their standing posture might also suggest that these people still refused to bow down and acknowledge Jesus as Lord, adding to their condemnation as wicked in their rejection of Him.

Apparently the people standing before the throne exist in their resurrection bodies (cf. Daniel 12:2; John 5:29; Acts 24:15; Revelation 20:5). The eternal nature of the resurrection body is an indication of the eternal nature of the judgment to follow. Just as Satan, the beast, and the false prophet receive eternal judgment, so will their followers (cf. Matthew 25:46; 2 Thessalonians 1:9).

The Basis

John sees some open books. Such books are associated with divine judgment (cf. Daniel 7:10). The resurrected dead standing before the throne were "judged from the things which were written in the books according to their deeds" (Revelation 20:12 NASB). (That is, on the basis of what they had done with their lives.) Such a judgment would, first of all, assure their condemnation, because "all have sinned, and come short of the glory of God" (Romans 3:23).

Also, "according to their deeds" suggests that the judgment of the wicked at the Great White Throne will determine degrees of punishment based on individual actions. This same truth appears to be taught by Jesus in Matthew 11:20-24 where He asserts that "It shall be more tolerable for Tyre and Sidon at the day of judgment, than for you" (verse 22) and "it shall be more tolerable for the land of Sodom in the day of judgment, than for thee" (verse 24). In other words, the principle that "the greater the rejection, the more severe the judgment anticipated" would apply at the Great White Throne as well. Because the eternal destiny of all of those who have rejected God's gift of grace in Christ is eternal separation from Him, then the judgment at the Great White Throne according to their deeds is simply the time at which the actual degrees of judgment are finally announced. The expression "the punishment fits the crime" is an apt description of what will take place as the dead stand before the throne to receive judgment on the basis of what they have done.

The Extent

Just as the expression "the great and the small" includes all the wicked dead, so also Revelation 20:13 reinforces the reality that each individual will be judged according to what he or she has done. "And the sea gave up the dead which were in it, and death and Hades gave up the dead which were in them; and they were judged, every one of them according to their deeds" (NASB).

That "death and Hades gave up the dead" once again suggests the all-inclusive nature of this final judgment. According to the Old Testament, those who died would have been in Sheol, called "Hades" in the Greek translation of the Old Testament. The idea that Hades is the place of the unregenerate dead while they await their resurrection and final judgment is reflected in the incident recorded in Luke 16:23. That passage pictures the rich man as suffering torment in Hades, in contrast to Lazarus who was enjoying the comfort of Abraham's bosom. Revelation 1:18 mentions Jesus as having "the keys of death and of Hades" (NASB), pointing to his authority over all the dead. In Revelation 6:8 (NASB), "Hades" is pictured as following the rider named "Death." This fourth rider brings extensive death to the earth; Hades appears to be the destination of the wicked dead in these New Testament texts.

The mention of the fact that "the sea gave up the dead" suggests the completeness of this final judgment. The foundation for the use of this image may lie in Isaiah 27:1 where Leviathan, the fleeing serpent, is associated with the sea. The prophet's denunciation of Leviathan was probably an attack on the false religions of Isaiah's day and would have been proclaiming Jehovah's authority and judgment of all evil, even the Leviathan of pagan mythology. Job 3:8 also mentions Leviathan in a negative light (cf. Job 41:1). The mention therefore of the sea giving up the dead points to the fact that even a place often associated with evil and the control of evil would ultimately be conquered by God and brought into submission. This association is supported by the fact that the beast that comes out of the sea (Revelation 13:1) is the Antichrist. Nonetheless, Revelation 5:13 asserts that "every created thing which is in heaven and on the earth and under the earth and on the sea, and all things in them" (NASB) will praise the Lord. Revelation 7:1-3 uses the terms "earth" and "sea" to refer to the totality of the earth's surface being protected until the appropriate time. There are no exceptions; God is in control of all. Even their own stronghold could not hide the wicked dead from the judgment of the Great White Throne.

With this final judgment of the wicked, death and Hades were cast into the Lake of Fire, where the devil, the beast, and the false prophet had already been consigned to be tormented forever and ever. All of the wicked dead would join with those they had followed in their rebellion against God. There they also would pay the penalty for their rejection of the God who created them, who loved them, and who, despite their sin and rebellion, wanted to save them from their sin. Their judgment is everlasting (Daniel 12:2; Isaiah 66:24; Matthew 3:12; 25:46; 2 Thessalonians 1:9). In fact, Daniel 12:2 uses the same word to describe the everlasting life of the righteous as it does to describe the everlasting disgrace and contempt of the wicked.

It is the enormity of the sin of rejection of God that leads to the enormity of final eternal judgment. To have anything less than the eternal judgment described in the Scriptures would minimize the significance of sin against the God of the Bible. Sin against the infinite, loving God demands eternal punishment. This punishment is exclusion from the presence of God and consignment to the Lake of Fire with all of those who have similarly rejected the infinite love of the infinite God.

The Book of Life

Revelation 20:15 states, "And if anyone's name was not found written in the book of life, he was thrown into the lake of fire" (NASB). This verse certainly supports the idea that the wicked dead would be thrown into the Lake of Fire, because the Book of Life seems to be related to believers throughout its use in Scripture. None of the names of these wicked dead would be found in the Book of Life. Yet, because John has already stated that the wicked dead were judged from the books, why would this additional statement be necessary?

Although it is generally assumed that the Book of Life records the names of all the saved throughout all of history, it might be better to see it as containing the names of all the saved living on earth at any particular time. This under-standing would help explain Exodus 32:32-35. In that context, those who sinned would have been judged by physical death rather than by loss of their salvation, and Moses would have been requesting that God take his life if He would no longer go with His people. Again in Revelation 3:5 some in the church at Sardis were in danger of having their names erased from the Book of Life. Relating this to temporal judgment rather than to loss of salvation would fit well with the teaching of other passages such as 1 Corinthians 11:30.

Because the Great White Throne appears to be the final judgment mentioned in Scripture, the presence of the Book of Life may intimate that the righteous who have lived through the millennium and have resisted the attacks of the enemy at the end of the millennium will, like all believers before them, stand before the Lord to be judged according to their works (Romans 14:10; 2 Corinthians 5:10). Certainly believers who had lived through the millennial period would need to receive their resurrection bodies in order to enter into the blessings of the new heavens and the new earth and enjoy perfect, eternal fellowship with the Lord and, like all other believers, give an account "for his deeds in the body" (2 Corinthians 5:10).

Application of Judgment

This final judgment of Revelation 20:11-15, then, brings to a close this present human sinful existence. It establishes God's holiness and emphasizes the reality of the horror of sin and the enormity of rejecting Christ. Such a reality ought to give us far greater sensitivity to the terror that awaits those who reject Christ and the importance of sharing the good news of the gospel and the grace of God.

One's relationship to Christ is a serious matter. Only those who have experienced the grace of God will enter into an eternity of perfect fellowship with the One who created them and loved them so much that He sent His own Son to pay the penalty for their sin. Those who reject the good news of the grace of God will experience eternal separation from the God who loves them and spend eternity with the one who has sought to destroy them and with all those who have rejected God's love. The options for mankind are two: either an eternity with our loving Creator, God, or an eternity with the one who hates God and God's greatest creation—humankind.

And I saw a new heaven and a new earth: for the first heaven and the first earth were passed away; and there was no more sea.

REVELATION 21:1

Get that very clear in your minds—heaven is a place. I used to think of it as a state of being in a disembodied condition (perhaps here) and as a little boy I shuddered and shrank from becoming a ghost, and thought how cold and bleak and uncomfortable it must be. When I confided all this to someone, I was told that I could be an angel if I were good and have wings and a harp. Let's get these unscriptural notions out of our minds. Heaven is a place, a "prepared" place, which means a suited place. I believe that *there is in man a nostalgia for heaven.* Forgive me for reminding you that the word *nostalgia* comes from two Greek words: *nostos* meaning "return home"; and *alos,* meaning "pain." It meant originally homesickness as an incurable malady; incurable by anything—except, of course, by *home.*

—C.I. Scofield

CHAPTER 20

Heaven and Eternity Future

Charles U. Wagner

Of all the subjects considered in prophecy, without a doubt the one most cherished is heaven. All we know about heaven is found in God's revealed Word—the Bible. What we read and learn is encouraging and comforting. Christ and the apostles preached and taught about heaven as a real place—the final residence of all who know Christ as Savior. Echoing this thought, D.L. Moody said:

> I'd like to locate heaven, and find out all about it I can. I expect to live there through eternity. If I were going to dwell in any place in this country, if I were going to make it my home, I would want to inquire all about the place, about its climate, about what kind of neighbors I was going to have, about the schools for my children, about everything, in fact, that I could learn concerning it.[1]

As we come to the last chapter of *Countdown to Armageddon,* the words of Moody ring in our ears and burn in our hearts motivating us to see what the Bible has to say about heaven, our future home. In our brief study we will include heaven as it is today, which we will call "heaven today," and then the new heavens and the new earth, which we will call "heaven tomorrow—eternity future." Just the mention of heaven brings about many erroneous concepts which a lot of believers have embraced as biblical truth.

About these concepts, J. Dwight Pentecost writes:

> Most believers have a nebulous concept of heaven. None of us have been there. People don't vacation there and return with slides to show their friends. Much of our concept of heaven has been fashioned by hymn-writers or cartoonists. The hymnwriters portray heaven as a place where believers sit in the shade with soft breezes keeping them cool as they relax day after day. The prospect seems monotonous. The cartoonist pictures the saints sitting on the edge of a cloud with their feet hanging over into nothingness about to slip off into space.[2]

Heaven Today

Heaven Is a Place

As we turn from human imagination to God's inspired Word, it becomes very clear that heaven is a place. A few references ratify this truth. Scripture is clear that God created heaven (Acts 4:24). Heaven belongs to God (Psalm 115:16). It is the place where God dwells (Matthew 6:9). Christ promised a divine, heavenly home and said, "I go to prepare a *place* for you" (John 14:2, emphasis added). We are clearly told that Christ is seated in heaven at the right hand of God (Hebrews 1:3; Ephesians 1:20). Peter affirms that heaven is a real place where the inheritance is kept with care for the child of God (1 Peter 1:4). Also we read that God will create a new heaven and a new earth (Isaiah 65:17).

The biblical teaching of heaven being a place transforms our concept of the future. The great Bible teacher, C.I.

Scofield of the *Scofield Reference Bible,* wrote concerning this place:

> Get that very clear in your minds–heaven is a place. I used to think of it as a state of being in a disembodied condition (perhaps here) and as a little boy I shuddered and shrank from becoming a ghost, and thought how cold and bleak and uncomfortable it must be. When I confided all this to someone, I was told that I could be an angel if I were good and have wings and a harp. Let's get these unscriptural notions out of our minds. Heaven is a place, a "prepared" place, which means a suited place. "Let not your heart be troubled: ye believe in God, believe also in me. In my Father's house are many mansions: if it were not so, I would have told you. I go to prepare a place for you" (John 14:1,2). These words can convey to our minds only ideas of locality and substantial entity. This at least Heaven is, spiritu-alize as you please. On the other hand, we are not to suppose that heaven is a place full of bricks or stone houses. That would be a very crude and fleshly con-ception of it. I don't know what glorified architecture is like, but I do know that the Christ who has sown this earth with flowers, and lifted into it majestic mountains, and set the continents in the tossing seas, and filled the upper air with drifting clouds is the same Christ whose Hand is shaping the eternal love Home of His bride. *I go to prepare a place for you* is enough for me.[3]

It is important to note that actually there are three heavens. The "atmospheric" heavens, which includes the space that surrounds the earth. Scriptures speaks of this heaven many times (Isaiah 55:9-11). Secondly, there is the "celestial heavens," which includes the sun, moon, the planets, and the stars (Genesis 1:14). Then, there is "the abode of God"! "For thus saith the high and lofty One that inhabiteth eternity, whose name is Holy: I dwell in the high and holy place, and with him also that is of a contrite and humble spirit..." (Isaiah 57:15). The title "The LORD God of heaven" or "the God of heaven" is found numerous times (2 Chronicles 36:23; Nehemiah 1:5; Daniel 2:37). Interestingly, there are seven words used in the Old and New Testaments referring to heaven as a place, a dwelling, a habitation. Also, the Apostle Paul spoke of his experience when he was taken up to the third heaven, the dwelling place of God (2 Corinthians 12:2-4).

Again, by "heaven today" we simply mean that place that now exists, the residence of God and the home or residence of those who have died "in Christ." When a believer dies, he goes directly to this heaven. There is no truth to the idea that a believer dies and sleeps until the Lord comes, only then realizing heaven. Several passages make this clear. Paul said to the Philippians, "For to me to live is Christ, and to die *is gain.... For I am in a strait betwixt two, having a desire to* depart, and to be with Christ; which is far better" (Philippians 1:21,23, emphasis added). Again, "Therefore we are always confident, knowing that, whilst we are at home in the body, we are absent from the Lord: (For we walk by faith, not by sight.) We are confident, I say, and willing rather to be *absent from the body, and to be present with the Lord"* (2 Corinthians 5:6-8, emphasis added). When a believer dies, he or she is ushered instantaneously into the presence of the Lord. What a delight and comfort to those who have loved ones who have passed away—they passed into heaven—to be with Christ!

What Is Heaven Like, Today?

Although there are many questions that cannot be answered as to the state of believers now in heaven, the Bible does give us a glimpse into what Lewis Sperry Chafer called the "intermediate state." Concerning this state, Chafer writes:

> In theological usage, the term *intermediate state* refers to the manner of existence of the human soul and spirit in

the interval between death and resurrection. But for the translation of some of the saints, death and resurrection are universal; and, since death is never represented as an unconscious condition, the souls and spirits of all men, because they remain cognizant, are subject to both location and conditions.[4]

We are encouraged knowing that our saved loved ones are "with Christ." And that this is "far better" than anything experienced in this life. Judson Palmer wrote:

At the moment of death the child of God will be with Christ in heaven. Christ Jesus ascended into heaven and took His seat at the right hand of the Father on high in His resurrection body, a material body of flesh and bones (Luke 24:39), the Man in the Glory. He has been seen there since He ascended by three men in the flesh on the earth, on three different occasions. He is there this very moment, in the same body in which He ascended from Olivet.[5]

Also, Scripture seems to reveal that believers have some kind of intermediate body while there with their Lord. Chafer writes:

A declaration is made in 2 Corinthians 5:1-5, that should this "earthly house of this tabernacle" be dissolved, "we have a building of God, an house not made with hands, eternal in the heavens," and that the human spirit earnestly desires not to be unclothed or disembodied but to be clothed upon; and to this end a body "from heaven," eternal—with respect to its qualities as any body from heaven must be—awaits the believer who dies. He will thus not be unclothed or bodiless between death and the resurrection of that original body which will be from the grave. The body "from heaven" could not be the body which is from the grave, nor could the body from the grave serve as an intermediate body before the resurrection. Apart from the divine provision of an intermediate body, the believer's desire that he should not be unclothed or bodiless could not be satisfied.[6]

Many believers have been comforted with this Scripture. We know that they are in His presence as well as the presence of others who have gone on before and that they are happy. "Blessed [happy] are the dead which die in the Lord..." (Revelation 14:13).

As we think about the privilege of being with Christ in heaven, it gives us a type of nostalgia. A former great pastor of Westminster Central Hall in London, England, William E. Sangster, writes:

> I believe that *there is in man a nostalgia for heaven.* Forgive me for reminding you that the word *nostalgia* comes from two Greek words: *nostos* meaning "return home"; and *alos,* meaning pain." It meant originally homesickness as an incurable malady; incurable by anything–except, of course, by *home.* Now I believe that although it is hidden, ignored, overlaid, and even denied, there is in man a homesickness for heaven. Wordsworth, in his famous ode on "Intimations of immortality from recollections of Early Childhood," speaks with plainness of this secret reminiscence in the soul. He says: "Our birth is but a sleep and a forgetting: The soul that rises with us, our life's Star, Hath had elsewhere its setting, And cometh from afar: Not in entire forgetfulness, And not in utter nakedness, But trailing cloud of glory do we come, From God, who is our home. From God, *who is our home!*"[7]

What's Next?

The next event in God's timetable, according to the Word of God, is the Rapture of the church. The Scripture is clear on this subject. When a believer dies, the soul and spirit go to be with Christ. The body goes to the grave. But this is only temporary. We read:

> For the Lord himself shall descend from heaven with a shout, with the voice of the archangel, and with the trump of God: and the *dead in Christ shall rise first:* Then we which are alive and remain shall be caught up together with them in the clouds, to meet the Lord in the air: and so shall we ever be with the Lord. Wherefore comfort one another with these words (1 Thessalonians 4:16-18, emphasis added).

At this time, we will receive permanent bodies to be occupied through all eternity. We will have bodies like the Lord's own glorious body. The Apostle Paul states that our body of humiliation will be changed to a body "like unto his glorious body" (Philippians 3:21). Christ's resurrection is the firstfruits anticipating a coming resurrection for the believer in Christ. "But every man in his own order: Christ the firstfruits; afterward they that are Christ's at his coming" (1 Corinthians 15:23). Believers will be in heaven at the Judgment Seat of Christ to be rewarded, and then will return with the Lord to the earth to set up His Kingdom (1 Corinthians 3:12-14; 2 Corinthians 5:10; Revelation 19:11-16).

Heaven Tomorrow

By "tomorrow," we speak of that time after the millennium. Following the Time of Jacob's Trouble, the tribulation (which lasts for seven years), the Lord will set up His kingdom. After that 1,000-year period we are introduced to "a new heaven and a new earth" (Revelation 21:1). Remember, we have reigned with Christ during the 1,000-year millennium. The Great White Throne Judgment takes place, which is the judgment of the unsaved (Revelation 20:11), and Scripture tells us that the day will come when this heaven will be no more (Job 14:12; Isaiah 51:6). We are told that "all the host of heaven shall be dissolved, and the heavens shall be rolled together as a scroll" (Isaiah 34:4). This is followed by the eternal state. This eternal state, of the "New Heaven and the New Earth" is described vividly in the book of Revelation. (Heaven is mentioned 22 times in the book of Revelation.) The "throne" in heaven is referred to 36 times. John Walvoord states:

> ... having revealed the destruction of the old earth and the old heaven, John wrote that he saw what will take its place—a new heaven, new earth, and a New Jerusalem.... Scriptural revelation gives very little information about the new heaven and the new earth, except by inferring that it is quite different than our present earth. The only major characteristic mentioned is that there will not be any longer any sea in contrast to the present situation where most of the earth is covered by water. It is apparent as the narration goes on that the new earth is round because there are directions of north, south, east, and west (Revelation 21:13), but there is no indication as to whether the new earth is larger or smaller than our present earth.[8]

What Will Heaven Be Like?

Suppose we could be projected back in time and were able to explain to our forefathers something of what life is like on earth today. Now see yourself trying to explain a simple elevator to George Washington. You describe a black compartment with a cord on the top that pulls up the compartment to the third floor, and you are doing so with the benefits of electricity. He would be hard-pressed to understand. Or, how about explaining your computer with its online communications skill. I mention this only to state that if we knew all that God had provided for us in heaven—we probably could not fully comprehend it. It is no wonder that we know more about what will *not* be in heaven than we know what *will* be there. So, we read, "And God shall wipe away all tears from their eyes; and there shall be no more death, neither sorrow, nor crying, neither shall there be any more pain: for the former things are passed away" (Revelation 21:4). A little girl, hearing this verse read, said, "Mommy I think heaven is the place of "no mores." And so it is.

A Literal Place. Again, it is important to stress that we are speaking about a specific location. Some scholars seek to spiritualize the place called heaven and look at it in a non-literal way. Heaven is described beautifully for us in Revelation 21 as a city that comes down from the air with dimensions and even walls. Walvoord states:

> Beginning with Revelation 21:9, John describes the new Jerusalem as "the bride, the Lamb's wife." As stated before, although there has been scholarly debate on this point, the preferable interpretation is to regard the description of the city as meaning a literal city that is as beautifully adorned as a bride, rather than trying to suggest the symbolism of a bride who is represented by a city.[9]

Pentecost adds:

> The city will be spacious, built on a square, and the length is as large as the breadth. The measure of the city was 12,000 furlongs, which is approximately 1,500 miles. Some visualize this as a cube with four dimensions. Others view it as a pyramid with three dimensions. Whatever shape it is, it is spacious. Today 1,500 miles is not far, but it was in John's day. Christ was born in Nazareth, thirty miles inland from the Mediterranean Sea, but Scripture doesn't record that He ever saw the sea. He traveled the ninety miles from Galilee to Jerusalem because He was compelled to attend the feasts. When John spoke of a city 1,500 miles by 1,500 miles by 1,500 miles, he was speaking of that which was beyond comprehension. John was trying to communicate the spaciousness of the city, not necessarily its physical dimensions. The city will be big enough to

bring all of the redeemed ones of God into the Father's presence.[10]

The Glories and Blessings of the Place Called Heaven

Christ's Presence. The heaven of "tomorrow"–the new heaven, will have something in common with the heaven of today. There we will be in the presence of the Lord. We read, ". . . and God himself shall be with them, and be their God" (Revelation 21:3). The presence of the Lord characterizes heaven as it is and as it will be. "For now we see through a glass, darkly; but then *face to face*" (1 Corinthians 13:12, emphasis added). Did not Christ say, "I will come again, and receive you unto myself; that *where I am, there ye may be also*" (John 14:3, emphasis added).

What is it that makes heaven, heaven? It is the presence of our Lord Jesus Christ. Pentecost says it so well:

> Heaven, first of all, is the presence of God. This does not mean that heaven is not a place, for it certainly is; but heaven is more than that. We should think of it, first of all, as the place of God's revealed presence, where He displays His glory. John wrote concerning the redeemed: "they shall see his face" (Revelation 22:4).[11]

Rest from Our Labors. "And I heard a voice from heaven saying unto me, Write, Blessed are the dead which die in the Lord from henceforth: Yea, saith the Spirit, that they may rest from their labours; and their works do follow them" (Revelation 14:13).

Serving the Lord Forever. Don't misunderstand rest. This is not the proverbial "rocking chair" on heaven's "front porch." "And there shall be no more curse: but the throne of God and of the Lamb shall be in it; and his servants shall serve him" (Revelation 22:3). Think of serving the Lord and being used by him–and having it last eternally. No wonder we feel that serving the Lord today is just a "little bit of heaven." Full service will be a blessing indeed.

Oh Worship the King. What a wonderful combination, service and worship. "And after these things I heard a great voice of much people in heaven, saying, Alleluia; Salvation, and glory, and honour, and power, unto the Lord our God" (Revelation 19:1).

Glory. A life of glory—describes our life in heaven with Him. "For our light affliction, which is but a moment, worketh for us a far more exceeding and eternal weight of glory (2 Corinthians 4:17). Again, "When Christ, who is our life, shall appear, then shall ye also appear with him in glory" (Colossians 3:4). Pentecost has written:

> The glory of our expectation is that we shall be transformed into His likeness, being sinless, deathless, and experience the perfection of development.

> > Oh, Christ! He is the fountain,
> > The deep, sweet well of love!
> > The streams on earth I've tasted,
> > More deep I'll drink above:
> > There, to an ocean fullness,
> > His mercy doth expand,
> > And glory, glory dwelleth
> > In Immanuel's land.

> There is the danger that the redeemed one will become so occupied with the anticipation of his own experience of glory that the supreme glorification of the Godhead is lost. Our occupation in the eternal state will not be with our position or glory but with God Himself. John writes: "we shall see him as he is" (1 John 3:2). We shall be fully occupied with the One "that loved us, and washed us from our sins in his own blood, and hath made us kings and priests unto God and his Father" (Revelation 1:5,6), ascribing "Blessing, and honour, and

glory, and power, be unto him that sitteth upon the
throne, and unto the Lamb for ever and ever" (Revelation 5:13).[12]

Joy and Abundance. Certainly, there is joy in serving the Lord,
but can you imagine what it will be like in glory? "And God
shall wipe away all tears from their eyes; and there shall be
no more death, neither sorrow, nor crying, neither shall
there be any more pain: for the former things are passed
away" (Revelation 21:4). "I will give unto him that is athirst
of the fountain of the water of life freely" (Revelation 21:6).
  Walvoord writes concerning this blessing:

> The wonder of salvation by grace and drinking of the
> spring of the water of life are part of the wonderful pro-
> vision God has made for those who put their trust in
> Him. This refers to how abundant our new life in Christ
> is as indicated in the invitation of Isaiah 55:1 and that
> of Christ in John 4:10,13,14. The promise that all things
> will be inherited by those who overcome by faith and
> that God will be his God and he will be God's son is the
> illustration of the abundant grace that Christians have
> in Christ and how marvelous our inheritance is (cf. Mat-
> thew 5:5; 19:29; 25:34; 1 Corinthians 6:9,10; Hebrews
> 1:14; 9:15; 1 Peter 1:4; 2:19; 1 John 5:5).[13]

Fellowship with Others. To be sure, our greatest fellowship will
be with Christ. But, there will be fellowship with others as
well. Paul Rood writes:

> The saints of God will be in heaven. How thrilling it
> will be to meet Enoch, who "walked with God; and was
> not, for God took him"! How wonderful it will be to
> have fellowship with Noah, the preacher of righteous-
> ness who was faithful to his Lord in a time of apostasy!
> How interesting it will be to walk down the golden
> streets with Jonah, who had a post-graduate course in
> Fish College, and with Isaiah, who dipped his pen in

all the colors of the rainbow in order to depict the glories of the coming millennial reign of Christ! What shall we then say of John, the disciple whom Jesus loved, and Paul, the great apostle to the Gentiles? Shall we listen to John expounding his writings, and Paul, explaining the things that were difficult to understand? Martin Luther, the great reformer, John Wesley, the great organizer, Charles Finney, the great evangelist, Dwight L. Moody, the great soul winner, will all be in heaven. Our departed friends will be there...."[14]

Most of us have loved ones already in glory. Parting was difficult. But, what joy in knowing that someday we will be with them and share eternity with them in glory.

Thinking about this wonderful fellowship with others in our future home, heaven, the question comes, Who will populate heaven? Concerning this question, Pentecost writes:

"But ye are come unto mount Zion, and unto the city of the living God, the heavenly Jerusalem ..." (Hebrews 12:22). The emphasis here is on the city again. In this heavenly Jerusalem several groups are identifiable. First, he mentioned "an innumerable company of angels" (verse 22). This referred to all the unfallen angels who have faithfully served God from the time of their creation, having resisted the temptation of Lucifer, who sought to draw all the angels after himself. This heavenly city will be occupied by unfallen angels. Second, he mentioned the "general assembly and church of the firstborn" (verse 23). I believe this refers to the church of this age, the church that is Christ's body, which began at Pentecost and will continue until the Rapture. The second identifiable group of inhabitants is the church of this present age. The third group is "the spirits of just men made perfect" (verse 23). Evidently this refers to all Old Testament saints from the time of Adam to the inception of the church, and to tribulation saints from the Rapture to the second advent. It also includes all millennial saints, those born and redeemed in the millennial age. This is a third, separate, identifiable group. The church and the spirits of just men—the Old Testament saints and the New Testament saints—comprise the total body of the redeemed. They are all there by faith through grace, based on the death of Christ; but they are there in a different relationship to Christ. The church is there as His bride. The Old Testament saints are there as friends of the Bridegroom. They are related to Christ. They are within the body of the redeemed. God, the Judge of all, is in the city (Hebrews 12:23) and "Jesus the mediator of the new covenant" (verse 24) will also be there. Thus, along with the unfallen angels, the Old Testament saints, and the church saints, the Father and the Son are present. The redeemed who occupy this heavenly city are together in the presence of God.[15]

As we consider these great blessings the words of Wiersbe are very thought provoking:

Human history begins in a Garden and ends in a city that is like a garden paradise. In the Apostle John's day, Rome was the admired city; yet God compared it to a harlot: "that which is highly esteemed among men is abomination in the sight of God" (Luke 16:15). The eternal city of God is compared to a beautiful bride (Revelation 21:9), because it is the eternal home for God's beloved people.[16]

Finally, it is important to understand that heaven is a prepared place for a prepared people. Christ clearly states that trusting Him is the only way to heaven. After talking about heaven he said, "I am the way, the truth, and the life: no man cometh unto the Father, but by me" (John 14:6). If you have not trusted Christ, we urge you to do it today. Christ is the way to heaven; trusting Him makes our destination sure as we look toward the *Countdown to Armageddon*.

Seventy weeks are determined upon thy people and upon thy holy city, to finish the transgression, and to make an end of sins, and to make reconciliation for iniquity, and to bring in everlasting righteousness, and to seal up the vision and prophecy, and to anoint the most Holy. Know therefore and understand, that from the going forth of the commandment to restore and to build Jerusalem unto the Messiah the Prince shall be seven weeks, and threescore and two weeks: the street shall be built again, and the wall, even in troublous times. And after threescore and two weeks shall Messiah be cut off, but not for himself: and the people of the prince that shall come shall destroy the city and the sanctuary; and the end thereof shall be with a flood, and unto the end of the war desolations are determined. And he shall confirm the covenant with many for one week: and in the midst of the week he shall cause the sacrifice and the oblation to cease, and for the overspreading of abominations he shall make it desolate, even until the consummation, and that determined shall be poured upon the desolate.

DANIEL 9:24-27

The 70 Weeks of Daniel

Compiled by Thomas N. Davis

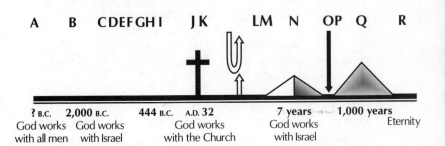

A B CDEFGHI JK LM N OP Q R

| **?** B.C. | **2,000** B.C. | **444** B.C. | A.D. **32** | **7 years** | **1,000 years** | |
| God works with all men | God works with Israel | | God works with the Church | God works with Israel | | Eternity |

A. The date of creation is unspecified in Scripture. No later than 3760 B.C. God works with all the descendants of Adam, but wickedness leads to Noah's flood.

B. Abraham was called out of the Gentiles around 2000 B.C. God now works primarily through his descendants, the Jews/Israel.

275

C. 605 B.C. Nebuchadnezzar of Babylon attacks Jerusalem the first time taking Daniel captive.

D. 597 B.C. Second Babylonian attack.

E. 586 B.C. Third Babylonian attack in which Solomon's Temple, which had stood for 375 years, is destroyed. Ezekiel watched the glory of God leave the Temple (Ezekiel 10-12).

F. 536 B.C. The Persians allow Zerubbabel and 49,897 Jews to return to repopulate Jerusalem. It has been 70 years since Daniel was taken to Babylon. Daniel realizes that Jeremiah 25:11 must be fulfilled.

G. 516 B.C. The Second Temple is completed and dedicated. It has been 70 years since the First Temple was destroyed.

H. 444 B.C. The Persians decree that Nehemiah may rebuild the walls of Jerusalem. According to Daniel 9, this is the starting point for the "70 Weeks of Daniel."

I. 395 B.C. By this time, the walls of Jerusalem are complete and the city is secure fulfilling the first "7 weeks" (49 years) of Daniel 9.

J. A.D. 32. After the next "62 weeks" (434 years) for a total of 483 years since 444 B.C., Messiah the prince is cut off (killed) and the people (Romans) of the prince who shall come (the Antichrist) destroys Jerusalem (A.D. 70, Daniel 9). The dating is based on the Jewish calendar, which was a lunar calendar of 360 days per year.

K. After Christ's return to heaven, having been rejected by His people Israel, God works through the Church, which was founded in Acts 2 and defined in the book of Ephesians. Paul, who was not one of the disciples trained by Christ for the offer of His kingdom during

Christ's public ministry, is selected to promote and define this new work of God among man.

L. The Rapture of the church from the planet occurs "at any moment," and cannot be dated, for no man knows the day or the hour when Christ returns (Mark 13:32; John 14:3). A pretribulational rapture is accepted because the church is promised deliverance from the period of time in which God's wrath is poured out on the earth (1 Thessalonians 1:10; 5:9; Revelation 3:10) and because this time of wrath is the "seventieth Week of Daniel" (7 years), which was for Daniel's people (Israel, Daniel 9:24). At the Rapture, the believers are given their rewards at the "judgment Seat of Christ" (1 Corinthians 3; 2 Corinthians 5:10), and then they enjoy the "marriage of the Lamb" (Revelation 19) and look forward to the "marriage feast," which will start the kingdom reign of Christ on the earth.

M. The 7-year period of tribulation is divided into two halves in Daniel 9, Matthew 24, and Revelation 11. Various designations are used such as 1,260 days, 42 months, and "time, times, and half a time."

N. The first half is "relatively peaceful" as the Antichrist begins to consolidate his power base in Europe (the territory of the old Roman Empire). The "7 years" is begun with the signing of a protection treaty with Israel that apparently also allows Israel to build the Third Temple (2 Thessalonians 2). A number of events occur at the mid-point, which radically alter the nature of the tribulation for the second half: (a) Satan is cast out of heaven by Michael (Revelation 12); (b) the Antichrist recovers from an initial military setback, perhaps even a mortal wound to his person, ascends out of the abyss (Revelation 13) to afflict Israel and the world, taking credit for defeating Gog (Ezekiel 38,39; Daniel 11:40-45); (c) the

"Two Witnesses," who had been protected and had performed miracles during the first half are now allowed to be killed by the Antichrist (Revelation 11); (d) the "One World Church" which had been manipulated by the Antichrist is now cast aside (Revelation 17); and (e) the Antichrist sets himself up as a god to be worshiped by all men (the "Abomination of Desolation" Matthew 24) causing them to receive his mark on the hand or forehead if they expect to buy or sell (Revelation 13).

O. Battle of Armageddon to defeat the Antichrist.

P. Daniel 12 talks of an additional 75 days added to the end of the 7 years, which are apparently for the sheep and goats judgment (Matthew 25) designed to ensure that only believers enter the kingdom, and also to prepare for the inauguration of the kingdom.

Q. Revelation 20 indicates six times that the initial phase of God's eternal kingdom will involve a 1,000-year reign of Christ on the earth. It is a return to the Garden of Eden to demonstrate that physical life on this planet can be "good." Lifespans will be lengthened to the apparent original ideal of one thousand years. Blessedness will characterize the period, although the sin nature of man will not be eradicated and therefore the rebel will be dealt with brutally by the Messiah (Isaiah 65).

R. After fulfilling the promised earthly blessings to Israel (Genesis 12) and also proving that even in a perfect environment man still is inclined to rebel (Revelation 20), God destroys the current heavens and earth and creates a "new heaven and a new earth," which will be the eternal abode of believers from all the ages of human history (Revelation 21,22).

Notes

Chapter 1–Profiting from Prophecy

1. Shakespeare, *Macbeth,* act 1, sc. 3.
2. C.I. Scofield, *Prophecy Made Plain* (London, England: Pickering & Inglis), p. 14.
3. Charles L. Feinberg, Editor, *Prophetic Truth Unfolding Today.* E. Schuyler English, *The Church on Earth* (Westwood, NJ: Fleming H. Revell Company, 1968), p. 22.
4. Lewis Sperry Chafer, *Systematic Theology, Volume IV, Introduction to Eschatology* (Dallas, TX: Dallas Seminary Press, 1948), p. 257.
5. David Breese, *The Marks of a Cult* (Eugene, OR: Harvest House Publishers, 1998), p. 165.
6. Warren W. Wiersbe, *Be Real* (Wheaton, IL: Victor Books, 1979), p. 164.
7. Roy B. Zuck, "Balancing the Academic and the Spiritual in Seminary." Edited by Stanley D. Toussaint and Charles H. Dyer, *Essays in Honor of J. Dwight Pentecost* (Chicago, IL: Moody Press, 1986), p. 92.
8. Benjamin Breckenridge Warfield, *Spiritual Culture in the Theological Seminary,* Princeton Theological Review, January 1904, p. 70.
9. Warren W. Wiersbe, *Real Worship* (Nashville, TN: Thomas Nelson Publishers, 1986), p. 81.
10. Elisabeth Elliot, *The Journals of Jim Elliot* (Old Tappan, NJ: Fleming H. Revell Company, 1978), p. 18.
11. John F. Walvoord, *The Revelation of Jesus Christ* (Chicago, IL: Moody Press, 1966), p. 273.
12. Charles Caldwell Ryrie, *The Basis of the Premillennial Faith* (Neptune, NJ: Loizeaux Brothers, 1953), p. 15.
13. Alfred p. Gibbs, *Worship, the Christian's Highest Occupation* (Kansas City, KS: Walterick Publishers, N.D), pp. 173-174.
14. Author unknown.
15. Wiersbe, *Real Worship,* p. 56.
16. Scofield, p. 19.

Chapter 2–How to Interpret Bible Prophecy

1. Stephen F. Olford, Editor, Charles L. Feinberg, *Prophetic Truth Unfolding the Prophetic Word* (Old Tappan, NJ: Fleming H. Revell Company, 1968), p. 127.
2. Roy B. Zuck, *Basic Bible Interpretation* (Colorado Springs, CO: Victor Books, 1991), p. 228.
3. *Ibid.,* p. 228–33.
4. Elliot E. Johnson, *Essays in Honor of J. Dwight Pentecost, Apocalyptic Genre in Literal Inter-pretation,* edited by Stanley D. Toussaint and Charles H. Dyer (Chicago, IL: Moody Bible Institute, 1986), p. 197.
5. Elliot E. Johnson, *When the Trumpet Sounds, Literal Interpretation: A Plea for Consensus* (Eugene, OR: Harvest House Publishers), p. 212.
6. Charles L. Feinberg, *Premillennialism or Amillennialism?* (Wheaton, IL: Van Kampen Press, 1954), pp. 207, 220.
7. F.F. Bruce, *Interpretation of the Bible; Evangelical Dictionary of Theology,* Walter A. Wells, Editor (Grand Rapids, MI: Baker), p. 566.

8. Wilbur M. Smith, *World Crisis and the Prophetic Scripture* (Chicago, IL: Moody Press, 1951), p. 55.

9. John F. Walvoord, *The Millennial Kingdom* (Grand Rapids, MI: Zondervan Publishing House), 1959, pp. 33-34.

10. Thomas D. Ice, *An Evaluation of Theonomic Neopostmillennialism* (Bibliotheca Sacra, Dallas Theological Seminary V. 145# July), 88.300.

11. David L. Cooper, *The World's Greatest Library Graphically Illustrated* (Los Angeles: Biblical Research Society, 1970), p. 11.

12. John F. Walvoord, *The Prophecy Knowledge Handbook* (Wheaton, IL: Victory Books, 1990), p. 17.

13. J. Dwight Pentecost, *Things to Come* (Findlay, OH: Dunham Publishing Company, 1958), p. 60.

14. Charles L. Feinberg, *Premillennialism or Amillennialism?* (Wheaton, IL: Van Kampen Press, 1954), p. 17.

15. *Ibid.*, p. 18.

16. *Ibid.*, p. 17.

17. John F. Walvoord, *Prophecy: 14 Essential Keys to Understanding the Final Drama* (Nashville, TN: Thomas Nelson Publishers, 1993), p. 20.

Chapter 3–The Times of the Gentiles

1. Norval Geldenhuys, "Commentary on the Gospel of Luke," in *The New International Commentary on the New Testament* (Grand Rapids: Wm. B. Eerdmans Publishing Company, 1975), p. 536.

2. Charles Boutflower, *In and Around the Book of Daniel* (Grand Rapids: Zondervan Publishing House, 1963), p. xv.

3. *Ibid.*, p. 47.

4. Edward J. Young, *The Prophecy of Daniel* (Grand Rapids: Wm. B. Eerdmans Publishing Company, 1970), p. 74.

5. Boutflower, *In and Around the Book of Daniel*, p. 34.

6. *Ibid.*, p. 25-26.

7. H.C. Leupold, *Exposition of Daniel* (Grand Rapids: Baker Book House, 1949), p. 117.

8. Boutflower, *In and Around the Book of Daniel*, pp. 26-28.

9. C.F. Keil, *Biblical Commentary on the Book of Daniel* (Grand Rapids: Wm. B. Eerdmans Publishing Company, 1959), p. 106.

10. Boutflower, *In and Around the Book of Daniel*, p. xvi.

11. Leupold, *Exposition of Daniel*, p. 118.

12. Boutflower, *In and Around the Book of Daniel*, pp. 29-30.

13. Samuel J. Schultz, *The Old Testament Speaks* (New York: Harper & Brothers, Publishers, 1960), p. 248.

14. John F. Walvoord, *Daniel* (Chicago: Moody Press, 1971), p. 73.

15. Boutflower, *In and Around the Book of Daniel*, pp. 31-32.

16. *Ibid.*, p. 45.

17. *Ibid.*

18. *Ibid.*, p. 46.

19. *Ibid.*, pp. 47-48.

20. *Ibid.*, pp. 46-47.

21. *Ibid.*, p. 25.

22. Much of the material in this chapter has been borrowed, with the permission of the author, from the following source: Renald E. Showers, *The Most High God* (Bellmawr, New Jersey: The Friends of Israel Gospel Ministry, Inc., 1982), pp. 12-25.

Chapter 4–Revival of the Roman Empire

1. For an in-depth study of the identification of these powers and the fulfillment of this prophecy see: Renald E. Showers, *The Most High God* (Bellmawr, NJ: The Friends of Israel Gospel Ministry, 1982).

2. Earle E. Cairns, *Christianity Through the Centuries* (Grand Rapids: Zondervan Publishing House, 1981), p. 185.

3. *Ibid.*

4. *Ibid.*, p. 187.

5. Emil Ludwig, *Napoleon* (New York: Boni and Liveright, 1926), pp. 85, 211, 238, 245-46.

6. *Ibid.*, p. 667.

7. *Ibid.*, p. 514.

8. *Ibid.*, pp. 227-28.

9. *Ibid.*, p. 566.

10. William L. Shirer, *The Rise and Fall of the Third Reich* (New York: Fawcett Publications, Inc., 1962), p. 133.

11. Arnold J. Zurcher, *The Struggle to Unite Europe, 1940-1958* (New York: New York University Press, 1958), p. 6.

12. Laura Fermi, *Mussolini* (Chicago: The University of Chicago Press, 1961), p. 216.

13. Benito Mussolini, *My Autobiography* (New York: Charles Scribner's Sons, 1928), p. 130.

14. Roy MacGregor-Hastie, *The Day of the Lion* (New York: Coward-McCann, Inc., 1963), p. 237.

15. Fermi, *Mussolini,* p. 361.

16. Shirer, *The Third Reich,* p. 1295.

17. *Ibid.*, p. 1296.

18. Zurcher, *Unite Europe,* p. 19.

19. Shirer, *The Third Reich,* p. 1340.

20. Zurcher, *Unite Europe,* p. 21.

21. *Ibid.*, pp. 22-24.

22. John Gunther, *Inside Europe Today* (New York: Harper and Brothers, Publishers, 1961), p. 263-64, and editorial, "Birth of Unity for Europe," *Life,* April 8, 1957, p. 36.

23. Gunther, *Inside Europe Today,* p. 18.

24. Konrad Adenauer, *World Indivisible, with Liberty and Justice for All* (New York: Harper and Brothers, Publishers, 1955), pp. 49-50.

25. *Ibid.*, p. 53.

26. Zurcher, *Unite Europe,* p. 172.

27. Scott Sullivan, "The Czar of Brussels," *Newsweek,* February 6, 1989, p. 32.

28. Andrew Phillips, "A European Revolution," *Maclean's,* December 5, 1988, p. 43.

29. Scott Sullivan, "Who's Afraid of 1992?" *Newsweek,* October 31, 1988, p. 34.

30. Caspar W. Weinberger, "1992 Is Closer Than We Think," *Forbes,* April 17, 1989, p. 33.

31. Robin Christmas, Producer, "Birth of a Superstate," Canadian television documentary, June, 1990.

32. *Ibid.*

33. David Israelson, "European Leaders Take 'Historic' Step to Unity," *Toronto Star,* December 15, 1990.

34. *Ibid.*

35. "Birth of a Superstate."

36. Sally Jacobsen, "Europe Finally to be United, but Federation is a Loose One," *The Arizona Republic,* October 13, 1993.

37. James K. Glassman, "New Coin of the Realm," *U.S. News & World Report,* May 11, 1998, p. 50.

38. *Ibid.*

39. *Ibid.*

40. *Ibid.*

41. "Birth of a Superstate."

42. Robin Knight, Fred Coleman, and John Marks, "Summer of Discontent," *U.S. News & World Report,* June 6, 1994, p. 48.

43. "Birth of a Superstate."

44. Nadji Tehrani, "Publisher's Outlook–Europe 1992–An Opportunity or Real Pitfall?" *Tele-marketing,* April, 1989.

45. Dresdner Bank, "What's Uncommon About the Common Market?" *Forbes,* October 21, 1991, p. 154.

Chapter 6–An Examination of "The Pre-Wrath Rapture" View

1. Robert Van Kampen, *The Rapture Question Answered* (Grand Rapids: Revell, 1997), pp. 41-44.

2. *Ibid.,* p. 39.

3. *Ibid.,* p. 49.

4. Marvin Rosenthal, *The Pre-Wrath Rapture of the Church* (Nashville: Thomas Nelson Publishers, 1990).

5. Robert Van Kampen, *The Sign* (Wheaton, IL.: Crossway Books, 1992).

6. Rosenthal, *Pre-Wrath,* pp. 34-35.

7. Van Kampen, *Rapture Question,* p. 42.

8. Ibid.

9. Rosenthal, *Pre-Wrath,* p. 111.

10. *Ibid.,* p. 176.

11. Rosenthal, *Pre-Wrath,* p. 176; Van Kampen, *Rapture Question,* pp. 3-24.

12. Robert L. Thomas, *Revelation 1–7: An Exegetical Commentary* (Chicago: Moody, 1992), p. 457.

13. Rosenthal, *Pre-Wrath,* p. 166-67.

14. Chart in *Ibid.,* p. 149.

15. Thomas, *Revelation,* p. 458.

16. Charles C. Ryrie, *Come Quickly, Lord Jesus* (Eugene, OR: Harvest House Publishers, 1996), p. 106.

17. Rosenthal, *Pre-Wrath,* p. 117.

18. Ryrie, *Come Quickly,* pp. 106-07.

19. Rosenthal, *Pre-Wrath,* p. 103.

20. *Ibid.,* pp. 103-08.

21. McLean, "Chronology and Sequential Structure of John's Revelation" in Thomas Ice and Timothy Demy, eds., *When the Trumpet Sounds* (Eugene, OR: Harvest House Publishers, 1995), p. 341.

22. Rosenthal, *Pre-Wrath,* p. 37.

23. *Ibid.,* p. 152.

Chapter 10–Israel's Title Deed to Palestine

1. Walter Kaiser, *Toward an Old Testament Theology* (Grand Rapids, MI: Zondervan, 1978), p. 82.

2. David Larsen, *Jews, Gentiles & the Church* (Grand Rapids, MI: Discovery House Publishers, 1995).

3. Louis Goldberg, *Turbulence over the Middle East* (Neptune, NJ: Loizeaux Brothers, 1982), p. 55.

4. Elwood McQuaid, *It Is No Dream* (Bellmawr, NJ: The Friends of Israel Gospel Ministry, Inc. 1993), p. 93.
5. Martin Gilbert, *The Arab-Israeli Conflict: Its History in Maps* (London: Weidenfeld and Nicolson, 1976), pp. 56,57,109.
6. George Will, "Israel has a right to its military." *The Glens falls Post-Star,* May 7, 1998, p. A4.

Chapter 11–Thy Kingdom Come: Christ's Title Deed to the Throne

1. See the excellent discussion in Keil and Delitzsch, *The Pentateuch, Vol. 1* (Grand Rapids, MI: Wm. B. Eerdmans Publishing Company, 1959), pp. 392-402.
2. Alan H. McNeile, *The Gospel According to St. Matthew* (Grand Rapids, MI: Baker Book House, 1980), p. 4.
3. For a full discussion see Frederick Godet, *A Commentary on the Gospel of Luke* (New York: Funk and Wagnalls Company, 1887), pp. 126-133.
4. *Ibid.,* pp. 128-129.
5. *Ibid.,* pp. 129-130.
6. Darrell Bock, *Luke* (Grand Rapids, MI: Baker Books, 1994), p. 923.

Chapter 12–The Coming World Religion

1. This is particularly noticeable in Ezekiel 28:2 where God addresses the "prince" (Hebrew, *nasi)* of Tyre but by verse 12 this is changed to the "king" (Hebrew, *melek)* of Tyre.
2. Walter Rauschenbusch (1861–1918) was a professor at Rochester Seminary. He wanted to clean up the slums of New York City. His book, *The Theology of the Social Gospel,* was a blueprint to reform society and make it into the "Kingdom of God."
3. Evangelist Jack Wyrtzen was fond of saying, "Before you get the man out of the ghetto, you have to first get the ghetto out of the man!"
4. Tara Center, "The Christ Is in the World," *USA Today* (January 12, 1987), p. 7A.
5. Norman L. Geisler, "The New Age Movement," *Bibliotheca Sacra* (January 1987), pp. 79-103.
6. David Spangler, *Reflections on the Christ,* p. 39.
7. On the World Wide Web: <http://www.shareintl.org/maitreya.html>.
8. Marjory Roberts, "A Linguistic 'Nay' to Channeling," *Psychology Today* (October 1989), pp. 64-65.
9. Brooks Alexander, "Theology from the Twilight Zone," *Christianity Today* (September 18, 1987), p. 25.
10. In June 1992, Harvard psychiatrist John E. Mack, MD and M.I.T. physicist David E. Pritchard, PhD held the Abduction Study Conference at M.I.T. The researchers at the five-day conference included Temple University historian David Jacobs, PhD; California physician John G. Miller, MD; Sacramento psychologist Richard J. Boylan, PhD; and Budd Hopkins, who claims to have investigated more than 1,200 abduction cases and has written two books on the subject.
11. Yankelovich Monitor, *American Demographics* (August 1998), p. 61. Between 1976 and 1997, the percentage of Americans who believe in spiritualism rose from 12 to 52 percent; faith healing: 10 to 45 percent; astrology: 17 to 37 percent; UFOs: 24 to 30 percent; reincarnation: 9 to 25 percent; and fortune telling: 4 to 14 percent.
12. Greenhaven Press, Inc., San Diego, CA.

Chapter 13–The Tribulation

1. J.B. Smith, *A Revelation of Jesus Christ* (Scottdale, PA: Herald Press, 1961), p. 136.

2. Henry Alford, *The Greek New Testament* (London: Rivingtons, 1875), 4:622.
3. Henry M. Morris, *The Revelation Record* (San Diego: Creation-Life, 1983), pp. 303-04.

Chapter 14—The Abominable Antichrist

1. Walter K. Price, *The Coming Antichrist* (Chicago: Moody Press, 1974), pp. 100-131.
2. David Larsen, *Jews, Gentiles & the Church* (Grand Rapids, MI: Discovery House Publishers, 1995).
3. Alexander Hislop, The Two Babylons (New York: Loizeaux Brothers, 1943).
4. Paraphrase of a comparison made by James Fleming, Biblical Resources, Jerusalem.
5. D. Edmond Hiebert, *The Thessalonian Epistles* (Chicago: Moody Press, 1971), p. 125.

Chapter 15—The Campaign of Armageddon

1. The *NIV Study Bible* (Grand Rapids: Zondervan, 1985), p. 1944 (note on Revelation 16:14).
2. While writing this in the summer of 1998, I saw an ad for a movie called *Armageddon.* The blurb describes it by saying that the lead actors "drill a hole in an asteroid while it's zooming toward earth and plant a nuclear device to blow it off course."
3. E. Nestle, "Har-magedon," *A Dictionary of the Bible,* James Hastings, editor (Edinburgh; and T. Clark, 1910), 1:304,5.

Chapter 16—The Judgment of the Nations

1. Thomas J. Finley, *The Wycliffe Exegetical Commentary: Joel, Amos, Obadiah* (Chicago: Moody Press, 1990), p. 84.
2. J. Dwight Pentecost, *Things to Come* (Grand Rapids: Dunham Publishing Co., 1964), p. 417.
3. Geoffrey Bromiley, *Theological Dictionary of the New Testament,* edited by Kittel and Friedrich (Grand Rapids, MI: Eerdmans, 1992), p. 201.
4. J. Dwight Pentecost, *The Words and Works of Jesus Christ* (Grand Rapids, MI: Zondervan, 1981, p. 409.
5. Arnold G. Fruchtenbaum, The Footsteps of the Messiah (Austin, TX: Ariel Ministries Press, 1993), p. 260.
6. John F. Walvoord, *Major Bible Prophecies* (Grand Rapids, MI: Zondervan, 1991), p. 386.
7. Fruchtenbaum, p. 259.
8. Joseph Dillow, *The Reign of the Servant Kings* (Hayesville, NC: Schoettle Publishing Co., 1993), pp. 73-82.
9. *Ibid.,* pp. 140-143.
10. Finley, p. 87.

Chapter 17—The Marvelous Millennium

1. Charles Ryrie, *The Basis of the Premillennial Faith* (Neptune, NJ: Loizeaux Brothers, 1953), pp. 145,146.
2. Lewis Sperry Chafer, *Systematic Theology, Volume IV, Eschatology* (Dallas, TX: Dallas Seminary Press, 1948), p. 265.
3. *Ibid.,* p. 265.
4. David L. Larsen, *Jews, Gentiles & the Church* (Grand Rapids, MI: Discovery House Publishers, 1995), p. 307.
5. Ryrie, *The Basis of the Premillennial Faith,* p. 12.
6. J. Dwight Pentecost, *Thy Kingdom Come* (Wheaton, IL: Victor Books, 1990), p. 316.
7. J. Dwight Pentecost, *Things to Come, A Study in Biblical Eschatology* (Grand Rapids, MI: Zondervan Publishing House, 1958), p. 477.
8. *Ibid.,* p. 480.

9. John F. Walvoord, *The Millennial Kingdom* (Grand Rapids, MI: Zondervan Publishing House, 1959), p. 307.

10. Larsen, *Jews, Gentiles & the Church*, p. 314.

11. Ryrie, *The Basis of the Premillennial Faith*, pp. 149, 150.

12. Pentecost, *Thy Kingdom Come*, pp. 316,317.

13. Ralph H. Alexander, *Ezekiel, The Expositor's Bible Commentary* (Grand Rapids, MI: Zondervan Publishing House, 1986), pp. 950, 951.

14. Horatius Bonar, *The Coming and Kingdom of the Lord Jesus Christ* (London: J. Nisbet & Co., 1889), pp. 222, 223.

15. John L. Mitchell, *Animal Sacrifices in the Millennium*, unpublished thesis (Dallas, TX: Dallas Theological Seminary, 1947), p. 42.

16. Larsen, *Jews, Gentiles & the Church*, p. 320.

17. Pentecost, *Things to Come*, pp. 492,493.

18. Lewis Sperry Chafer, *Systematic Theology, Volume V* (Dallas, TX: Dallas Seminary Press, 1948), pp. 373, 374.

Chapter 18–The Final Revolt

1. J. Dwight Pentecost, *Things to Come* (Grand Rapids, MI: Dunham Publishing Company, 1958), p. 475.

Chapter 19–The Great White Throne Judgment

1. Warren Wiersbe, *Classic Sermons on Heaven and Hell* (Grand Rapids, MI: Kregel Publications, 1994), p. 10.

2. J. Dwight Pentecost, *Prophecy for Today* (Grand Rapids, MI: Discovery House Publishers, revised edition 1989), p. 192.

3. C.I. Scofield, Prophecy Made Plain (London, England: Pickering & Inglis, date unknown), pp. 165-166.

4. L.S. Chafer, *Systematic Theology*, Volume 4 (Dallas, TX: Dallas Press, 1948), p. 413.

5. Judson B. Palmer, *In the Meantime... What Happens Between Death and the Rapture?* (Schroon Lake, NY: Word of Life Fellowship, Inc., 1984), p. 4.

6. Chafer, *Systematic Theology*, pp. 414-415.

7. Wiersbe, p. 50.

8. John F. Walvoord, *The Prophecy Knowledge Handbook* (Wheaton, IL: Victor Books), p. 632.

9. John F. Walvoord, *Prophecy: 14 Essential Keys to Understanding the Final Drama* (Nashville, TN: Thomas Nelson Publishers, 1993), p. 171.

10. Pentecost, *Prophecy for Today,* pp. 208-209.

11. *Ibid.,* pp. 202-203.

12. J. Dwight Pentecost, *Things to Come* (Findlay, OH: Dunham Publishing House, 1958), p. 582.

13. Walvoord, *The Prophecy Knowledge Handbook*, pp. 634, 635.

14. Paul W. Rood, *The Heavenly Home* (Grand Rapids, MI: Zondervan Publishing House), p. 14.

15. Pentecost, *Prophecy for Today,* pp. 205-206.

16. Warren W. Wiersbe, *Be Victorious* (Wheaton, IL: Victor Books, 1985), p. 145.

Contributing Authors' Biographical Sketches

Dr. Paul N. Benware

An author, pastor, and former professor of Bible and Theology at Moody Bible Institute, Dr. Benware graduated from Los Angeles Baptist College and holds a ThM degree from Dallas Theological Seminary and a ThD degree from Grace Theological Seminary. He has served as pastor in churches in California, Indiana, and Illinois, and his teaching ministry includes several months at the Lutsk Regional Bible Institute and Odessa Theological Seminary in the Ukraine. He and his wife, Anne, have four children.

Dr. Mark L. Bailey

Dr. Bailey is the vice president of academic affairs and academic dean at Dallas Theological Seminary where he has taught since 1985. He is a graduate of Southwestern College and holds MDiv and ThM degrees from Western Conservative Baptist Seminary and a PhD from Dallas Theological Seminary. He has pastored several churches, served as a tour guide for numerous trips to Israel, and is an author. Currently he is also the senior pastor of Faith Bible Church in DeSoto, Texas. He and his wife, Barbara, have two sons.

Dr. David Breese

A graduate of Judson College and Northern Seminary, Dr. Breese has taught philosophy, apologetics, and church history. He is the President of Christian Destiny and publisher of the *Destiny Newsletter,* a periodical presenting a Christian view of current events. He is also producer of the syndicated radio and television commentary, *Dave Breese Reports.* He has authored several books, pamphlets, and magazine articles and is active in a ministry to college and university students.

Dr. Thomas N. Davis

Dr. Davis is a graduate of Word of Life Bible Institute, Lancaster Bible College, and Grace Theological Seminary. He completed a year of graduate work at Jerusalem University College and holds an EdD degree in computer and information technology from Nova Southeastern University. He pastored churches in Pennsylvania and Indiana before joining the staff of Word of Life Bible Institute in 1978 where he is academic dean and professor. He and his wife, Susie, have five daughters and a son.

Dr. James "Jimmy" DeYoung, Jr.

Since 1991, Dr. DeYoung has resided in Jerusalem as a fully credentialed journalist. He appears regularly on the television program, *Day of Discovery,* and on radio, with political, biblical, and prophetic reports and commentary that are broadcast over several networks. He has produced several audio and video productions and publishes the *Until* newsletter. Dr. DeYoung also ministered with Word of Life Fellowship for 12 years and for five years was the general manager of a Christian radio station in New York City. He and his wife, Judy, have four children and three grandchildren.

Dr. Thomas O. Figart

A graduate of Philadelphia College of Bible and Johns Hopkins University, Dr. Figart holds ThM degree from Dallas Theological Seminary and a ThD degree from Grace Theological Seminary. He served as a professor of Bible at Baltimore School of the Bible before joining Lancaster Bible College as academic dean and is currently a Distinguished Professor. Dr. Figart is an author of several books and articles and for many years was a visiting professor at Word of Life Bible Institute. He and his wife have been married for 53 years; they have four children, nine grandchildren, and one great-grandson.

Dr. Thomas D. Ice

Dr. Ice is executive director of The Pre-Trib Research Center, which was founded in 1994 with the purpose to research, teach, and defend the pretribulational rapture and related Bible prophecy doctrines. He has coauthored several books and magazine articles and served as a pastor for 15 years. He is a graduate of Howard Payne University and holds a ThM from Dallas Theological Seminary and a PhD from Tyndale Theological Seminary. He and his wife, Janice, have three sons.

Dr. Elwood McQuaid

Following undergraduate studies, Dr. McQuaid accepted a call in 1953 to pastor a church in Virginia. Over the next 24 years he pastored three churches and founded a Christian school. In 1977 he joined The Friends of Israel ministry and later served Moody Bible Institute before rejoining The Friends of Israel as executive director in 1989. He has authored several books and currently is the editor of *Israel My Glory* magazine and host of the daily radio program, *Friends of Israel Today*.

Dr. Joe Jordan

After coming to Christ as a teenager on Word of Life Island, Dr. Jordan went on to graduate from Tennessee Temple University with a BA in Bible and Theology. He also attended Philadelphia College of Bible and Lynchburg College and holds a DD from Tennessee Temple University. In 1969 he founded and directed the ministry of Word of Life in Argentina for the following 20 years. The ministry expanded from there to include every Spanish-speaking country in Latin America and several others around the world. Dr. Jordan is now the director of Word of Life Fellowship. He and his wife, Melva, have three children and one granddaughter.

Dr. John R. Master

Dr. Master is chair and professor in the Division of Biblical Education at Philadelphia College of Bible. Before joining the faculty there in 1987, he was academic dean at Baptist Bible College and taught at Baptist Bible Theological Seminary and Word of Life Bible Institute. He has written Sunday School material for Union Gospel Press and Regular Baptist Press. He graduated from Houghton College and holds ThM and ThD degrees from Dallas Theological Seminary. He and his wife, Janet, have three sons.

Dr. J. Dwight Pentecost

A Distinguished Professor of Bible Exposition at Dallas Theological Seminary, Dr. Pentecost has taught at the seminary since 1955. He is a graduate of Hampden-Sydney College and holds ThM and ThD degrees from Dallas Theological Seminary. A noted speaker, his teaching ministry has influenced believers in more than 25 countries around the world. He has authored several books and was featured on the video series, *The Words and Works of Jesus Christ.* He and his wife, Dorothy, have two children and two grandchildren.

Dr. Charles C. Ryrie

Dr. Ryrie graduated from Haverford College and holds ThM and ThD degrees from Dallas Theological Seminary. He also has a PhD from the University of Edinburgh and a

LittD from Liberty Baptist Theological Seminary. He has taught at Westmont College, served as president of Philadelphia College of Bible, and as chair and professor of systematic theology at Dallas Theological Seminary. He has authored numerous books, pamphlets, magazine articles, and the Ryrie Study Bible. He is an adjunct professor at Philadelphia College of Bible and visiting professor at Word of Life Bible Institute.

Dr. Renald E. Showers

A graduate of Philadelphia College of Bible and Wheaton College, Dr. Showers holds a ThM in church history from Dallas Theological Seminary and a ThD from Grace Theological Seminary. He has served as a pastor; as a member of the faculties of Lancaster Bible College, Moody Bible Institute, and Philadelphia College of Bible; and as a visiting professor at Word of Life Bible Institute, Calvary Bible College, and Baptist Bible Seminary. He is currently on the staff of the Church Ministries Division of The Friends of Israel and teaches in the ministry's Institute of Biblical Studies. He has authored several books and numerous magazine articles. He and his wife, Ellie, have two daughters.

Dr. Charles U. Wagner

Having held pastorates in Michigan, New Jersey, and Washington, Dr. Wagner is currently the senior pastor of Calvary Baptist Church in Covington, Kentucky. He is a graduate of Detroit Bible College and holds a DD from Los Angeles Baptist Seminary. He has served as president of Northwest Baptist Seminary and Grand Rapids Baptist College and Seminary. He is an adjunct professor at several colleges and seminaries and visiting professor at Word of Life Bible Institute. He has authored several books. He and his wife, Ruth, have two children and seven grandchildren.

Dr. John F. Walvoord

A theologian, pastor, and author, Dr. Walvoord graduated from Wheaton College and holds ThB, ThM, and ThD degrees from Dallas Theological Seminary and a LittD from Liberty Baptist Seminary. He joined the faculty at Dallas Theological Seminary in 1936 and later became president in 1953 and chancellor in 1986. One of the most influential dispensational theologians of the twentieth century, Dr. Walvoord is prominent in prophetic conferences advocating a pre-tribulational rapture, a literal thousand-year millennium, and the distinction between Israel and the church.

Other Good
Harvest House Reading

Final Signs
Ed Hindson

Hindson offers fast-moving, intriguing background on more than two dozen of the most amazing prophecies in Scripture, including the desire for a world government, the rapture of the church, and the rise of Antichrist and the false prophet.

Fast Facts on Bible Prophecy
Thomas Ice and Timothy Demy

An A to Z end-times resource, *Fast Facts on Bible Prophecy* includes more than 175 in-depth Bible prophecy definitions, backgrounds on different interpretations of prophecy, outlines on the timing of prophetic events, and much more. A compilation of the Pocket Prophecy series.

Is the Antichrist Alive and Well?
Ed Hindson

The author turns to Scripture to discover the truth about the master deceiver we call the Antichrist. Along with compelling evidence that every age has an Antichrist ready to take control, you'll discover how you can further Christ's kingdom during this crucial time before Antichrist's rise to power.

Jerusalem in Prophecy
J. Randall Price

Jerusalem has a rich and fascinating history spanning more than 3,000 years, but this city's most significant days are still to come. The stage is now set for both a terrifying destruction and an amazing deliverance! Discover what the Bible says about Jerusalem as J. Randall Price, an expert on prophecy and the Middle East, takes you on an informative and exciting journey through *Jerusalem in Prophecy*.